Arise

'Jane Holgate is a brilliant thinker. By centring her thesis on power, this book contributes to our understanding of what strategies and mechanisms enable workers to stand a chance at achieving justice.'
—Jane McAlevey is an organiser, scholar and author of *No Shortcuts: Organizing for Power in the New Gilded Age*

'A must-read – by a top-class scholar, union educator and activist, and written with exceptional clarity. Readers will come away with a deeper understanding of the world and with the tools to change it.'
—John Kelly, Emeritus Professor of Industrial Relations at Birkbeck College University of London

'Part history text, part employment relations research; Jane Holgate's book critiques decades of union renewal strategies in the UK and questions assumptions from both the left and right over how to regain collective power rather than just recruit new members.'
—Dave Smith is a blacklisted construction worker and co-author of *Blacklisted: The Secret War Between Big Business and Union Activists*

'A brilliant treatise on how to think about worker power in the context of sweeping structural change. It is well past time for labour scholars to return to this fundamental question and Jane Holgate has made an indispensable contribution to the canon.'
—Janice Fine, Professor of Labor Studies and Employment Relations, Rutgers University and Director of Research and Strategy at the Center on Innovation in Worker Organization

'An excellent review of the leaps forward and setbacks for workers and their unions, and an invaluable read for Jane Holgate's astute analyses. But that's not what the book is about. It is about power. Power for workers, which is the reason for organising, and which is too often forgotten in the daily struggle. We can continue on the current path to oblivion, with unions becoming little more than legacy politicians, or remember our roots and aggressively organise in new ways with workers in an evolving economy.'
—Wade Rathke, founder and Chief Organiser of ACORN International

'In examining the problems that we have to face to rebuild the movement, this analysis of power, who has it and how to build it, is a must-read for aspiring activists. An essential book for those who are committed to the idea that trade unionism is a vehicle through which we can organise to delivering transformative change for all workers.'
—Wilf Sullivan, Race Equality Officer for the Trades Union Congress (TUC)

'Jane Holgate's experience as an academic and a union activist has given her unique insights that make this book an important read for anyone who wants to understand where unions have been, where they are now and where they need to go'
—Arnie Graf, community organiser with the Industrial Areas Foundation and author of *Lessons Learned. Stories from a Lifetime of Organizing*

Wildcat: Workers' Movements and Global Capitalism

Series Editors:
Immanuel Ness (City University of New York)
Peter Cole (Western Illinois University)
Raquel Varela (Instituto de História Contemporânea [IHC]
of Universidade Nova de Lisboa, Lisbon New University)
Tim Pringle (SOAS, University of London)

Also available:

Choke Points:
Logistics Workers Disrupting the Global
Supply Chain
Edited by Jake Alimahomed-Wilson and
Immanuel Ness

The Cost of Free Shipping:
Amazon in the Global Economy
Edited by Jake Alimahomed-Wilson and
Ellen Reese

Power Despite Precarity:
Strategies for the Contingent Faculty
Movement in Higher Education
Joe Berry and Helena Worthen

Dying for an iPhone:
Apple, Foxconn and the Lives of China's
Workers
Jenny Chan, Mark Selden and Pun Ngai

Just Work?
Migrant Workers' Struggles Today
Edited by Aziz Choudry and Mondli
Hlatshwayo

Wobblies of the World:
A Global History of the IWW
Edited by Peter Cole, David Struthers and
Kenyon Zimmer

Augmented Exploitation:
Artificial Intelligence, Automation and Work
Edited by Phoebe V. Moore and
Jamie Woodcock

Organizing Insurgency:
Workers' Movements in the Global South
Immanuel Ness

Southern Insurgency:
The Coming of the Global Working Class
Immanuel Ness

Amakomiti:
Grassroots Democracy in South African
Shack Settlements
Trevor Ngwane

Workers' Inquiry and Global Class Struggle:
Strategies, Tactics, Objectives
Edited by Robert Ovetz

The Spirit of Marikana:
The Rise of Insurgent Trade Unionism in
South Africa
Luke Sinwell with Siphiwe Mbatha

Solidarity:
Latin America and the US Left in the Era of
Human Rights
Steve Striffler

Working the Phones:
Control and Resistance in Call Centres
Jamie Woodcock

Arise

Power, Strategy and Union Resurgence

Jane Holgate

PLUTO  PRESS

First published 2021 by Pluto Press
345 Archway Road, London N6 5AA

www.plutobooks.com

British Library Cataloguing in Publication Data
A catalogue record for this book is available from the British Library

ISBN   978 0 7453 4403 4   Hardback
ISBN   978 0 7453 4402 7   Paperback
ISBN   978 0 7453 4406 5   PDF
ISBN   978 0 7453 4404 1   EPUB
ISBN   978 0 7453 4405 8   Kindle

This book is printed on paper suitable for recycling and made from fully managed
and sustained forest sources. Logging, pulping and manufacturing processes are
expected to conform to the environmental standards of the country of origin.

Typeset by Stanford DTP Services, Northampton, England

Simultaneously printed in the United Kingdom and United States of America

Contents

For John, who for nearly 40 years has
fought for social justice by my side

Abbreviations

ACAS	Advisory, Conciliation and Arbitration Service
AFL-CIO	American Federation of Labor-Congress of Industrial Organizations
APEX	Association of Professional, Executive, Clerical and Computer Staff
CSOs	civil society organisations
CWU	Communication Workers Union
EU	European Union
FBU	Fire Brigades Union
GMB	General, Municipal, Boilerworkers and Allied Trades Union
HRM	human resource management
ILO	International Labour Organisation
IWGB	Independent Workers of Great Britain
LCDTU	Liaison Committee for the Defence of Trade Unions
NAFF	National Association for Freedom (now the Freedom Association)
NCB	National Coal Board
NGA	National Graphical Association
NIRC	National Industrial Relations Court
NUJ	National Union of Journalists
NUM	National Union of Mineworkers
OA	Organising Academy
PCS	Public and Commercial Services Union
RMT	Rail, Maritime and Transport Union
SEIU	Service Employees International Union
TGWU	Transport and General Workers' Union (now Unite)
TUC	Trades Union Congress
USDAW	Union of Shop, Distributive and Allied Workers
UVW	United Voices of the World

Series Preface

Workers' movements are a common and recurring feature in contemporary capitalism. The same militancy that inspired the mass labour movements of the twentieth century continues to define worker struggles that proliferate throughout the world today.

For more than a century, labour unions have mobilised to represent the political-economic interests of workers by uncovering the abuses of capitalism, establishing wage standards, improving oppressive working conditions, and bargaining with employers and the state. Since the 1970s, organised labour has declined in size and influence as the global power and influence of capital have expanded dramatically. The world over, existing unions are in a condition of fracture and turbulence in response to neoliberalism, financialisation and the reappearance of rapacious forms of imperialism. New and modernised unions are adapting to conditions and creating a class-conscious workers' movement rooted in militancy and solidarity. Ironically, while the power of organised labour contracts, working-class militancy and resistance persist and are growing in the global South.

Wildcat publishes ambitious and innovative works on the history and political economy of workers' movements and is a forum for debate on pivotal movements and labour struggles. The series applies a broad definition of the labour movement to include workers in and out of unions, and seeks works that examine proletarianisation and class formation, mass production, gender, affective and reproductive labour, imperialism and workers, syndicalism and independent unions, and labour and leftist social and political movements.

Acknowledgements

This book was written in the midst of the Covid-19 global pandemic. Being locked down in March 2020 and restricted from meeting people outside one's own household provided plenty of time for reflection on my work on the organising of workers into labour unions. It also afforded the opportunity for lengthy discussions with my partner, John Page. We would rise at 5 a.m. each day and walk around our local park and the wonderful Abney Park Cemetery in north London, talking about our understandings and experiences of organising in the UK. The pandemic was a traumatic time for many people as loved ones died or became sick, and I valued our daily conversations about the issues in my book as a welcome distraction. I lost my father as a result of the Covid-19 virus in the middle of writing the book, and travel restrictions prevented me from attending his funeral, but experiencing the arrival of spring and summer on our daily walks provided a sense of hope and illustrated the potential for change, despite the sorrow of the seemingly ever-growing daily death tolls.

My heartfelt thanks are extended to John, for his love, care and companionship throughout this time, and for reading and commenting on each chapter as it was completed. His insightful comments have enriched the book immensely. Thanks also to Professor John Kelly, one of the most articulate, thoughtful and unassuming academics I have been fortunate to know. As one of the most renowned industrial relations scholars of our time, I benefited from his extensive knowledge of the ins and outs of the labour movement and his wise counsel in suggesting amendments. Heartfelt thanks are also due to Janice Fine, Jane McAlevey, Wade Rathke, Arnie Graf, Dave Smith and Wilf Sullivan, who all provided wonderful endorsements for the book – thank you for taking the time to read the book prior to publication.

I would also like to thank the many colleagues with whom I've collaborated over the last few decades in research, writing and presentations at conferences and seminars, and whose conversations have helped sharpen my thinking about trade unions and industrial relations in general. In particular, thanks to Gabriella Alberti, Maite Tapia, Janice Fine, Melanie Simms and Ian Greenwood.

I am indebted to the trade unions that have provided access for my research and for all the conversations I've had with trade unionists, both officials and members, who have given their time so freely as we explored the problems facing the labour movements at a time when our neoliberal enemies have been working so hard to undermine our efforts to rebuild power for workers. While many unions have been challenged by a political agenda that has shifted the economic balance of power quite dramatically in favour of capital and have struggled to readjust to the changing nature of work and employment over the last 40 years or so, I firmly believe that there are opportunities for change and a resurgent labour movement. Workers have always fought injustice, and will continue to do so. There are many examples in the current period of unions fighting and winning, and sometimes winning big. Power is not static, it's a relationship that can change in unpredictable ways. We have witnessed the inventiveness of capital in adapting over the last couple of hundreds of years, but we have also seen that it relies on the labour of workers to survive. If there is a willingness to adapt, to strategise and to equip workers with a political education to realise their collective power, I believe there can be a powerful resurgence of worker struggles. I hope my book both adequately conveys this message and acts as a siren call for that change.

What you are running here is not a factory, it is a zoo. But in a zoo there are many types of animals. Some are monkeys who dance on your fingertips, others are lions who can bite your head off. We are the lions, Mr Manager.

(Jayaben Desai, strike leader, Grunwick, 1976)

Rise like lions after slumber
In unvanquishable number!
Shake your chains to earth like dew
Which in sleep had fallen on you
Ye are many – they are few!

(Percy Shelley, The Masque of Anarchy, written following the Peterloo Massacre in Manchester, 1819*)

---

*   In 1819, a crowd of 60,000 women, children and men gathered in Manchester for a peaceful anti-poverty and pro-democracy protest. The event became a massacre when the protest was attacked by armed forces and police on horseback wielding sabres and clubs. The crowd was charged, and 18 people were killed and another 700 seriously injured.

1

Looking to the Past to Understand the Present

> Both the working class and the labour movement ... have been passing
> through a period of crisis, or, if you prefer to be mealy-mouthed about it,
> of adaptation to a new situation.
>
> (Hobsbawm 1978, p. 279)

These are the words of labour historian Eric Hobsbawm in an influential
(and controversial) article called 'The forward march of labour halted?',
drawing from a speech he gave in 1978 in which he discussed the changing
structure of British capitalism in the post-Second World War period and
the detrimental effect it was having upon workers. The same words could
have been written today, except current labour movement analysts would
more likely talk in terms of global capitalism and the widespread neoliberal
hegemony that has curtailed the power of the working class.

Similar words, however, could also have been written in the late eighteenth century, when the Industrial Revolution transformed both the form
and place of work, leaving craft workers facing unemployment. The growth
of a new manual industrial working class at that time was spectacular. It
concentrated workers into factories, mines and mills, such that by the early
1900s over three-quarters of the British labour market was comprised of
industrial manual workers. A consequence of this changing format and
structure of employment was that it facilitated the organisation of these
workers into combines or trade unions, due to their concentration in larger
workplaces and industrial sectors. Alongside this developed a common
understanding of shared interests. There was a strong internal cohesion to
this new working class, an understanding of common everyday experiences,
and shared geographical networks that could be utilised to change their
working lives for the better. Together, this 75 per cent majority of workers
had lots of ideological common ground: they were manual workers with

similar pay and conditions, living in the same communities alongside craft workers and agricultural labourers, they had strong regional similarities with regional accents and support for town football teams – all reinforcing a sense of class identity. And there were the 'others' – the bosses, factory owners and the landed gentry who had a different ideological perspective on how society should be run. People were acutely aware of their class position and on which 'side' they were located. They also recognised the extent to which it mattered to their material conditions.

As Hobsbawm said: 'a century ago the working class was deeply stratified, though this did not prevent it from seeing itself *as a class*' (1978, p. 281; emphasis added). There was, he said, a 'common style of proletarian life' where people were drawn together through a growing class consciousness that had arisen through articulated political demands (e.g. education, health, social security, local government) alongside economic demands for a greater share of the profits from capitalism. Industrial structures were such that workers understood the nature of power and how they could, when combined in unions, re-balance that power in favour of their class and their own material interests. This is why membership of unions grew rapidly in the late nineteenth and early twentieth centuries and workers were able to fight for, and win, better pay and working conditions. One of the key disputes that demonstrated workers' power and gave rise to the growth in union membership was that of the 100,000 dockers who went on strike in 1889 for an increase in pay to 6 pence an hour, which they won. Even if people did not expressly articulate an understanding of power analysis, they knew it was possible to effect change by acting in concert with others.

The advance of the working class, or in Hobsbawm's phrase, the forward march of labour, had begun to slow in the late 1940s/early 1950s. The collective sense of 'us' began to break down or dissipate for a wide range of social, political and economic reasons. Understanding that unionism was for all workers whatever their background or industry (as had been the case in the 1880s period of 'new unionism') had begun to change in the post-war period as the focus on sectional interests became the more dominant practice in some unions. This led to stratification among workers between those who were earning a 'good' industrial wage and who had structural power as a result of their ability to extract concessions from employers by withdrawal of labour (sometimes, if contentiously, referred to as the 'labour aristocracy') and those who had much less, or even no, collective bargaining power.

While these potential power differentials among workers and employers had always existed due to the nature of the work undertaken, there was a widening gap in the post-war period between these two sections of the labour force where different groups of workers were ideologically pitted against each other at the expense of class solidarity (Taylor 2018). Added to this was the simultaneous growth of the 'service sector' or white-collar and professional occupations. The sense of who was included in, or belonged to, 'the working class' was thus beginning to change. A classic example of this is bank workers, once considered a very middle-class profession, but one which has been effectively proletarianised. Importantly, and despite wage/earnings differentials between workers being much narrower in the post-war period than they are today, people began to *feel* differently about class identification. There was an increasing identification with a growing 'middle class', which, in some sense, was more a cultural affinity (Wets 2019), as these 'new' workers didn't have any ownership or control over the means of production. They were still, in Marx's term, members of the proletariat – they owned little more than their ability to sell their labour, but it increasingly mattered that they did not *feel* working-class, that they felt separation from the class.

The conclusion of Hobsbawm's (1978) analysis of the declining power of the union movement and the crisis this created for workers was that, despite the impact of the changing structures of employment being unfavourable to the ability of workers to extract benefits from employers, the labour movement needed to look carefully at its own actions and lack of forward-thinking strategy:

> if the labour and socialist movement is to recover its soul, its dynamism, and its historical initiative … [we need] to recognise the novel situations in which we find ourselves, to analyse it realistically and concretely, to analyse the reasons, historical and otherwise, for the failures as well as the successes of the labour movement, and to formulate not only what we would want to do, but what can be done.
>
> (p. 286)

The aim of this book – some 40 years after Hobsbawm's article was written – is to do just that, and it will begin by doing so in the context of a review of the approaches to organising and revitalisation in the UK union movement over the last 20–30 years.

We will start by highlighting some of the key debates around union renewal and the 'turn to organising' that took place following the instigation by the Trades Union Congress (TUC) of an Organising Academy in 1998 (detail about this will follow later in the book). The aim in establishing a training programme for a new wave of organisers was to kick-start a renewal initiative across unions so that there would be cross-union discussion about strategy and tactics. How this worked in practice has been discussed elsewhere in a review from authors who had followed the Organising Academy's effectiveness over 15 years (Simms et al. 2013), but this book will take a much broader perspective with a focus on the missing element of power. This initial context will help to set the scene to show how narrow the debate around union organising has been, focusing primarily, as it has, on recruitment, tactics and individual campaigns rather than a strategic review of where power lies and how it can be (re-)created. Viewed from this perspective, the trade union and labour movements' approach to organising and union renewal has never seriously considered the potential for *transformational* change through an understanding of, and commitment to building, different concepts of power. There are therefore a number of key questions the book hopes to answer: what strategically, if anything, are unions trying to achieve alongside membership growth, why has organising in the UK not succeeded in revitalising unions, and does unionism in the twenty-first century require a fundamental rethink about the structure and strategy of trade union organising?

This introductory chapter will lay the groundwork to consider these questions, and will also ask what *should* unions be organising for? Is there an alternative vision which at its heart is building the capacity of workers to increase their collective control over the conditions and rewards for their labour? But also, is there a renewed role for trade unions to reconnect with the communities in which their members live? Jane McAlevey (2003) talks about the importance of 'whole worker organising' as a means to build deep solidarity and as a way to embed unionism in the social and cultural arenas of society. It will be argued that the lack of any serious consideration of these last two questions is what has led unions to adopt policies and practices that have, over the last 30 years, largely proven incapable of delivering a strong and growing union movement. The book will draw upon almost 20 years of my research into union organising strategies, but also my own experiences as a union activist. Being part of the labour movement, and at the same time viewing it though an academic lens, has provided an opportunity to combine theory and practice, and to understand how difficult it can be to effect change in large organisations. Undertaking research with a number of unions, and the many conversations and interviews with trade unionists, has allowed for a privileged insight into a wide range of views on organising strategy and tactics at different levels within the organisations, and I am grateful to all who have provided their time so generously.

BRIEF OVERVIEW: KEY DEBATES ABOUT UNION ORGANISING

There have been thousands of academic research papers and books from both scholars and practitioners on the questions of union decline, union organising and efforts to revitalise the union movement (for a series of recent writings that provide an overview of this literature, see Ellem et al. 2019; Heery 2015; Ibsen and Tapia 2017; Kelly 2015; Murray 2017; Simms et al. 2013). Many of these focus on individual case studies as unions seek to implement new tactics to recruit new groups of workers. Others are more concerned with institutional organisational change designed to facilitate innovation in strategic approaches. All tend to have a similar objective: to find out what has worked, what has not and what needs to be done, and these will be considered in more detail in a moment.

The collective data on this topic is vast, yet the union movement is still struggling to adopt an adequate response to the decline in union membership and power. But time is running out. In 2020, trade union membership (6.35 million) in the UK stands at 23.4 per cent of all employees, and collective bargaining, a proxy indicator for union power, is just 26 per cent overall, yet only 14.7 per cent in the private sector where the majority (83.5%) of workers are to be found (Department for Business, Energy & Industrial Strategy 2019). Today, however, with union density so low and bargaining power so weak, unions find it increasing difficult to achieve significant gains on behalf of their members, and in truth, much collective bargaining often takes place in name only. Compare this to 1979, when trade union membership stood at 13.2 million, or 58.3 per cent of all employees, and when the proportion of workers who were covered by collective bargaining agreements was 70 per cent. In just a decade, union membership dropped by

25 per cent (Machin 2000), in part due to the Conservative government's anti-union stance, but also due to more conservative social attitudes and the changing nature of the labour market (Laybourn and Shepherd 2017).

In the post-war period, up until 1979, workers were acutely conscious of the power of unions. Trade union leaders were widely recognisable figures who appeared regularly on the daily news, and were often seen meeting with government ministers. As one commentator explains:

> such were the numbers in the union movement come the 1960s and 1970s that not only were trade union general secretaries household names, but prime ministers, Labour and Conservative, feared and respected them in equal measure. This was the era of 'beer and sandwiches' where governments, unions and employers sat down together to discuss economic matters.
>
> (Gall 2018)

High-profile industrial disputes were then a common occurrence, but these were unlike the more 'symbolic' disputes witnessed today: they were highly visible and often very effective in achieving union demands. To put the changing scale of industrial action into context, the highest annual total for working days lost to strike action was 162.2 million in 1926. This was exceptional, as it was the year of the general strike, but since then:

> there have only been three years when the annual total of working days lost has exceeded 20 million:
>
> - 23.9 million in 1972, due mainly to a strike by coal miners
> - 29.5 million in 1979, due mainly to the so-called 'winter of discontent' (a number of strikes in the public sector in the winter of 1978 to 1979)
> - 27.1 million in 1984, due mainly to a strike by coal miners.
>
> (Office for National Statistics 2019)

Since 2000, the highest annual total of working days lost was 1.4 million in 2011, due mainly to two large public-sector strikes. The latest figures from the Office from National Statistics (2018) are 273,000 working days lost involving 39,000 workers. And of these, 66 per cent of all working days lost to strike action were largely accounted for by university lecturers and professional staff (including myself) striking over detrimental changes to their pensions – a dispute that is still ongoing at the time of writing this book, but one that, as yet, and despite 22 days of discontinuous strike action in 2018–19, did not extract sufficient significant concessions from the employers, and nor did the follow-up 14 days of strikes in 2020, perhaps demonstrating very clearly that associational power is not always sufficient to win industrial disputes.

WHEN UNIONS WERE ABLE TO WIELD POWER:
LOOK BACK IN AWE

So what have been the recent responses from unions in terms of attempts to rebuild and to regain the power that has diminished over the last 40 years, and what have academic studies had to say about the different approaches? Before answering these questions, it's necessary to look back to the time when UK unions were fully aware of their structural power. Much of the effective industrial actions and civil disobedience in the 1960s and 1970s was in opposition to government-imposed incomes policies and attempts to regulate union activities, especially the power of strikes and secondary picketing. In 1969, the then Labour government produced a White Paper (*In Place of Strife*; Castle 1969) setting out a proposal for legislation to replace voluntary collective bargaining with forceful state intervention and a formal system of industrial relations. Government minister Barbara Castle proposed the creation of the Commission on Industrial Relations, giving it legal powers to facilitate improved industrial relations and regulate collective bargaining. This included ballots before undertaking strike action and a 28-day cooling-off period before action could be taken. Further, it gave the government powers to enforce settlements in inter-union disputes and unofficial disputes, and to enforce penalties for non-compliance. Needless to say, the unions were vigorously opposed to any form of intervention in their activity. In the end, that particular legislation was never enacted, as the Labour government lost the general election in 1970.

These failures by Labour and the trade unions to resolve their differences produced a public mood that became hostile to what was seen (or constructed) as abuse of union power – an issue that succeeding Conservative governments from the 1970s onwards exploited. In addition, the media helped to embed this increasingly dominant discourse such that large sections of the working class, and trade union members themselves, adopted this viewpoint. The new incoming Conservative government pledged to challenge union power by introducing the National Industrial Relations Act in 1971, which aimed to regulate strike action through the National Industrial Relations Court (NIRC). The opposition to this in the trade union movement was immense. Many unions refused to co-operate with the legislation, and the TUC called a day of action over the issue, with one union, the Amalgamated Engineering Union, calling 1.5 million of its members out on a one-day strike.

There were also the national miners' strikes of 1972 and 1974 that were significant turning points in attitudes to trade unions and the extent to which they were able to wield power in the future. In 1972, the mineworkers challenged the government's pay restraint and demanded a significant wage increase as they argued their pay had fallen behind that of other workers. The employer, the National Coal Board (NCB), offered an increase of 8 per cent, but this was rejected and a national strike began in January 1972. Using militant tactics by sending pickets from site to site across the country, the miners were able to block the movement of coal to the power stations. A consequence was that the country was faced with electricity power cuts – an issue that focused the minds of the NCB and the government. A crucial point in this dispute was the miners' blockading of the Saltley coke plant in Birmingham. The miners were determined to shut down any fuel depots still supplying industry and the national power grid. They correctly identified this as where their power was strongest. Cutting off fuel supplies would incapacitate the country and force the employer to settle. The local police chief reportedly said any blockade would happen 'over my dead body'. But faced with 30,000 trade union pickets (from a range of unions who were there to support the miners), the police were overwhelmed and the gates to the plant were locked. At that point, the dispute was won – this was working-class power in defiance of the state. By the end of February, the employer capitulated and the miners won and had demonstrated their power: they squeezed over £116 million from their employers and the average miner's earnings rose between 17 and 24 per cent.

But it was the imprisonment of five dockers – 'the Pentonville 5' – who refused a court order to appear before the NIRC in relation to unlawful picketing that led to even more civil disobedience and unrest and the eventual defeat of the Industrial Relations Act in 1974. This event occurred just months after the Saltley gate dispute just mentioned. Beside an ongoing picket of the prison where the five dockers were held, their arrest provoked a wave of strike action in the docks and elsewhere, and the Trades Union Congress general council called a one-day general strike on 31 July 1972. A consequence was that the solicitor general intervened and the dockers were quickly released. As a show of union power, this was highly significant, but for the government it now appeared that unions were above the law, and this reinforced the view that action needed to be taken to restrain the unions. But the 1970s continued to be a period of union militancy, and this strained the union movement's relations with the Conservative government to breaking point.

In 1974 there was another national miners' strike, but this time it brought down the Conservative government. The miners walked out in January that year demanding a 35 per cent pay increase (high inflation and government-imposed wage restraint had seen the pay of workers falling). In December 1973 the government had imposed a three-day working week to conserve energy as a result of the miners' ongoing overtime ban, which had resulted in low coal stocks. The country was in crisis such that two days after the strike started, the prime minister, Edward Heath, called a snap election with the slogan 'Who governs Britain?' It was a call for the electorate to decide where power should lie – with the unions, or with the government and the state. Heath believed that the public would side with the Conservatives on the issues of strikes and union power. However, he lost the election, and the Labour Party was back in government. The unions were awarded a 35 per cent pay increase by the new government, and the strike was called off.

Yet the relationship between the Labour Party and the unions became increasingly acrimonious. The unions initially agreed to work with the government on its economic policy and accepted a voluntary incomes policy in return for increasing public control over the private sector and improvements in social welfare, but this consensus soon broke down as a result of rapidly rising inflation and unemployment. The Labour government tried to control the economy by imposing wage restraint – a limit on the amount employers were able to increase the pay of workers – but also implemented cuts to public expenditure. The unions felt the government had reneged on its commitment to the 'Social Contract', and when inflation overtook wage increases, the unions reasserted their right to free collective bargaining and demanded increases in pay for their members. The result was the onset of the so-called 'Winter of Discontent' in 1979 which saw mass strikes and demonstrations with 1.25 million public-sector workers taking industrial action. This structural power resulted in significant pay increases – up to 25 per cent for some workers.

THE BREAKING OF UNION POWER

Despite these events, such demonstrations of power were not to last much beyond the decade. After the 1979 general election, Margaret Thatcher's promise to reduce the influence of the trade unions began to be implemented, and union membership started to fall. It did so almost continually for the following 40 years, to the extent that today there are only half the numbers there were at the start of the 1980s (with 2.5 million members lost in the first five years of the Thatcher government). Along with a raft of anti-trade union legislation between 1980 and 1993, which included banning secondary action, restricting picketing and the calling of industrial action, and restricting use of the 'check-off' (deduction of union subscriptions by employers), the Conservative government introduced legislation in 1990 and 1992 to abolish the 'closed shop' (an agreement requiring all employees in a workplace to join a union as a condition of their employment). A consequence was that workers now had a choice whether or not to join a union rather than it being a condition of their employment. This meant that workers who didn't join could now 'free-ride' and secure the same benefits from collective bargaining as union members. The perception that unions were dinosaurs, looking to hold on to the past, and were only concerned with sectional interests in contrast to being concerned about all workers – a critique that held some substance – had gained considerable traction (Laybourn and Shepherd 2017). Now, unions needed to appeal to workers who were influenced by these narratives and to try to win them over.

One of the first responses from the UK's trade union federation, the TUC, to the changed political and economic climate of the 1980s was to adopt a new industrial relations approach that recommended dispensing with the type of militancy that had become common in the 1960s and 1970s – flying pickets and mass demonstrations – and looking toward a more collaborative approach with employers and government (Fairbrother and Yates 2003). The notion of partnership was espoused and packaged as the new 'new unionism' (Heery 1996).[1] The feeling was that industrial militancy was having a detrimental impact on the way unions were perceived, and was contributing to an ongoing decline in union membership. It was at the beginning of the Conservative government's anti-trade union onslaught that the TUC adopted what it referred to as 'new realism' in 1983 – a pragmatic approach to new forms of engagement with employers, or as one writer commented, a 'capitulation to employer strategies' (Stirling 2005, p. 46) – and later looked toward labour–management partnership deals via the establishment of the Partnership Institute in 2001. The thinking was that given the ascendency of capital and its ability to rebalance the rate of exploitation in the favour of employers, and the resulting weakening of labour power (perceived to be as a result of globalisation and the opening up of financial markets), unions needed to move beyond adversarial industrial relations. In a number of cases, and in order to survive, unions had become 'increasingly dependent on their ability to engage in cooperative industrial relations with employers' (Kelly and Badigannavar 2011, p. 6). The partnership approach thus rejected adversarialism and mobilisation in exchange for dialogue and co-operation. The extent to which this was to provide a way forward for trade unions was a topic of extensive debate and research.

The two authors just mentioned asked whether or not labour–management partnership really would help unions to revive their membership strength, and they compared this approach with the contrasting 'organising model' approach, which was simultaneously adopted by the TUC when it established the Organising Academy in 1998. The organising approach stems from a belief that rank-and-file workers need to be actively engaged in building the union from the bottom up, often using radical tactics to encourage people into membership and force the employer to recognise the union (Heery et al. 2000a; 2000c). Running these two very ideologically different and contrasting strategies side-by-side perhaps suggests there wasn't consensus among the TUC affiliated unions about which was the best way forward in terms of union revitalisation (Heery 2002). These conflicting approaches to union strategy were also reflected and debated in the many academic writings on this topic (Danford et al. 2002; Heery 2002; Kelly 1999; McIlroy 2008; Terry 2003).

The pro-partnership strategy stems from a belief that hostile employers make union organising more difficult, thus a more conciliatory and collaborative approach to the employment relationship could lead to less hostility, and perhaps membership growth. This resonates with research that shows that employer hostility is a significant factor determining the confidence of workers to unionise (Dundon 2002; Murphy 2016). A body of literature argues that given the weakness of unions, there is little option other than to follow the partnership model, and case study examples are provided to show how this can work in practice (Geary and Trif 2011; Johnstone and Wilkinson 2016). However, partnership will only work in situations where there is already a degree of receptiveness, as truly hostile employers are unlikely to engage voluntarily unless they are forced to by powerful unions. Even militant or radical unions would probably accept that collective bargaining 'wins' often involve at least some element of mutual gains or integrative bargaining strategies – through a form of labour–management cooperation, if not 'partnership' itself. There is a view that an organising approach needs to precede partnership to be effective, and as such:

> organizing to build membership strength is a precondition for a meaningful partnership, either formally, in the recognition agreement itself, or informally through 'integrative' bargaining post-recognition. According to this view, it is only when the union bargains from a position of strength rather than weakness that the 'mutual gains' of labour–management cooperation are likely to materialize.
>
> (Kelly and Badigannavar 2011, p. 10)

These authors found that 'union representatives in partnership workplaces were more likely to report management indifference to the union and an unwillingness to engage in meaningful negotiations' (Kelly and Badigannavar 2011, p. 21), perhaps showing the ineffectiveness of unions when the balance of power is not in their favour. Another more biting critique has stated: 'the partnership route offers no guarantees for UK trade unions and may well constitute a dangerous approach' (Terry 2003, p. 504), by which it's meant that unions risk losing independence and autonomy and perhaps become weaker still (Jenkins 2007).

While the partnership approach was perhaps an acknowledgement of the lack of union strength, and a pragmatic attempt to stop further decline, it failed to think through the fundamental issue in the employment relationship in the adoption of this method – that of power and its imbalance between the parties. There are examples of progressive employers embracing trade union voice and a pluralist approach, but in the main, capitalism is about extracting the greatest profit at the expense of workers, and to do that, employers are generally reluctant to willingly concede the power they hold. Understanding this point perhaps helps explain the limitation of partnership as a way of revitalising the labour movement. Indeed, it might actually further its decline as unions come to be seen as instruments of management. Other approaches include organising as a way of reigniting grassroots activism in unions – finding the issues around which workers have the greatest concerns, then providing them with the tools and tactics to engage with their fellow workers to collectivise and to take action. The writing on this topic, from both academics and practitioners, is vast, from journal articles to books to instruction manuals, and there is lots of common ground as well as much disagreement on tactics, or even what constitutes 'organising'. Given this, there isn't the space here to do justice to the nuances in the many debates on the topic – readers who are interested in the detail have plenty of scope to read more widely on this topic (Ibsen and Tapia 2017; Murray 2017; Simms et al. 2013). But it is useful nevertheless to highlight some of the key issues.

Firstly, there was a view that unions would not spontaneously grow. Unionisation campaigns in new workplaces needed kick-starting, and this needed to be done by organisers being sent in by unions to 'educate, agitate and organise'. The Employment Relations Act of 1999 introduced by the new Labour government brought in a statutory right to union recognition for collective bargaining where a majority of workers in a proposed bargaining unit are in favour (Brown et al. 2001). It was felt that this would be a springboard to further union organising campaigns resulting in increased membership for the movement. New industries were going to be organised not on the basis of workplace militancy, but on the basis that unions – whether operating a partnership model or not – would have a legal right to recognition and the membership dues that came along with it from servicing members by dealing with grievances and disciplinary actions etc. Five years after the Act was introduced there were almost 3,000 new recognition deals (and 128 de-recognition cases) with employers, and although this resulted in around 846,000 new union members (Gall 2006, p. 15), 42,000 were lost through de-recognition, and the growth in numbers tailed off drastically after this period, so it was never the magic bullet for renewal some may have imagined (Gall 2007). Similarly, it was argued that the Union Learning Fund – a scheme introduced by the government in 1998 to encourage workplace learning – could contribute to revitalisation by enhancing relationship-building with members, potential members, employers and government (Findlay and Warhurst 2011). Yet despite claims by unions that the union learning has increased union membership (Stuart et al. 2010), there has been little empirical evidence to demonstrate these claims apart from in a few small-scale examples (Heyes 2009).

A SHIFT TOWARD AN ORGANISING APPROACH

Organising, however, was a major initiative introduced to facilitate union renewal, and was central to TUC strategy in 1997:

> New Unionism aims to put the drive for membership growth at the top of unions' agenda and create a new organising culture. ... A shift in the power imbalance between employers and workers through the creation of new rights will help too. But ultimately there will need to be a significant and sustained investment of resources – finance and people – if unions are to make a lasting impression.
>
> (Healey and O'Grady 1997, p. 176)

It involved the establishment of an organising training programme and expressly required a more diverse range (than was then the case) of new union officials to be recruited and trained in practices associated with the, perhaps ill-defined 'organising model' of trade unionism. The belief was that organisers needed to look (and behave) more like the workers they were hoping to recruit. The TUC led on this initiative by establishing the Organising Academy in 1998. Academic and practitioner interest in this strategy was intense (for an overview of this literature, see Kelly and Frege 2004; Simms et al. 2013). Decades of research followed, analysing every aspect of policy, practice and resulting gains (and losses) from the approach. Individual unions were scrutinised and case studies were picked apart to evaluate which aspects of organising tactics were working and which weren't.

In short, much of the debate has been quite narrowly defined around tactics and impact, not just upon 'wins' (however these are defined – whether this is in terms of union recognition or, more importantly, in terms of actual material gains for employees), but also the extent to which organising has created change within the unions themselves (Heery et al. 2000b; Simms and

Holgate 2010b). Most of the literature and research has tended to focus on the tactics of organising rather than its strategic vision, politics or its potential for transformative change, and it's this approach that has led to a focus on recruitment and membership growth, rather than an analysis of where different forms of power lie and what that means for building the capacity of workers to increase their collective control over their employment conditions and rewards for their labour. As Simms and Holgate (2010a) note:

> organising has, perhaps understandably given the level of unionisation, been talked about in terms of membership growth, renewal or revitalisation, with little common agreement of what is meant by these terms and no common understanding of where a cultural shift towards a 'new' organising agenda might lead the union movement.
>
> (p. 158)

In a word, the vision was limited. Instead of envisaging transformational change to shift power and renew the union movement, many leaders were concerned with a cost-benefit analysis of whether the investment in organising was paying off in terms of membership gains. While clearly an important consideration, this narrow perspective on organising resulted quite quickly in a shift from organising to recruitment. The distinction here is important – especially in relation to power.

As already mentioned, deep and transformative organising is about building capacity and self-reliance among workers so they are able to use their own agency to effect change through collective action – or at least the credible threat of it. Holgate et al. (2018) define deep organising as a process that:

> involves engaging and activating people who may not initially agree but who, through a process of collective organizing and the development of grassroots leaders, begin to self-identify as part of a community with a shared objective in seeking to challenge injustice.
>
> (p. 600)

This latter point about identifying as a workplace community that has shared objectives is key in distinguishing different levels of commitment from members to their union, and the extent to which they are passive or active within the union. Those who are 'organised' on the basis of an instrumentalist approach – i.e. 'What can the union do for you?' – tend to see the union as a service provider when there is a problem in the workplace. Central to a *deep* form of organising is that workers increase their numbers by recruiting their colleagues to become active to increase the potential for power. Recruitment on its own (which, confusingly, is also sometimes referred to as 'organising') – just signing up new members on the basis of individual instrumentalism, but not engaging them in the process contributing to changing their material circumstances through collective action – leaves them passive and largely ineffectual, and perhaps even vulnerable to anti-union sentiments. They then become members who expect a service from their union when they find they have a problem at work, which in turn requires greater resources from the union, leaving little time for union organising for union renewal. This has led to the many debates about 'servicing' versus 'organising' (i.e. whether one or the other, or both, are necessary). While this debate has lost focus and is unresolved, the distinction between the two was used to argue explicitly that 'organising' was necessary for union renewal, and that this couldn't occur through recruitment alone.

While it is evident that the TUC's initiative resulted in a 'turn to organising' for a number of affiliated trade unions, and it's undoubtedly the case that union membership would have declined much further had organising not taken place, it hasn't been the panacea that was hoped for. It's argued here that this is because the 'organising model' was largely a toolbox of tactics focusing primarily on recruitment and individual campaigns, rather than a strategic review of where power lies and how it can be (re-)created. In the main, organising was reduced to an attempt to grow membership to improve the financial stability of unions. This way of thinking about organising and union renewal never seriously considered the potential for *transformational* change. Without a focus on power – the essential factor needed for workers to effect change to improve their terms and conditions of employment – unions have adopted policies and practices that have proven incapable of delivering a strong and growing union movement.

There are a number of questions to consider at the end of this chapter: What should unions be organising for if they wish to remain relevant over the next couple of decades? Is there an alternative vision of the labour movement which is about building the capacity of workers to increase their collective control over the conditions and rewards for their labour? If so, what is this, and is it possible? These questions are unanswerable without a proper understanding of power and its different forms. The next chapter will explore this issue by looking at different conceptualisations of power and how these apply to the union movement and the way it operates (or needs to operate) in a labour market of increasing precarity where many workers are unsure who actually employs them – or whether they are 'employed' at all.

2

Let's Talk about Social Power

The workers' strategies constructed in the industrial age have been under-mined not because globalisation has eviscerated labor power but because it weakened old labor strategies and spurred aggressive new elite strate-gies with which labor has yet to cope.

(Fox Piven and Cloward 2000, p. 414)

The quote above highlights that the loss of worker power is not an inevita-ble consequence of globalisation and the neoliberal agenda that has been in ascendancy for the last 50 years. Workers and trade unions remain active agents capable of effecting change. Workers have the potential for power, even if not yet realised, because capital and employers depend upon them. The key issue emphasised by these two labour scholars is that too often the strategies deployed today are formed out of past conflicts by leaders and organisations that have 'cultural memory and habits' carried over from previous struggles or even different times. That they might have been suc-cessful in the different circumstances of the past, and led to great wins being achieved, doesn't necessarily mean those strategies are appropriate to the changed industrial climate of today. Understanding the nature of the power resources available, and their application in industrial disputes, is essential when fighting to win:

The forging of new repertoires of struggle is always uncertain and con-tingent, depending as it does on agency as much as the unfolding of institutional trends. Still, it just may be that this is not the end but the beginning of a new era of labor power.

(Fox Piven and Cloward 2000: 427)

While this view might be considered overly optimistic given the perilous state of much of today's labour movements, some groups of the most precarious of workers are still managing to win concessions despite their seemingly weak bargaining power in certain sections of the labour market (Staton 2020). If workers are to enter a new era of labour power, they will need a much deeper understanding of the conceptualisation of power and its different forms – only then will they be able to adapt organising tactics and strategies that utilise this power to win their demands. But before we consider this point, let's think about why people don't act when their interests are not met: what holds people back from demanding a fair share? Workers are, after all, in the majority – employers are few in comparison – so, on a simplistic level, if all workers walked off the job, then employers could not function without them, and business would come to a halt. But, in the main, this doesn't happen. Insufficient confidence, fear and the lack of alternative conceptual frameworks hold people back. The internalisation of dominant values, or norms, can shape people's awareness and ultimate understanding of policies, practices and legal rights and prevent critical consideration of alternative ways of being.

CONTROL THROUGH IDEOLOGY

Antonio Gramsci, the Italian Marxist, posed this rhetorical question on the importance of independent critical thinking and the impact this has on a person's ability to act:

> Is it better to work out consciously and critically one's own conception of the world and thus, in connection with the labours of one's own brain, choose one's sphere of activity, take an active part in the creation of the history of the world, be one's own guide, refusing to accept passively and supinely from outside the moulding of one's own personality?
>
> (Antonio Gramsci, in Crehan 2002, p. 81)

Yet, for many, there is a taken-for-granted, or unchallenged, understanding of the way the world works – a 'natural' order of doing things that is learnt and deeply embedded in ideology. Gramsci explains this through his notion of ideological hegemony, the idea that sometimes control can be achieved through consent rather than force, and this is possible because what is sometimes referred to as 'invisible' power is constituted in the realm of ideas and knowledge. The famous quote from Marx expresses this well:

19

The ideas of the ruling class are in every epoch the ruling ideas, i.e. the class which is the ruling material force of society, is at the same time its ruling intellectual force. The class which has the means of material production at its disposal, has control at the same time over the means of mental production, so that thereby, generally speaking, the ideas of those who lack the means of mental production are subject to it. The ruling ideas are nothing more than the ideal expression of the dominant material relationships, the dominant material relationships grasped as ideas.

(Marx 1977, p. 176)

This contributes to our first consideration of one aspect of social power (ideological power), which is that workers – as well as employers, the state, the education system and the media – combine to produce a set of beliefs that express particular sets of power relations. These ideological power relations operate in social networks, in discourse, in culture, and are played out in actions. They position people in hierarchies of power – some in places of security and wealth, and others in poverty and precarity. The power of ideology is therefore strong and controlling, derived from within individuals, as well as being reinforced by outside influences in wider society. As such, sometimes people are unaware of their own true interests (the power of the unquestioned), and they become implicated in the system that exploits them; they become grateful, they get a wage, a chance to earn a living, and the price of this is subjugation – a phenomenon that has been well documented in racial or imperial contexts. Control over the ideological apparatus by the groups just mentioned is important in securing acceptance of a particular social and political order – it's the way the ruling class secures consent, and why workers often feel they don't have the right, or the power, or the understanding, to effect change that would benefit their material conditions.

This is not to say that people are unable to resist the ideological power of rulers by developing their own frames of reference; they can, and have done this repeatedly over time. Sometimes this is done by workers in subtle or covert ways, for example through sabotage, theft or slow-downs, or it might be expressed overtly through strikes or other forms of industrial action, which can be costly. They can be smart in figuring out the cost-benefits of non-cooperation with employers, and if they feel, instinctively or expressly, that the balance of power is not in their favour, then they may be more reluctant than they otherwise would be to take action. The power of ideology is often in inverse relation to workers' self-organisation, because when workers combine, they will likely generate alternative narratives that redefine the notion of 'us' and 'them'. In doing so, their struggles will often create a powerful alternative to the erstwhile 'dominant' narratives. But let's pause here and take a step back to define what is meant by power by considering its different forms, and how it might be deployed for the benefit of workers and their collective organisations.

HOW DO WE THINK ABOUT POWER
IN THE EMPLOYMENT RELATIONSHIP?

Robert Dahl (1957) explains power in this way: A has power over B to the extent that A can get B to do something B would otherwise not do. This simple definition of power hides its complex nature and the various forms it takes. But it does establish that conflict is part and parcel of power relationships. A (or let's name it by a source of power we know well – the employer) has the ability through influence, authority, coercion, force or manipulation to get B (workers) to accept a course of action, a rate for the job or set of instructions either against their will when they are coerced, or because they have been persuaded that the instructions are 'reasonable'. In the absence of brute force, they may comply, either because the employer has created or reinforced social and political values and/or institutional practices (i.e. they are manipulated to acquiesce against their own self-interest), or they feel powerless in the face of authority.

We are made aware by Kathy Davis's work on gender and power that power is both enabling and constraining. For example, sanctions can be applied to force people to do things they would not choose to do, but also rewards within the control of power holders can be used as a form of inducement to get people to do what is wanted. Davis notes that 'any analysis of power, then, will entail sorting out both of these dimensions and how power is connected to constraint and enablement in specific instances of social interaction' (1991, p. 74). It is this social interaction which is central to understanding power. Power is a relationship. It is at the same time a dialectical relationship whereby opposing forces are required to work together. The parties in power relationships are not equal, they compete for control over the resources at their disposal, but their relationship is reciprocal, by which it is meant that

21

there is autonomy and dependence on both sides. While one side might have more power, it seldom has total power. There is generally a sharing of power (however unbalanced), which means the least powerful have, given the right circumstances, the ability to act to alter the power relationship. In the example of ideology above, we can understand power as the capacity to influence judgement. To have power is to have control over others, and by its nature it is asymmetrical, which is why in common parlance (and especially in the employment relationship) we talk about 'the balance of power'. Steven Lukes (2004, p. 70) writes about the power as a 'potentiality', by which he means it's possible to *have* latent power, but not necessarily the ability to *exercise* power: 'power is a capacity, and not the exercise or vehicle of that capacity'. For example, having the *means* of power is not, claims Lukes, the same as being powerful. In many cases, employers don't need to demonstrate power; they are automatically assumed to have power as that is what workers are educated to believe, and what experience teaches us. It has been built into common understandings of what is 'right', or what Gramsci refers to as 'common sense', through both our practical experience and the existence of rules and procedures (Crehan 2016).

Bertrand Russell explains that what he terms 'traditional power' resides in some organisations, and this is often perceived to be more benign than newly acquired power because it is accepted as 'part of the rules of the game': 'where ancient institutions persist, the injustices to which holders of power are always prone to have the sanction of immemorial custom' (Russell 1986, p. 19). As such, power in this sense can be understood as being either authoritarian or paternalistic. It arises through the establishment of status and deference and, at least on the surface, is not contested, and has the capacity to influence judgement by convincing the oppressed that their grievances are illegitimate. Power need not be exercised (or even displayed) to have an effect. There can be times where there is no *observable* evidence of its existence, yet it can still be present and pervasive. As Lukes (2004, p. 1) noted, 'power is at its most effective when least observable'. Because the value frames with which people view the world are enforced or policed through ideology, power in the hand of superiors is considered legitimate and reasonable, which is why workers often unquestioningly accept rules, policies and taken-for-granted day-to-day practices (including their pay and other terms of the contract of employment).

Gramsci (1971) says that it is only at times of crisis, when control through such hegemonic structures fails, that power is exercised directly, and forcefully, in order to restore control. This was to be seen most starkly during the UK's 1984–85 miners' strike in the police brutality meted out to pickets and their supporters. Reflecting on what happened at 'the battle of Orgreave' on 18 June 1984, 30 years later, newspaper reports suggest that the violence from the state was orchestrated in advance. Four and a half thousand police officers from different forces nationwide were there to police the 8,000 workers picketing at the coking plant. It was claimed by union officials that what happened was a planned operation to crush the strike, and this seems to be corroborated by at least one police officer who said the plan was to inflict a significant defeat on the miners (Conn 2012). The police are rarely perceived as being a paramilitary presence in communities, but when 'the gloves are off', they can exercise brutal violence on behalf of the state. An ITV News journalist who witnessed the events at Orgreave that day reported:

> The scenes there were reminiscent of the English Civil War and, in some senses, it was an ugly, bloody skirmish in another civil war. Had the miners succeeded in shutting down the coking plant they might have prolonged the dispute; they might even have gone on to win. It was a decisive battle neither side could afford to lose but the government of Margaret Thatcher won and the NUM [National Union of Mineworkers] didn't. As Michael Mansfield QC said: 'They wanted to teach the miners a lesson – a big lesson, such that they wouldn't come out in force again.'
>
> (Stewart 2016)

This was an extreme case of control and expression of power by violent means. The miners had recent memory of being able to shift the balance of power in their favour from two significant disputes in the 1970s, but not all workers had this degree of militancy and class understanding that would have enabled them to challenge the dominant ideology of subservience. While some workers may reject management's right to issue directions and the ideological control that is held over them, and while this perhaps leads to resentment, it doesn't automatically lead to workers taking action to change their circumstances and to challenge the balance of power in the employment relationship. In order for that to happen, workers need to be able to articulate their dissatisfaction as collective interests – views also held by their colleagues – and to have a process to be able to frame the discontent as not only legitimate, but in such a way that it is attributed directly to managers or employers (on mobilisation theory and the factors necessary for workers to move into action, see Kelly 1998). When this occurs, leaders, however defined, in the workplace are able to put forward a counter-hegemonic and direct challenge to the ideological power of the employer. Whether or not this encourages workers to take action then depends on an assessment by those workers of the effectiveness of that action, for example through strikes, slow-downs or work to rules. An unspoken or even subconscious 'risk register' may include a calculation of possible financial and personal costs – including whether action will make the workplace a more or less attractive place to work – but also consideration of the danger of counter-mobilisation and the economic power of the employer. In these circumstances, when workers do decide to collectively reject the authority of their employer and refuse to comply with instructions, then the fight begins and there's a direct challenge to the balance of power in the employment relationship. Until then:

> One man has another in his power when he holds him in bonds: when he has disarmed him and deprived him of the means of self-defence or escape; when he has inspired him with fear, or when he has bound him so closely by a service that he would rather please his benefactors than himself, and rather be guided by his benefactor's judgement than by his own.
>
> (Spinoza 1677, quoted in Lukes 2004, p. 86)

IDEOLOGY, POLITICAL CONSCIOUSNESS AND POWER

In order to change the balance of power between bosses and workers, there is a need for a political or class consciousness among the latter group that can provide people with the confidence to act to change their circumstances. By analysing the power structures that hold them in bonds and finding weak points of resistance, workers are able to overcome the apathy, inertia and fatalism that prevents them from taking action. Political education is central to this, not necessarily in a formal classroom sense, but education that arises from real-life examples of where the dominant ideology has led to real injustice or where collective struggles have met with success. Politics and education provide legitimacy, confidence and the tools to understand what actions are necessary for change to occur. As Wrong (1979, p. 13) has said: 'politics includes both a struggle *for* power and a struggle to limit, resist and escape *from* power' (emphasis added). Breaking the dead weight of coercive ideology is a prerequisite for collective resistance as it creates the potential for the asking and answering of new questions, and allows for an understanding on the part of these workers themselves of how power can shape the participation of those who may have thought they were relatively powerless.

In order for workers to successfully challenge holders of power, there is a need to interrupt the process of internalisation of powerlessness that stops people from taking action to change their circumstances. There is a dialectical inter-relationship between consciousness and participation: participation *leads* to consciousness, but also participation is a *result* of consciousness. But previous defeats, fatalism and passivity can lead to quiescence. Although workers have seen and experienced struggles failing, and the 1984–85 year-long miners' strike is one such infamous and tragic example, these defeats can feed into a belief of powerlessness; although the individual memory of this defeat may not loom large in the personal consciousness of those under the age of 50, the institutional memory of these events, and other notable defeats (e.g. at Grunwick, Warrington and Wapping)[1] is probably still present in the memories of those in leadership positions of today's unions. This particular example – the 1984–85 miners' strike – felt for many like an attack on the soul and confidence of the UK trade union movement. The once mighty power of the mineworkers, as shown in the 1972 and 1974 strikes (and outlined in Chapter 1), was no more. The union was crushed and its power dissipated. Many workers felt that if these strongly collectivised workers who had brought down the government could be defeated, what hope was there for the rest of the working class? Such an internalisation of the powerlessness of the oppressed is an ideology that drives fatalism and passivity. It then becomes more difficult to challenge managerial prerogative, the dominant ideology of the state and the views held in wider society.

Yet power is not static nor one-dimensional. The relationships of power can be subject to change depending on social, political and economic circumstances. This is the pattern of history, but it's also a guide to the present and the future as workers learn to change their circumstances and rebalance power relationships. The labour movement was once strongly committed to the value of providing political education as a means of developing critical thinking to challenge these dominant ruling-class ideas in society (Bridgford and Stirling 1988; Fisher 2005). Unfortunately, this type of worker education has, to all intents and purposes, been abandoned by the UK trade union movement (Bridgford and Stirling 1988; Ross 2012; Seal 2017), and without this, there are fewer ways in which learning can take place to contest the structures of ideological domination that hold workers down.

Political education is a way to challenge ideologies that divide workers and prevent them realising their power, and it is often key to levels of participation in workers' struggles as it can provide the development of different frames of reference that help convince people there are alternative forms of action workers can take to rebalance or change the power relationship in which they find themselves.

If we accept that power is integral to all social interactions and is also intrinsic to human agency (i.e. what we do and how we do it), then we need to figure out, by undertaking a process of practical power analysis, how relationships of dependency and autonomy work in society – whether this be in the workplace (between bosses and workers) or the wider communities in which workplaces are located. This we will come back to later, but before that, let us consider other sources and uses of power and how they are used to control workers, but also how they can be challenged by workers.

POWER RESOURCES AND WORKERS

We have already established that power does not exist *in and of itself* – it is manifest or brought into being through the economic, political and ideological relationships between classes, groups or individuals. As such, power can be realised in different ways through various forms of control. Ideological influence has already been discussed, absorbed as it is through education, lived experience, dominant narratives and the media, but we can also explore the control of information as a source of power in ways specifically relevant to workers and their place in the employment relationship. 'Knowledge is power' is a phrase commonly used: the ability to constrain access to sources of information is important not only in maintaining hegemony, but also, if employers are able to restrict access to information, they can use this to advance a particular cause, or form of action, or it can be used to attack or defend a particular status quo. When employers deny workers access to information, this reduces the ability of employees, and their unions, to challenge specific decisions that are detrimental to terms and conditions of employment. If workers and their representatives have limited or no access to information about how an employer is functioning, or why it is making decisions, then the potential power of workers will also be limited. When employers decide to make redundancies or refuse a pay increase or decide to reduce the terms and conditions of employment, the reasons are often presented as necessary for the effectiveness or survival of the business. Sometimes they may be, but other times they are about increasing the profit for the owners, or ensuring a more quiescent workforce. The control of information thus provides employers with a means of power to minimise or nullify dissent.

When the UK government introduced the European Union's Information and Consultation of Employees Regulations in 2005, which marginally improved upon previous legislation,[2] this was hailed by the Trades Union Congress as a great step forward enabling workers to have access to employer information on a range of topics, including a business's economic situation, its employment prospects and decisions that were likely to lead to substantial changes in work organisation or contractual relations. Needless to say, the response from employers and their organisations was less favourable, and they opposed the introduction of this legislation (Hall 2005). Perhaps understandably, the employer body the Confederation of British Industry was concerned to defend the power of employers, recognising that this comprehensive statutory framework giving employees the right to be informed and consulted by their employers on a range of key business, employment and restructuring issues could reduce this particular source of power for employers.

Let's also not forget the power the state holds in relation to its citizens. While it could be argued that globalisation of financial wealth has weakened this form of power, nevertheless the police, courts and legislature – all arms of the state – are still able to control or limit the actions of people and organisations. In the employment context, labour law is the main area of legislation that regulates the relations between employers, workers and trade unions. For most of the twentieth century, the UK had a mainly voluntarist system of employment relations (Heery 2011). This meant that the regulation of the employment relationship was supposedly based on mutual trust, largely enabling trade unions and employees to regulate their own relations without interference from the state or other public bodies. Free collective bargaining between the parties, through negotiation and established proce- dures and rules, was the dominant process of dispute resolution. This was the preferred method for most trade unions and for many employers. While it wasn't the case that there was always a 'hands off' approach to the state's involvement in the employment relationship, intervention was relatively minor until the 1960s and 1970s, when the voluntarist approach came under challenge. But it wasn't until the election of Margaret Thatcher in 1979 that this system began to be dismantled.

Through a raft of labour law over successive parliaments, the Conserva- tive Party sought to shift the balance of power away from workers and over to employers and the state. This was done by the dismantling of statutory support for collective bargaining, which had been one of the functions of a government body, the Advisory, Conciliation and Arbitration Service. Other changes to labour law introduced by the Conservatives from 1979 until the Labour party was elected in 1997 included the outlawing of com- pulsory union membership – the 'closed shop', whereby union membership was a condition of employment – and the promotion of non-unionism. It restricted the legitimacy of industrial action and increased penalties for unlawful action. Social security measures that provided a basic income floor when wages were lost through strike action were withdrawn, as were the protections afforded by individual employment rights, which were seen as placing unacceptable burdens on business – for example, the scope of unfair dismissal legislation was reduced and the qualifying time extended. And finally, there was intervention in union activity through the regula- tion of internal union government. Altogether, the aim was to enhance and extend managerial prerogatives, to increase the relative power of employers and to further reduce that of workers (Dickens 2008). As Margaret Thatcher put it: 'We must neglect no opportunity to erode trade union membership wherever this corresponds to the wishes of the workforce. We must see to it our new legal structure discourages trade union membership of the new industries' (Downing Street papers 1983).

'Money is power' – a phrase that sums up what control can be exercised by those holding the purse strings. Disparities in wealth have always provided those with money with the possibility of influence over others, but the widening gap between rich and poor has created a huge chasm, with those at the bottom feeling they have very little ability to change their circumstances. The financial power of huge transnational companies is, in this current era, immense – often surpassing that of nation states. This means that companies are able to override or influence government regulations, avoid taxes, set their own standards and determine the working conditions of people across the world. This power can be exercised by creating bogus systems of employment ('self-employment'), complex supply chains and umbrella companies to complicate and confuse workers as to whom their grievances should be targeted against. In 2020, Halliburton, the global mining and energy company, reported a gross income revenue of $14 billion. Apple, the global electronics company, dwarfed Halliburton's figure by grossing $275 billion in the same year. Yet both of these companies seem like small fry compared to the global retail chain, Walmart, which made a $524 billion profit in 2020. Such companies are powerful. They can control markets, politicians, consumers and, of course, the workers they either employ or control through supply chains:

> The transnationalisation, or de-nationalisation, of production and finance has created new and growing opportunities for firms to shift production, participate in complex global value chains that are difficult to regulate, and circumvent state attempts to regulate and tax corporate activities. As a result, big business has developed a profound structural power position on the global scale. This implies a permanent transformation of the relations between state and capital, especially in international politics. State and corporate power are no longer exclusively exercised in the iron cage of the nation state, but in the overarching sphere of global capitalism.
>
> (Babic et al. 2017, p. 21)

The mechanisms of nation states, or transnational bodies like the United Nations, or the International Labour Organisation (ILO), become impotent when faced with the huge power of these huge organisations. The corresponding transnational bodies of labour – the global union federations – have been similarly ineffective in challenging these global corporations. As one writer has commented, this shift in power has created a 'global governance gap that defies standard and simple solutions' (Ruggie 2018, p. 329). As discussed above, the *modus operandi* of these mega-corporations helps to consolidate power in the hands of employers and weakens the challenges from workers. Yet as long as workers are oppressed and feel aggrieved and exploited, they retain the latent power, either when pushed too far or because of a change in consciousness, to react. This will either be spontaneous or planned, through organised labour machinery or not, but at some point, workers figure out that collectively they *do* have the power to challenge the bosses. At this point, workers will likely take action, whether this is through the withdrawal of labour, through sabotage, through slow-downs, through reputational damage to the company or by some other means, but when they decide not to submit to being humiliated any longer, that's when they will begin to assert their power. The next section will take a look at the different forms of power available to workers and the strategies they can apply in using that power.

WORKERS' USE OF POWER

Workers increase their power by combining with their work colleagues to take action to change the exploitative circumstances in which they find themselves. This *associational power* is at the heart of what trade unions are about. Simply defined, it is the capacity of union members and their leaders to act collectively. It also includes the 'various forms of power that result from the formation of collective organisation of workers' (Wright 2000, p. 962). By acting in concert, the members of a union are able to challenge the power of employers. It's the realisation by workers that they have *strategic capacity* – through their own actions – that makes the union powerful, not merely the existence of collectivism itself. Unions need to be able to develop and implement tactics and strategies that have the support of the members, because without the latter, 'members can be an obstacle to their own union' (Ellem et al. 2019) through their passivity, their lack of confidence, or because of an unsupportive leadership.

Union density – the percentage of a workforce that are union members – is often used as a proxy for associational power, but as one author notes, it:

> fails to inform us about three crucial things: the relative strength of any given group within unions, the ability of this group to use the trade union power, and the extent to which union members belonging to the group would advance the interests of the entire group by using this power.
>
> (Koçer 2018: 153)

Density is thus a weak predictor of associational power in particular work-places or sectors. It does not even tell us how strongly the members identify with their union. Other more useful measures, depending on specific cir-cumstances, could include total membership in particular areas, number of active union representatives, and their strategic capacity for mobilising members, bargaining success and industrial action, as well as the implemen-tation of strategic plans; political influence and bargaining power, and the extent to which unions are able to build coalitions with other social justice organisations (Kelly 2015). So, by combining together in unions, workers have taken the important first – but certainly not the last – step to develop the capacity to express or realise the opportunities to alter the power rela-tionship between themselves and their employer. The fact that employers and workers rely on each other in different ways (employers need people to perform tasks, and workers need to earn money to survive) binds them together in a dynamic and dialectical relationship. Marissa Brookes, in her work on union organising, argues that 'these two factors – workers' embed-dedness and employers' dependence – interact to produce three other types of labor power: structural power, institutional power, and coalitional power' (2019, p. 17).

Once the basis of associational power (which includes working in coali-tions) is understood, it allows for consideration of what other forms of power resources are available, and how they can be used to the benefit of workers. *Structural power* arises from the position of workers in the economic system; it's their ability to bargain in the labour market and workplace (Silver 2003). This could be as a result of a particular body of knowledge, skill or under-standing being scarce and in demand in the labour market – when this is the case workers and unions have leverage to claim higher wages for their labour. Or it could be that certain types of work are grounded in place – or what geographers refer to as 'spatially fixed' (Herod 1997; 1998). When this is the case, it helps to increase the structural power of workers, as what they do can't easily be off-shored.

In the workplace, the labour process can be disrupted by workers with-drawing their labour or creating stoppages or slow-downs. Workers are embedded in complex employment practices, and while this creates struc-tural power for employers, it does so for workers as well. It should be noted, however, that structural power cannot be disconnected from associational power, and vice versa. If unions have strong associational power – high union membership and density – this does not necessarily mean they also have structural power. An example of weak structural power might be a union organising homeworkers across a city where there is an oversupply of labour; the union has managed to get a significant membership of home-workers, but doesn't have a central employer with which to bargain, and instead is faced with scores of small traders which can take the work else-where. In contrast, in places where just-in-time production is dominant (e.g. car plants) or where products have a short shelf life (e.g. fruit and vegeta-bles), it may take only small numbers of workers who are, perhaps, without strong associational power to shut down production by utilising their struc-tural power of disruption. Some commentators have argued that one of the main factors contributing to union decline from the 1970s onwards has been the diminishing structural power of workers that has resulted from neoliberalism and financialisation, and has helped to weaken market-based bargaining power (Schmalz et al. 2018).

Another form of power resource available to workers is *institutional power*. This is the capacity to hold employers to account through laws and regulations at transnational, national and local levels. These might include ILO conventions, social dialogue procedures, labour legislation, and work-place rules and procedures. As discussed earlier, in the past, the UK's system of industrial relations was based on voluntarism – where state interven-tion was minimal. Yet, since the 1960s, this approach gave way to a rapid increase in the introduction of labour law. While some of this was restrictive to trade union operations, other pieces of legislation provided positive indi-vidual (and collective) employment rights, such as the minimum wage, and the right to union recognition. Union leaders have sometimes been able to use such institutional power to the advantage of their members, for example by negotiating with multi-national companies via International Framework Agreements. But this has often proved to be a double-edged sword because the inter-governmental and other supposedly 'co-determination' institu-tions involved are, in reality, set up to favour capital against labour. One of the wonders of the capitalist class and those who operate on its behalf is its ability to take advantage of institutional rules and regulations for its own benefit. The challenge of institutional power is that it is ultimately a com-promise that militates against open disputes between labour and employers. The trade union power inherent within institutional power is effectively power 'borrowed' from more traditional bases. If the laws are enforceable, then monitoring can be powerful, but if the laws are merely setting 'norms' as opposed to obligations, then monitoring their compliance can be nothing more than measuring how far short employers are falling. Primarily, the power of trade unions within institutions rests on their ability to enforce change. If that power has been eroded, then their institutional power will, in general, also decline.

However, as Schmalz et al. have noted, 'trade unions can continue to use institutional power resources even if their associational and structural power is shrinking' (2018, p. 122). This is often the case in poorly organised sectors such as the garment industry. Here, the global union federations will work with the International Labour Organisation (through its tripartite structures) to secure changes through international framework agreements. For example, when the Rana Plaza factory in Bangladesh collapsed in 2013 killing 1,132 workers, the global union, IndustriALL worked with partners to create the 'Bangladesh Accord', a legally binding safety agreement covering more than 180 brands from 20 countries. As a result, 2 million workers were covered by enhanced, albeit minimal, safety standards.

This ability of workers to take their fights outside the workplace and to link up with supporters in the wider community expands their power resource. By forming coalitions with supporters in other organisations, unions build *associational power*. The capacity to mobilise external support can increase leverage and put pressure on employers. When businesses adopt a commitment (whether or not in truth or practice) to corporate social responsibility, there is the possibility that workers can hold up a mirror to the organisation when its ethical practices fall short. Union members can bring to bear reputational damage on companies, particularly where they are dependent on public use for their profits – which is particularly the case in the hospitality, retail and service sectors. Unions can now draw upon the increasing use of the Internet and social media to cause reputational damage by asking the public to become activists in their cause, and if this happens, economic harm can be caused to businesses by reducing the willingness of customers to deal with them. The Internet has the potential to transform aspects of worker organisation by increasing associational power. It facilitates new forms of collective action, especially as information is easily shared with potentially large numbers of people outside the workplace and the unions. A recent example of this is the 2020 University and Colleges Union dispute, where UK university staff were on strike over pay, pensions, workloads, gender and ethnic pay gaps and casualisation. A leaked report from university vice-chancellors during the 2020 strikes showed that they were worried that the casualisation of staff contracts was leading to reputation damage as their exploitation of staff employed on insecure contracts became more widely known outside universities.

Amanda Tattersall, in her book *Power in Coalition: Strategies for Strong Unions and Social Change* (2010), draws on a number of examples of where associational power has benefited union members. She shows that coalitions can be a source of power and renewal for unions, and that this possibility is enhanced when reciprocal coalition-building respects the rights and values of all the coalition partners. There are many examples of unions working in coalition with other organisations to increase their power (see, e.g., Clawson 2003; Rose 2000), one of which is the wonderful story of the environmental activism of the New South Wales Builders Labourers' Federation in Australia. In the 1970s, union members linked up with environmental activists and residents to stop construction work by developers on environmentally sensitive or historic sites. They placed 'green bans' on areas by refusing to work on construction sites in these areas – an effective boycott that was incredibly successful. The willingness of union members to fight for workers' dignity, as well as wages and conditions, and to link this to environmentalism by working with residents, demonstrated the real strength of associational power (Burgmann and Burgmann 1998). Coalitions can therefore be a source of increased associational power for unions, including by helping to renew the union through increasing member activism while demonstrating the union has a broader social justice purpose and a willingness to engage the wider community.

While the forms of power just discussed are often thought of as key sources of power for workers, there are in fact many more power resources that can be drawn upon and utilised. These other forms are often inextricably linked to structural, institutional and associational power, which as we have already noted, need to be considered as interconnected and working in relationship with each other. Trade unions are often primarily thought of as economic actors, but they also draw upon *political power* through their links with political parties and governments. The UK's Labour Party grew out of the trade union movement, and it retains close links today through the affiliation of unions. Unions use this connection to advance the rights of workers through input into policy and by using their membership to influence votes within the party's structures. These privileged links are a way of enabling unions to sometimes achieve their industrial objectives more effectively and efficiently through political instead of industrial means (through electoral support for the party most sympathetic to their demands), particularly when their structural power is weak (Streeck and Hassel 2003).

Similarly, one of the key leverage points of the living wage movement has been its moral persuasiveness. This use of *moral power* draws upon a person's or organisation's moral standing in society, which in turn allows them to accept the righteousness of a particular cause: 'Moral power is a function of whether one is perceived as morally well intentioned, morally capable, and whether one has moral standing to speak to an issue' (Winship and Mehta 2010, p. 425). Classic examples of people perceived as holding these traits are Rosa Parks, Malala Yousafzai, Mahatma Gandhi, César Chávez and Martin Luther King. When leaders are able to uphold each of these values, they can command respect and followers. In talking about different types of power and the effectiveness of moral power, Winship and Mehta state:

> It is difficult to argue that the power of blacks and black leaders as understood in its traditional sense was the key factor in pushing through this [civil rights] legislation. Rather, it was, at least in part, the moral arguments made by Martin Luther King and others that were critical. Furthermore, it was not just the arguments that King and other clergy made, but their moral status and standing as ministers that was influential.
>
> (2010, p. 426)

As the authors go on to argue, 'persuading people to do or not do something because it is right is a far more effective form of influence than outright coercion'. Moral power can be a means to overcome dilemmas involved in collective action and to motivate members to action. A person's position in an organisation's structure can give them authority within it. Then there is personal power arising from the skill and ability to influence people and events whether or not the person exercising that power has any formal authority – the person's positional power is derived from their leadership skills and the degree of respect, or moral standing, they command. However, moral power begins to fall down when there are inconsistencies between what you ask from others and what you are willing to do yourself.

Union members cannot easily draw on the power resources so far mentioned unless they consider what Schmalz et al. refer to as *discursive power*. By this, they mean the ways we think and talk about a subject, and how this has an influence on, and reflects, the ways we act in relation to that subject. The authors say that the 'discursive power of trade unions is only effective, however, if it is in line with prevailing views of morality ... and can be built to politicise feelings of unjust treatment' (Schmalz et al. 2018, p. 124). To do this, unions need to be able to frame their social justice claims in a way that resonates with wider circles of people and shows they have a believable strategy for winning:

> If the trade unions fail to produce new patterns of interpretation to make these politically effective, the foundations of their coalitional and discursive power quickly crumble and in turn the opportunity to deploy them in the battle for hegemony.
>
> (Schmalz et al. 2018, p. 124)

A good example of the use of discursive power is the Justice for Janitors organising campaign in the USA. While the workers and their union drew strongly on associational and political power, it was through the framing and messaging around the injustice of the exploitation of workers in comparison to the big companies that employed them that created a narrative that gave them power to win. Political power is increased when it can be shown that an issue is widely and deeply felt and also it's manifestly obvious that there is injustice taking place – that something is morally wrong. Workers can therefore use discursive power to win wider support for their cause (e.g. by building supportive coalitions in the community), and it can be a key weapon in their power repertoire. This is when politicians, who wish to remain in position or be re-elected, start to listen and act. Taking control of the narrative, whether for positive or negative change, can be hugely powerful. We only need to consider the messaging around the issues of Brexit in the UK (both before the vote and afterward) to see how slogans such as 'take back control' or 'get Brexit done' were able to tap into feelings that provided the instigators with the power they needed to get the results they wanted.

This discussion on discursive power takes us back to the start of this chapter – the importance of ideas and the way these are used to control workers and keep them quiescent. Hopefully, it is clear that understanding on the part of workers the nature of different power resources (and their interaction) is essential for trade union strategising. For workers to be powerlessness is an injustice, and the reversal of this position is surely the *raison d'être* of trade unions, but the last 40–50 years has seen a growing weakness in the structural power of the labour movement. Much of the thinking about trade union renewal, both at academic and practitioner levels, has tended to assume that increased associational power should be the *key focus*, but the evidence suggests that people in leadership positions in unions have tended to think about power in very narrow ways, and this has constrained approaches to revitalisation. Further, many union activists have become locked in traditional ways of operating and have failed to develop new 'repertoires of contention' (Tilly 1995) that can be fitted to new and changing circumstances. As Ellem et al. (2019, p. 19) have claimed, union renewal strategies have not been effective because union leaders haven't taken into account cycles of power and how they intersect with one another as the labour market and the labour process have changed. There is a need for a greater understanding of power and how it can be used by union and community leaders, but with this on its own – without also a discussion among all concerned of the strategy and required tactics to actually harness power to win – the unions will continue to squander the power resources open to them. This issue of what Murray and colleagues (Lévesque and Murray 2010) refer to as the 'strategic capabilities' of unions, which we will return to in Chapter 8.

Working-class people need to re-focus on challenging the ideas that keep them in their place and that help prevent them from seeking to effect change in their own interests. This is key to union renewal. If workers are unable to see the broader picture of structural inequality, then they will not act to change their circumstances. Political education – another missing ingredient in union renewal strategies – is required to connect workplace concerns with other issues of control. When this occurs, the power resources discussed in this chapter can be linked to develop more sophisticated strategies for rebuilding the labour movement, but before this, the key question to be answered is 'What are unions organising for?' Until the purpose of a union is clear to its members and potential members themselves, any future strategy for renewal is likely to be flawed.

3

Harnessing Power in the Late Nineteenth-Century–Early Twentieth-Century 'Gig Economy'

The purpose of the chapter is to consider the growth and power of unions in the UK in the late nineteenth–early twentieth centuries, when work was almost universally casual and workers had no employment rights. How did workers succeed in collectivising despite the difficult economic and political circumstances of the time, and when there was no labour law to protect workers from the considerable exploitation and threats they faced? There isn't the space in a short chapter such as this to explore the whole development of trade unionism – that history can be found elsewhere (Clegg 1985; Pelling 1963), but it is important to contextualise how modern trade unions came into being in the late nineteenth century in order to understand the difficulties faced in organising workers, many of whom were in extremely precarious employment without any employment protection, and with no social welfare security when they were out of work.

Henry Pelling's *History of Trade Unionism* (1963) traces early worker organisations to the sixteenth century, when journeymen (skilled workers with a trade) would form small social societies to enforce work arrangements of mutual advantage. These self-help groups were the forerunners of the Friendly Societies that were developed by workers from the 1700s onward as mutual aid organisations to provide financial assistance in times of hardship (due to death, unemployment and illness). Many of these metamorphosed into pressure groups advocating on behalf of workers who wanted a means to bargain over wages and to restrict entry into craft trades to only skilled workers as a means to protect their jobs and rates of pay. The response from employers and the government was to introduce legislation in 1721 preventing workers from collectively bargaining. Anti-trade union legislation – although workers' organisations weren't yet called trade unions – followed in the form of the 1799 and 1800 Combination Acts, which made it unlawful for workers to come together to agitate for better pay and conditions:

> A penalty of three months' imprisonment was specified for those that formed an association of workers that had the purpose of: raising pay, reducing hours or interfering in any other way with the employers' business or the employment of workers.
>
> (Barrow 1997, p. 5)

Despite this threat, workers were not deterred; they continued to agitate, and in so doing, causing social unrest. Partly as a consequence of this, and partly due to social reformers and others who thought that the state should withdraw from interference in employment relationships, the Combination Act was repealed in 1824. So we see that even before the formation of trade unions as we know them today, social, political and economic measures were at work in determining the extent to which workers should be allowed to organise and the punishments they would face if they ignored the law.

Predictably, employers did not give up their opposition to workers forming their own organisations to improve their working lives, and invoked other pieces of legislation to prevent this happening. The Masters and Servants Act 1832 – which made it unlawful to strike for improved wages and conditions – meant that individual workers could be personally open to prosecution. Similarly, the Unlawful Oaths Act of 1797 was infamously used against six agricultural labourers, the Tolpuddle Martyrs, in 1834 to deter people from setting up secret organisations. Workers trying to avoid revealing that they were organising required members to sign an oath of secrecy and loyalty to the union, but the Act deemed this seditious and punished the six men by sentencing them to transportation to Australia for seven years in March 1834. The response to this from workers and their early combines was remarkable given the level of state repression. There was a concerted campaign to fight for the release of the six labourers across the country. One of the biggest events was a 100,000-strong protest in London in April, just four weeks after the convictions, and despite government attempts to quell the growing protests, workers and their organisations continued with the agitation for the men's release, including submitting a petition signed by 800,000 people.[1] A number of liberal MPs constantly raised the unfairness of the convictions in the Houses of Parliament until they forced the home secretary, in June 1835, to issue a conditional pardon to the men. The six refused this, and it wasn't until 14 March 1836 that they received a full and free pardon and were allowed to return home. This was an incredible achievement from the fledgling trade union movement – demonstrating on this occasion the political power of collective organisation.

In another less well-known case, three years after the Tolpuddle Martyrs, six women in Dundee, Scotland were sentenced to ten days' hard labour for walking off the job and demanding a pay increase of half a penny (Boston 1987, p. 20). Undeterred by attacks such as these, workers continued to organise into unions – although at that time women workers organised separately as they were largely excluded from the unions run by and for men. In some parts of the textile industry, where women formed around 70–80 per cent of the workforce in the late 1830s, women attempted to form unions – and it was here that mixed organising took place. These mixed textile unions in the north of England campaigned for and won equal pay for women by arguing for a fixed rate for the job rather than being paid according to sex. As Sarah Boston notes, if other unions had followed the textile unions, the union movement could have been very different, and perhaps would have developed greater power by uniting as a class, rather than acquiescing to the gendered divide-and-rule tactics of the employers:

> The politics of the textile unions of having a mixed membership and of negotiating a rate for the job were unique. They led a large and active female membership. ... No other unions of the period followed their example, but there is no doubt that if they had, the history of women workers in the trade union movement would have been very different.
>
> (Boston 1987, p. 23)

The power of these workers arose from the fact that instead of organising on sectional craft lines, the textile unions recognised that the unorganised 'unskilled' workers could easily be used to undermine them. As such, they were the first unions to combine skilled and 'unskilled' workers. This provided greater power to the workers, and employers were less able to dismiss workers and replace them. In addition, demands were gendered, in the sense that male journeymen petitioned on behalf of female workers, interestingly using moral arguments from the Bible to embarrass employers into making concessions.

However, in the main, male workers (and their exclusive unions) accepted the dominant ideology of the time that promoted the view that women were second-class citizens and should receive half the pay of men, and that they should be kept out of 'skilled' employment. There was therefore little room for them in the craft, or even in many of the newly forming general unions.

There was a strong intersection between economic and political demands of workers at this time, expressed through the Chartist movement after the Reform Act of 1832 limited the franchise to men with property. The working class felt betrayed – they didn't have a political voice, so they organised where they could, in their communities, in their workplaces and through their places of worship. In 1839, the Chartists had gathered signatures of 1.3 million workers calling for the right of men to vote and to stand as members of parliament. It is interesting to note that the original Charter, drafted by William Lovett, had included universal suffrage (for both men and women), but Lovett had been outvoted on the basis that others considered it unrealistic (British Library 2020). It wasn't long before workers used the strike weapon, as calls for the implementation of the Charter were included alongside demands for the restoration of wages to previous levels before the economic depression of 1842. The level of organisation of the Chartists was remarkable at that time, when many working-class people could not read or write and when there were limited opportunities to travel. The question, then, is: how did this happen? What organising methods were used, and how did workers expand their reach into workplaces and communities when there was nothing like the modern methods of communication and social networks we have today?

The answer is that it was largely through face-to-face conversations and small meetings where someone who could read would read aloud a pamphlet to fellow workers and neighbours. In the early 1800s, there were few communal spaces for workers other than the chapel and public beer houses. There is much (often unread) material languishing in trade union archives that demonstrates how early trade union leaders were influenced by words they had read in their Bibles and heard in their chapels. They used this information to provide a 'legitimate' challenge to the dominant narratives of the capitalist class, whose counter-narrative legitimised the holding of workers in poverty and servitude. Robert Moore describes how Methodism provided an education and training ground for an outstandingly large proportion of trade union leaders: 'whatever orthodox Methodists may have preached, the chapel was a school for democrats and a source of popular leaders' (Moore 1974, p. 13). It provided, in effect, the early trade union political education of its day.

George Loveless, along with two other Tolpuddle Martyrs, was a Wesleyan Methodist lay preacher who drew upon lessons learnt from religious teachings to talk about the poor conditions and treatment of the working class. Richard Wearmouth has written extensively on the influence of Methodism on the working-class movements of England during the nineteenth and twentieth centuries, and while he argues that the attitude of official Methodism to trade unionism can be described as 'non-committal or neutral, neither hostile or sympathetic', this was often not the case on the ground, where there was often great local support for trade union activity (Wearmouth 1937; 1948; 1954; 1957). He quotes from Dr Rattenbury, author of theologian John Wesley's legacy, who stated: 'Methodists flocked to the flag of trade unionism without forsaking the flag of Methodism. No body of people in England have been more conspicuous in their oneness with labour aspirations and propaganda that the Primitive Methodists' (Wearmouth 1937, p. 204). Home Office papers of the time report on activities of Methodists in various parts of the country; the Reverend Westmoreland from a village near Wakefield informed the authorities that 'the greater part of the people called Methodists are united with the Radicals. They assemble in the evening in certain cottages in the country under the pretence of religious worship' (Wearmouth 1937, p. 204). The workers were organising locally in one of the few places where they could – their communities.

Many organic leaders in their localities took advantage of the opportunity to address their fellow workers, friends and family on a regular basis. Besides the influence of Methodism on working-class activism, other religions and faith-based organisations involved themselves in the concerns of the labouring poor. The Labour Church Movement founded by John Trevor in 1891 was 'dedicated to the idea that the emancipation of the working classes from capitalism was a religious movement' (Pierson 1960, p. 463). Pierson explains how it was while listening to Ben Tillett, a Christian Socialist and one of the leaders of the 1889 London dock strike, speaking at a Unitarian conference that Trevor had the idea of a forming a radically new kind of Church to appeal to those sections of the working-class that were part of the growing labour movement. Trevor described the labour movement as the 'greatest religious movement of our time', and it was not long before 50

Labour Churches sprang up, first in the industrialised areas of Lancashire and Yorkshire, followed by other parts of England. The Labour Churches were a response to the dogmatism and middle-class domination of orthodox Churches, and as such they were stripped of the many of the rituals and trappings of Christianity: 'the typical [Labour] church had no priest, no pulpit and no bible' (Bevir 1997, p. 54). The *Labour Prophet*, the newssheet produced by John Trevor, reported how sermons in the Labour Churches mainly dealt with labour and social problems, and well-known socialist and labour leaders were invited to speak to audiences of 400–500 or more. Along with the Salvation Army, the Labour Church raised money for workers and their families in times of industrial unrest, most notably during the 1889 dock strike – during the time of 'new unionism', the period of union organising to which we will now turn. But it's also worth noting that a number of high-profile union leaders of this time used their religious upbringing or beliefs in their trade union organising. One was J.T. Murphy, a well-known radical trade unionist who became leader of the Shop Stewards' Movement in 1917 and was in his earlier years religious and became a preacher in the Primitive Methodist Church, where he would argue with his work colleagues about the importance of religion. Others include Keir Hardie, Ben Tillett, Henry Broadhurst, Ben Pickard and Arthur Henderson, to name a few (Holgate 2013).

THE 1870S: THE START OF NEW UNIONISM

The small craft unions of skilled workers continued to grow and consolidate throughout the 1800s, but these were very localised organisations. Despite many attempts to amalgamate trades into national bodies, many of the early attempts failed, and it wasn't until the 1880s – the period dubbed 'new unionism' – that we see the organising of so-called 'unskilled' workers, the formation of more general unions, and a significant increase in the size of the labour movement. As James Hinton recounts:

> Between the 1870s and the First World War a mass labour movement was formed in Britain. Trade union membership grew from about half a million in the mid 1870s to over 4 million by 1914. By 1914 nearly a quarter of the occupied population belonged to trade unions, compared with a mere 4 percent in 1880 ... trades councils, previously confined

mainly to the larger industrial towns, spread rapidly over the whole country, reflecting the growing identification amongst working-class activists with a national movement, broader and more political than mere sectional trade unionism.

(1983, p. 24)

This move from the sectional trade unions of the skilled craft workers, who had been successful by restricting entry into the trades in order to protect their own more privileged labour market position, began to give way to more general unions that were open to all workers regardless of their skills or occupations. But before taking a look at how this occurred, it is important to have some understanding of what was happening in the economic and political spheres at the time, as working-class organisation doesn't happen in a vacuum – it was usually a response to deteriorating employment conditions, including precariousness, unemployment, cuts to wages, etc. as well as a political consciousness and confidence in collective organisation that gives workers a belief in their own power to effect change.

From 1873 to the end of the century, Britain's pre-eminence as an economic powerhouse began to change. The Great Depression of this period led to uncertainty and 'undermined faith in the inevitability of economic progress, creating a receptive audience for elimination of poverty' (Hinton 1983, p. 26). The structure of the labour market was also changing rapidly – there was considerable movement of workers from the rural areas to towns and cities as agricultural employment declined by half in a 30-year period from 1871 onward, and sectors like transport and manufacturing increased considerably as people moved from land to factory. But it wasn't just internal rural to urban migration that was occurring on a significant scale. Immigration from Ireland saw people fleeing poverty and the Great Famine, such that by 1861 it is estimated that 600,000 people had travelled and set up home in England (Musson 1959). The vast majority of these immigrants were classed as unskilled workers, yet they helped build canals, reservoirs and railways that were so important to the development of British capitalism. They also joined the newly forming unions in the 1880s and were instrumental in organising to improve the lot of workers, as did the immigrant Jewish population, fleeing from pogroms in Russia, whose number had increased from around 50,000 to 200,000 between 1880 and the start of the First World War. Another significant presence of overseas labour in the UK was that of the 70,000 lascars (seamen) from India who worked on British ships. All of these migrant workers were playing a vital role in the economy of the time, yet were subjected to very poor working conditions, often much worse than those of the local workforce.

These signs of unity among workers were, however, not universal. There was considerable racism and antisemitism in sections of the working class at this time. This was evident in the so-called 'race-riots' of 1919 (Jenkinson 1981), which demonstrated the devastating effects of the dominant ideology of racism that was prevalent at the time, and in statements against Jews and immigration in the labour movement (Judd and Surrige 2013, p. 242). Despite a rise in working-class militancy, the First World War had uncovered and nourished a reservoir of xenophobia. The riots represented a manifestation of the way in which some workers, as a result of prevailing orthodoxy of xenophobia and petty nationalism, rejected what was in their own interests – unity against their employers – and resorted to attacking those worse off than themselves. Indeed, elements of the labour and socialist movement had not only absorbed popular racism, but were actively promoting it. In the immediate aftermath of the war, some trade unions called for jobs for 'whites before blacks', and the 1919 TUC Congress had passed a resolution condemning the recruitment of Asiatic labour, maintaining that preference should be given to British white workers. We will return to the significance of these issues to union formation later.

Meanwhile, a consequence of ever-increasing technological advances in the industrial sphere, the move from rural to urban and immigration was that greater numbers of workers concentrated in large workplaces, working in close proximity to each other – all providing the potential for workers to collectively organise to improve their conditions at work, sometimes peacefully, other times less so. Reports from the time describe how riots took place in areas with heavy concentrations of basic industries like coal, iron and steel, engineering and shipbuilding when periods of unemployment were high (13 per cent in 1886), but the economic conditions during the period of the Great Depression were mixed, as Musson notes:

> There is no doubt that, on the whole, the condition of the working classes improved during this period. Real wages rose considerably, there was a redistribution of the national income in favor of wage earners, pauperism declined, deposits in savings banks grew steadily, and consumption

per head of foodstuffs, beer, tobacco, and similar products rose, but it is doubtful whether the working classes *felt* better off. It was not only in the capitalist Parliament and press that there were complaints of distress, but also in trade-union reports and socialist publications. Although, as a contemporary remarked, the standard of living was actually rising, conditions 'did not seem to be improving', since money wages were reduced in many trades in the early years of the depression.

(1959, p. 200)

While real wages may have risen and conditions of labour marginally improved, unemployment, sickness and old age were not provided for by the state, such that the fear of finding yourself and family in a situation of hardship held terror for workers. Therefore, many workers did not feel that their material conditions were improving, and even those who did were nevertheless becoming more aware, through political education, of the unfairness and inequality between workers and their employers. A number of socialist intellectuals entered the labour movement, some influenced by newly formed organisations such as the Socialist Democratic Federation (founded 1881), the Fabians (1884), the Socialist League (1885) and the Independent Labour Party (1893). Tom Mann, Will Thorne and Ben Tillett, in particular, played key roles as organic leaders in the evolution of new unionism, and were members of one or other of these groups. Socialist ideas, promoted by these organisations were fermenting and being discussed among new groups of workers who were beginning to collectivise. Unlike their counterparts in the craft industries, who were able use their ability to restrict entry into skilled trades to force increased benefits, many of these newly industrialising workers had little opportunity to do the same as they could easily be replaced by other workers or the unemployed. Further, the Masters and Servants Act, which was introduced in 1823 and criminalised breach of contract (including strike action), was updated in 1876 and was used to counter the growing unionisation of workers. It is reported from a number of sources that employers were using this Act extensively in response to workers taking strike action, with figures suggesting convictions for breach of contract up to 10,000 a year (Barrow 1997, p. 9). This is a report from a barrister of the time talking about one particular case:

Forty-one men in the employment of Messrs Shaw, Johnson and Reay, of the Moor Iron Works, Stockton, were on Saturday charged before the Stockton Magistrates, under the Master and Servants' Act, with illegally absenting themselves from service on the 9th instant, and the prosecutors claimed 17s 6d as compensation in each case. A complaint had been laid by the men as to the quality of the coal supplied for puddling purposes, and it is affirmed that a better article was being provided, but the men, instead of submitting their grievance to the Board of Arbitration and Conciliation, of which both they and their masters were members, struck work, and hence these proceedings. The magistrates ordered the 'night shift' men to pay the 17s 6d each, or go to prison for a month. The cases against the 'day shift' and 'off shift' men were adjourned.

(*Bolton Evening News*, 25 November 1872,
quoted in Jones 1867, note 8)

So the penalty for organising was high. Yet workers continued to do so, and unionisation was beginning to spread, particularly among the so-called 'unskilled' general workers. This increased after the passage of the 1871 Trade Union Act, which legalised trade unions for the first time and removed some of the obstacles to organising such that the 'restraint of trade' doctrine in common law could not be applied to trade unions, therefore de-criminalising some trade union activity. Many of the new workers flocking into unions were considered 'for one reason or the other, difficult to organise' (Hinton 1983, p. 78) – a phrase often used today to describe workers in precarious jobs. These workers were classified as 'unskilled', they were migrants, the lowest paid, worked the 'lump' (were self-employed) or were employed as day labourers, paid one day at a time with no promise of future work beyond the day. But to what extent were these jobs different from many of the unorganised sectors of today's labour market, and why were unions able to expand so quickly in such a short time? The next section will look at a few examples of how, where and why this happened.

THE 'GIG ECONOMY' OF THE 1880S

The new general unions forming in the late nineteenth century represented a new way of thinking about unionism. While they were an alternative to the sectionalism and protectionism of the craft unions in the way they were

opening up unionism to non-craft work, they also signified changing attitudes to the form and structure of unionism as well. As one analyst of this
period has written: 'attitude, not skill, was to be the basis of the difference
between old and new trade unionists' (Laybourn 1997, p. 71). A figure
closely associated with this change in attitude and the development of new
unionism was Tom Mann, a member of the Amalgamated Society of Engi-
neers who advocated for the introduction of an eight-hour day in 1886. This
campaign 'offered a new conception of the role of trade unionism which went
out to organize all workers in an aggressive manner rather that to simply
defend, in a sectarian way, the wage levels of [some] workers' (Laybourn
1997, p. 70). It was the framing of this campaign in terms of a broad idea of
social justice that gave it popular appeal and helped bring together workers
and unions under a common strategy; it also connected with unemployed
workers who were at the time protesting against the impact of poverty – an
important tactic from which unions could learn today.

Working conditions for many at this time were harsh: long days, no
holidays, low pay, dirty and unsanitary conditions, and levels of precarious working much higher than in today's 'gig economy'. Many employers
exploited the system of day labouring, where workers were hired and paid
by the day (or less) with no promise of future work. There were few rights
for workers in the late nineteenth and early twentieth centuries, either collective or individual,[2] and those that came about later had to be fought for
one-by-one against employers who were determined to keep workers cowed.
Precarious working like this made organising into unions exceedingly difficult because employers could hire and fire at will. On the face of it, most
workers in these conditions had little power – yet still they organised and
won, and in doing so, transformed the nature of unionism, improving the
future lives of millions of workers. While it's true that most of the growth in
trade union membership actually took place in the already organised workplaces where workers had some semblance of power (Hinton 1983, p. 44),
the contribution of the new unions was to organise some of the most precarious of workers in the unorganised sectors where there was seemingly little
labour power.

One impetus for the growth in the new unions was the increased activity
of the established unions which were at this time demonstrating what collective labour power could achieve. By 1889, unemployment had begun to
fall from its high in 1886 such that levels were now very low and groups

of workers were more confident in taking action to challenge the power of employers. The militancy of already established organised workers in the mines, steel, cotton and railways saw massive increases in membership in the last decade of the nineteenth century. James Hinton reports that membership of coal mining unions increased 'by three or four times in the five years following 1887', and on the railways membership tripled in 1889, with strikes taking place in the cotton industry, the building industry, in engineering, docks, print and the shoe industries (Hinton 1983, pp. 46–47). This began a momentum for the unorganised workers to follow suit.

In explaining the growth of the new general unions at this time, many accounts look to the success of the London gas workers' strike in June 1889 and the London dockworkers' strike, which began a couple of months later, as the beginning of the period of new unionism. Without doubt these were extremely important events, and though we will come back to these in a moment, it's imperative that we begin by considering the significant contribution of the matchwomen's strike in east London that took place a year before – particularly as women are so often 'hidden from history' (Rowbotham 1975). Most accounts of this time either completely pass over this important event or relegate it to a passing sentence, but it's worthy of note that women played a leading role in starting the process of unionisation of workers in this period. I have too little space in this chapter to do this strike justice, but a much more comprehensive telling of this story can be found in Louise Raw's book *Striking a Light: The Bryant and May Matchwomen and Their Place in History* (2009). It has already been noted in this chapter that the early trade unions movement was mainly a male preserve. It was only the Lancashire textile unions that made a serious effort to organise women prior to this time, and it was the opposition to mixed craft unions that spurred on women to form their own organisations and to join the newly forming general unions that took a more enlightened approach to women members. Barbara Drake reports that:

> Of a dozen or more general unions [in the period of new unionism], practically all include women, and two are all-women's societies. The aggregate female membership, which was little more than 20,000 in 1914, had risen to 216,000 at the end of 1918, women forming about one-quarter of the total membership.
>
> (1984, p. 181)

49

The 1,400 women and girls who took strike action at the Bryant & May match factory in East London in July 1888 provided an example for other women and men to follow their lead.

1888 MATCHWOMEN'S STRIKE

This strike was about solidarity, improving working conditions, and respect – the common foundations of trade unionism. The origins of the strike came when a woman was sacked for allegedly disobeying an order from a manager; she was then joined by five other workers who walked out in solidarity. Many of the workers were discontented because of the company's practice of fining workers for minor misdemeanours, and harsh bullying treatment from overseers. Raw's account of the strike's development suggests that the five women stayed around the factory gates until break time, when other workers came out, and then recounted what had happened to their colleague. They persuaded fellow workers to join them by walking out of work in protest. Taking the company by surprise, the women were not in any mood to compromise, and given the support they received from other workers, they increased their demands, refusing to go back until these were met. The strikers quickly organised picket lines, such that by 6 July, four days after the initial woman was sacked, the whole factory was standing idle. The women strikers held a large protest march, 11,000 workers strong, and a mass meeting at its end – 'organized as it would seem, completely spontaneously' (Raw 2009, p. 135).

The strikers spoke at meetings detailing the appalling working conditions they had to endure, and garnered support from influential figures in progressive and socialist organisations to publicise their cause. They formed deputations to appeal to MPs to back their cause, as well as urging the London Trades Council to get support from its affiliated unions. For the first time ever, the Trades Council proposed a levy on its members to provide financial aid to the strikers if the strike continued, and the women themselves went out collecting donations in the wider community. Following 16 days of strike action, the company conceded the strikers' demands, including taking back the sacked worker, but further, the company agreed:

to 'provide a breakfast room for the girls so that the latter will not be obliged to get their meals in the room where they work' and to the formation of a union 'so that future disputes, if any, maybe officially laid before the firm'.

(*The Eastern Post*, 22 July 1889, quoted in Raw 2009, p. 141)

What is evident from the strike is that this was an exceedingly well-organised group of 'unorganised' workers. They walked off the job without the support of a union, and surpassed even their own demands through their militant action, including winning some of the first welfare institutions in Britain for industrial workers, including the provision of an on-site dentist. The women faced severe health complications from working with white phosphorus, most notably a condition known as 'phossy jaw', an often terrible condition which began with pain and swelling in the jaw. The bones in the jaw would literally die and begin to rot, progressing to brain damage, organ failure and death, so this was not an insignificant win for this group of workers. The Beckton gas workers' strike and well-documented London dock strike, which are most often credited with kick-starting new unionism, took place the following year. The east end of London, where the women match-workers were employed, was a tight-knit community with many recent Irish and Jewish immigrants – including many of the women strikers, who were of Irish descent. The women matchworkers had husbands, brothers, fathers and other male relatives, many of whom worked in the docks and at the gas works, and the lessons they learnt during the strike were quickly disseminated through the community via an informal political education that took place in churches, pubs, socialist groups and, more generally, on the street. A brief overview of the two 1889 strikes will provide a further understanding of how the 'gig economy' workers of this time were able to organise successfully and build effective unions. More importantly, we need to understand how they were able to identify the power resources at their disposal to effect the changes needed to improve their pay and working conditions.

THE 1889 GAS WORKERS' AND DOCK WORKERS' STRIKES

Just 11 months following the strike at Bryant & May, the gas workers at Beckton, also located in east London just a few miles away from the match factory, took decisive strike action and, in turn, sparked the impressive win which came out of the London docks strike two months later in August 1889. A few months before the strike began at the Beckton Gas Works in

June, workers had been laid off by their employer. Workers agitated and arranged a meeting with other gas workers in London to discuss what to do. They came together and decided to form a union to protect themselves from the power of their employer. One of the speakers at the meeting was Will Thorne, who later became the general secretary of the union. Thorne was born in Birmingham, started work at six years old, working a 12-hour day, and had to walk 5 miles to and from work each day. He moved to London and began work at the gas factory in Beckton. He was a young organic leader, just 28 years old, speaking up on behalf of his fellow workers. His political education, developed through his involvement with the forerunner of the Labour Party the Social Democratic Federation, equipped him with the skills to understand power, tactics and the framing of workers' demands so as to harness widespread collective support, even though he was barely literate at this time.

By the time the strike started in June, the union had only been in place for a matter of months and had organised 20,000 workers into membership – 800 joining on the first day (Raw 2009, p. 162). Thorne argued with fellow workers that their key demand should be for an eight-hour day (a reduction of four hours) on a three-shift system, and six working days (instead of seven) rather than an increase in pay. His reasoning was that reducing hours would also create more jobs for the large number of people who were currently unemployed or threatened with redundancy, which would in turn 'reduce the inhuman competition that was making men more like beasts than civilized persons' (Thorne 2018). Addressing his fellow workers, he said:

> I pledge my word that, if you will stand firm and don't waver, within six months we will claim and win the eight-hour day, a six-day week and the abolition of the present slave-driving methods in vogue not only at the Beckton Gas Works, but all over the country.
>
> (Thorne 2014, p. 68)

They did stand firm: almost immediately, the company gave in to the demands. Workers quickly understood the potential of their own associational power, as well as structural power arising from their position in the economic system. The employers were at this particular moment operating in a tight labour market with narrow profit margins, and they could not afford their plant being brought to a standstill. But the union's leaders also understood that with reduced hours, workers would have more time for political education, leadership development and organising. Branches of the union were established across the country and also succeeded in securing the eight-hour day and the raising of wages.

The victory of the gas workers spurred on dockers to make similar demands. But it wasn't just from the gas workers that dockers learnt to organise their union: many of the workers at the London docks were related to the matchwomen, and they approached the Union of Women Matchmakers to ask for advice on setting up their own unions. The Port of London was a massive employer in the area, with 90 per cent of workers being employed on a casual basis through hundreds of different companies. Men would turn up daily at the dock gate to wait to see if they would be given work that day. If you were considered an agitator, then you were easily excluded from employment by the overseers and it would be difficult to find work in the area – so union organising had serious repercussions. Nevertheless, organise they did.

There was already a union presence on the docks prior to 1889 – mainly among the skilled workers such as stevedores and lightermen – but the mass of dockers were deemed to be 'unorganisable' because of their so called 'unskilled' and casualised status. This was a group of workers that had considerable grievances, they were poorly paid, just 4 or 5 pence an hour, the work was intermittent, and they had to turn up daily not knowing if they would be given work that day. Following the success of the gas workers, the dock workers were becoming increasingly militant and began formulating demands, but at this stage didn't have a union to speak on their behalf. A group of union leaders linked to socialist organisations came together to articulate on behalf of the workers. Ben Tillett was one of these. He worked on the docks and had formed a small union of tea warehousemen in 1887, and four years later became a founding member of the Independent Labour Party. He had begun to develop a reputation as a union organiser who could rally workers to the cause and help frame demands that had mass appeal. He was also critical of the sectional nature of much of the established trade union movement and its general passivity in the face of considerable exploitation of the majority of workers. Along with Tom Mann, also a socialist, union organiser and fellow leader of the dock strike, they were advocating for a new form of unionism:

workers actually have a greater commitment to organising once the process has begun. We can see echoes of this in some sectors of today's 'gig economy', where the most 'difficult to organise' – in the traditional union member sense – groups of workers are beginning to organise, for example in Deliveroo, Uber, McDonald's, outsourced cleaners etc. But it's also important to recognise that this organising is largely taking place outside the mainstream unions, in small independent unions specifically organising in these areas. Another often overlooked feature from the period of new unionism is that it wasn't the case that unions went into these workplaces to organise workers; rather, workers rebelled against their exploitation and went on to organise unions. This distinction between top-down and bottom-up organising is important. It was often organic leaders from among the workers that led these successful strikes. They might not have had experience as organisers, but they understood – either instinctively or as a result of exposure to the economic arguments of socialist propaganda groups – the power of collectivising, and what withdrawal of labour had the potential to achieve.

One of the 'explanations' put forward for the difficulty of union organising today is that workers are too individual; society is structured such that people simply don't develop an understanding of the power of collective action. There is, it is argued, a breakdown in the notion of solidarity or community – a fractured society divided into discrete layers with the marginalised, poor and migrants at the bottom of the pile. Yet in the 1880s, when the new unions were forming, the workers that led the revolts were often made up of a combination of first-generation internal migrants from the rural areas and external migrants from around the world. While lacking a collective identity that originated from specific place-based histories, these disparate and marginalised workers came together and built new communities of solidarity.

One final reflection on the similarities and differences in union organising today: in the late nineteenth century, there was little employment protection, and workers were hired and fired at will. There was no recourse to labour law – not that this provides much protection for most workers even today – so if you were to challenge the power balance in the employment relationship, the only effective means was through collective action, and most often this was through the withdrawal of labour. In many ways, not much has changed in the capitalist system over the last 150 years. Or perhaps things did change for the better in the immediate 1945 post-war period, as strong unions moved power toward employees, but that process has been reversed since the 1980s as weakened unions have failed to prevent power moving back toward the employers. For example, the growth of 'bogus self-employment', precarious employment and zero-hours contracts has deliberately subverted hard-won legal protections for 'employees'. In any case, the withdrawal of labour remains the most effective weapon for unions to win power. A strike exerts power in two ways: first, it rebalances power in the (explicit or implicit) negotiations about the rate of exploitation, and secondly, it disrupts the 'circuit of capital'. Good union organising is about figuring out how to do this effectively by analysing the power resources available to workers and putting strategies in place to take power away from employers and use it to the advantage of the exploited.

What this chapter has shown is that when workers are able to understand their own power, when there are organic leaders who are able to articulate this in such a way as to frame a dispute so that it resonates with fellow workers and who are able to build strategic capacity and associational power throughout the wider community, there is a greater chance of winning. The next chapter will consider what we can learn from the times when workers have managed to use the levers of power at their disposal.

4

Understanding and Using Levers of Power in the Latter Half of the Twentieth Century

In the last chapter, we considered the hostile environment faced by workers in organising at the end of the nineteenth century, and how, despite the challenges of insecure work, criminal sanctions and lack of employment rights, they nevertheless identified and were able to mobilise the power resources at their disposal to effect positive changes to improve their lives. Yet the 1880s seem like the distant past – a history book away from where we are at the start of the third decade of the twenty-first century – way beyond the personal recollection of any worker in today's labour market. In this chapter, we will move to relatively more recent times, via a very brief reflection on how labour power developed at the start of the twentieth century, and how different levers of power were applied in 1945, before moving on to consider power when the UK union movement's strength was at its pinnacle in the first half of the 1970s. How was the power of the working class so strong at this time that it was able to bring down a government in 1974, and how did that power dissipate so quickly by the end of the 1970s? We will look at this from a range of perspectives – including the role community and local politics (municipal socialism) have played in union-building. We will also consider the influence of unions on control of the labour process, and the organising strategies of unions, taking into account the role of union members and the wider workforce, the function of leadership, and the linkages between the different levers of power located within economic, industrial, political and community spheres.

COMMUNITY IN THE UNIONS AND UNIONS IN THE COMMUNITY

Some of the most inspiring examples of working-class power are those that don't focus just on the workplace or the community as *the* locus of struggle,

58

but those that harness the relationships that exist between the two. Jane McAlevey (2016) uses the term 'whole worker organising' when discussing how to maximise the power of workers. This phrase captures the way people's lives are socially integrated. Organising in one arena without considering the scope for harnessing power in the other limits the possibility of making use of multiple resources of power that reside in each of these spheres. Drawing on a number of examples, we will explore where and how this approach to organising the working class has been particularly effective.

Over the last few decades, much has been written on union organising, reviewing its focus on its place in the community (Fine 2005; Holgate 2015; 2018; McBride and Greenwood 2009; Nissen 2004; Speer and Hughey 1995), yet there hasn't been much consideration of this from a historical perspective. Again, there isn't space here to spend much time on this, but it's worth considering an example of how and why this has been successful in the past, and the power that was utilised for improving the working and living conditions of workers. This is the union/community organising that took place in the London Borough of Battersea in the late 1880s, and the astounding successes achieved in the community by drawing on the combined use of political and structural or industrial power. Battersea was a predominantly working-class district with a noted militant tradition, with views that were often at odds with prevailing orthodoxy. During the 1880s, the working class in Battersea began to organise to secure for themselves better conditions of life – although working-class organisations in the borough can be traced to the establishment of collective self-help groups, such as friendly societies, from before the 1850s (Creighton 1999).

A considerable amount of industry was located in the area just south of the River Thames. The railways provided much work for the concentration of skilled workers. There was also an influx of less-skilled and 'unskilled' workers and farm labourers from all over Britain and Ireland in search of work, and many of these settled in the Nine Elms district of Battersea, which was consequently referred to as 'Irish Island'. This rapid growth in migrant labour resulted in overcrowding, and consequent bad housing conditions, but also the development of new unionism. In the harsh conditions of poor housing, overcrowding and unemployment, and combined with a local political leadership willing to organise the working class into action, it's perhaps unsurprising that a radicalism developed that was supported by large sections of the community. There were a number of elements that made this work.

First, there was the issue of leadership and a willingness to compete for and draw upon the positional power of politicians. There were numerous figures who played a significant role in establishing the Battersea labour movement, and the contribution of many of them has a part in explaining the consequent radicalism of the borough, and the effectiveness of trade union and community organising. One of these was John Burns, who was elected to parliament in 1892. He was widely known in Battersea as a member of the Social Democratic Federation and an organiser of unemployed marches, but it was his rise to fame in the 1889 dock strike and his election to the London County Council that gave him a wider profile. To support his election campaigns, he established the Battersea Labour League, which was a unique organisation comprised of a wide range of local bodies that came together to finance and secure his election and that of the Progressives candidates on the local vestry (council). Its aims were to promote 'unified action amongst all sections of the workers in all matters affecting their interests' as well as 'the diffusion of economic, social and political knowledge' (Wrigley 1974, p. 135). The significance of the educational element of these aims should not be overlooked. Another figure, who we have already met, was Tom Mann, Battersea resident and first secretary of the Independent Labour Party. He was instrumental in organising the first May Day demonstration in London in 1890, where 200,000 workers attended, with Mann chairing the meeting and Burns speaking from the platform.

Secondly, municipal socialism was developed in Battersea, with the vestry (and later the borough council) forming the first direct works department in the country after the Progressives swept into control in 1894, gaining 73 seats to the Moderates' 42.[1] It continued with radical reforms and public services that put it at the front of social provision for the whole community. For example, Battersea developed a whole range of social welfare measures, including:

Council housing, a municipal laundry, extra public baths and libraries, free school milk, a battalion of sanitary inspectors, its own cheaper electricity supply, and was the first borough to have health visitors and a local food analysis laboratory ... established in 1905 ... [it was the] only one of its kind in the country ... [the council] was further assisted by the canny introduction of an electoral registration office, the first of its kind in the country. The trades council repeatedly won concessions on trams fares for the local workforce.

(Rudder 1993, p. 7)

Battersea trade unionists formed the first trades union council in 1894 – a body made up of local unions to work together to maximise their power in working with the newly elected political leaders. Between them, they set up the first direct works department in the country, employing 2,200 people working on trade union rates. The decision by the vestry to use direct labour rather than private contractors was not only successful in saving money for the borough, but it provided work for local people on significantly better terms and conditions, and included the building of social housing for the working class. This early programme of the trades union council wasn't dealing just with members' pay and conditions, but embraced broader societal issues of concern to the whole community. The trades union council devised work plans to even out seasonal work in an attempt to reduce unemployment at certain times of the year. At the time, these significant contributions to the improvements in working people's lives stood in contrast to other boroughs that didn't have the same political and industrial organising on the ground, and earned Battersea the label of 'Municipal Mecca'. Needless to say, these policies received widespread support from the working people of Battersea. Importantly, they demonstrated that the election of working-class representatives provided a living example of how the combined use of positional or political power in the hands of elected representatives of the labour movement, backed by the unions' industrial power, could provide significant beneficial reforms. Community-based and trade union-based organising made this possible. It was in this climate of real wins that, despite the strength of racism of that time, Battersea elected a black mayor, John Archer, in 1913 and Indian Communist Shapurji Saklatvala as their MP in 1922. The Progressives' riposte to those who were horrified at the working class choosing an ethnic minority representative was: 'we do not recognise colour prejudice in Battersea, and Battersea does not care what people outside think'.[2]

ELECTORAL POLITICS: THE POWER OF THE WORKING CLASS

The political wing of trade union and co-operative movements began life when the Independent Labour Party (formed in 1893), and the Labour Representation Committee (formed in 1900), morphed into the Labour Party after the 1906 election with the idea of providing a political power resource for the benefit of the working class. In 1889, just after the dock strike, the Trades Union Congress passed a motion at its annual congress calling for the coming together of unions and socialist societies to form a political party for workers. It was to be seven years before the party was formed when 29 independent Labour members were elected to the House of Commons. A further spur to the party's formation was a legal judgment in 1901 when the Taff Vale Railway Company took legal action against the Amalgamated Society of Railway Servants in response to strike action. The courts held that a union could be sued for damages as a result of industrial disputes, which, in effect, abolished the strike as a weapon of organised labour – the key source of structural power for workers. As such, the unions turned to the Labour Party for redress, recognising that the working class needed to be able to leverage power in different arenas if they were to be effective. Legal restrictions on the ability of unions to organise precipitated a turn to gaining access to positional power with the object of overturning case law such as the *Taff Vale* decision. To ensure that the voices of the working class were heard and properly represented in parliament, it required working-class people to be elected. As Clement Attlee, leader of the Labour Party from 1935 and prime minister in the 1945 Labour government, noted:

> The pre-war [First World War] Parliamentary Party consisted entirely of working-class parentage and predominantly of Trade Union officials … it was not until 1922 that any person with the social background of the middle classes was elected a Labour member of Parliament. The Party was, in fact, predominantly the expression on the political field of the Trade Unions, and its members … it was a strictly working-class party.
>
> (Attlee 1937, p. 42)

As noted here, the party was at this time still primarily a trade union organisation that reflected its class composition of 1.5 million trade unionists affiliated through their unions (Attlee 1937, p. 42). Following the First World War, the party sought to more clearly articulate the connection between the practical struggles of workers and the ideology of socialism[3] by setting out a programme for a new social order that proposed 'democratic control of society in all its activities' and that 'embraced the whole range of human activity – political, religious, economic and cultural' (Attlee 1937, p. 67). In connecting the struggles of workers, the unemployed and citizens, the Labour Party was framing its demands and aspirations, consciously or not, in a way that had the potential to build discursive power – in essence, an understanding or belief in the notion or possibility of taking power for 'the common good'. The programme built upon the sense that change was possible given the collapse in confidence in the ruling class following the First World War, the 1916 Easter Rising in Ireland and the 1917 Russian Revolution. There was now a questioning of the current social order and a growing belief in the potential for change as people began to become more aware of their own class interests in opposition to those of their rulers:

> There was in the ranks of the governing classes a very lively fear of rev-olution. The existence of large numbers of unemployed ex-servicemen who demonstrated with discipline as well as enthusiasm held dangerous possibilities. The Trade Unions were strong in numbers and full of mil-itancy. Above all, the workers as a whole had been made to understand their importance. Behind all demands there loomed the menace of the general strike. The Triple Alliance of the Miners, Railwaymen, and Trans-port Workers was a powerful influence in inducing the Government to enact considerable measures of social reform, which were regarded as an insurance against revolution.
>
> (Attlee 1937, p. 51)

The vision of the Labour Party to unite the political and economic demands of the working class found its highest expression when Labour achieved positional power by winning the general election of 1945. The victory was dramatic, with Labour securing 47.7 per cent of the vote and 393 seats in the House of Commons – an increase of 364 MPs from 1906, with 31 per cent of its MPs sponsored by trade unions. The railway unions managed to secure the election of 22 of their 23 proposed candidates, the miners 35 of 35, and the Transport and General Workers' Union 17 out of 18 (Wrigley 2009). As such, the trade unions, as founders of the party and as financial backers, remained at the centre of Labour politics. Six trade union-sponsored MPs had places in the Cabinet, including Ernest Bevin, who had been general secretary of the Transport and General Workers' Union, George Isaacs, who had been chair of the TUC, and who became minister of labour, Aneurin Bevan, an ex-miner, union official and leading figure in the 1926 General Strike and architect of the National Health Service, and Ellen Wilkinson, minister for education, who had previously been a trade union organiser with the National Union of Distributive and Allied Workers, and was only the second woman to serve in Cabinet.

The prime minister, Clement Attlee, ensured that ministers consulted with the TUC and individual unions. Unions had now increased their access to the political levers of power, yet still had the independence to apply structural power in the economic sphere when necessary. It wasn't long before the unions saw the benefits of positional and institutional power for their members. The 1927 Trade Union Act – that placed restrictions on the ability of trade unions to strike and picket – was repealed in 1946, and a programme of social housing, and nationalisation of essential industries was embarked upon. But it was the implementation of a far-reaching welfare state, including the formation of the National Health Service in 1946, for which this government is best-known and celebrated. Not only that, union membership rose to from 7.8 million in 1945 to 9.5 million by 1951. The strategic choices made by unions to form the Labour Party and to devote resources to maintaining it were, at least in the context of the 1945 government, amply rewarded. No doubt there will be wide-ranging debates about exactly why subsequent Labour governments failed to deliver anything as far-reaching again, but those arguments do not undermine the *potential* of positional power demonstrated by the 1945 Labour government.

UNIONS' USE OF STRUCTURAL POWER

This section will consider how unions have used structural power: that is, their ability to bargain in the labour market and workplace to force employers to make concessions they would otherwise prefer to avoid. The main lever of structural power is the use, or threat, of industrial action, and predominantly that is strike action. The ability of workers to withdraw their labour until they have forced the employer to concede union demands is the most common form of industrial action, but it's not the only one: workers can be particularly inventive in their levels of disruptiveness. Structural power is dependent on a range of factors, including, for example, the strength of union resolve, leadership and strategic capacity, but also the state of the economy, the labour process, the ability of capital to withstand union action, and political intervention by the state. We will draw upon some examples of how unions have used various levers of power to understand their strength in different industrial settings.

One of the key areas of discussion about the decline of trade unions from the 1980s onwards concerns the anti-trade union legislation enacted by the Conservative governments that were in power from 1979 to 1997. The laws were clearly designed to restrict the power of trade unions, the outlawing of secondary action and flying pickets being a case in point. Workers taking industrial action in support of other workers had been a key strength of the structural power of unions. However, it's important to remember that despite such restrictions in the past, legislation need not necessarily impede industrial action. Take, for example, the government's introduction of the Munitions Act in 1915. The purpose of this legislation was to ensure wartime production was not disrupted by workers. Strikes in war industries were made illegal, and labour disputes were meant to be referred to compulsory tribunals. Yet from the time the Act was introduced to its repeal in 1919, there were 1,274 industrial disputes resulting in over 18 million days lost through strike action (Hinton 1973, p. 37). If the union movement is strong and workers have confidence, then it matters little what rules or regulations are in place – institutional power is never a match for *organised* workers' power. Workers have in the past been adept at understanding where the balance of power in the employment relationship resides and identifying the strategy and tactics needed to harness power for their own benefit. Also of interest is the fact that workers at times recognise they must respond to the conservatism in their own unions if they are to be effective:

> In the resulting battle to resist and push back the multiform pressures of industrial compulsion the trade union officials proved less convincing generals than the revolutionaries of the shop stewards movement. Above all else, it was the shop stewards who were responsible for the major victory over compulsion – the de facto maintenance of the right to strike.
>
> (Hinton 1973, p. 41)

As Laybourn (1997, p. 123) points out, 'there was widespread acknowledgement that some industrial power had been conceded to the trade unions in order to win the war'. He might more accurately have said power was conceded to the shop stewards' movement, as it was rank-and-file trade union members who were leading strikes and industrial action, often against the instructions of trade union officials:

> Confronted by employers, state and trade union officialdom, the shop stewards' movement saw all three forces as collaborating in the construction of the servile state. It is as a revolt against this emergent servile state that the political aspect of the shop stewards' movement is primarily to be understood.
>
> (Hinton 1973, p. 55)

As a result, for the first, but not the last time, union members organised themselves independently outside the official union structures. They co-ordinated and led militancy through local workplace committees – and in an era when most workers did not even have a landline telephone, let alone social media, co-ordinated these across industrial sectors by developing a delegate structure. This was a well-organised, politically astute group of workers who would not be cowed by their employers, the state or their trade union officials:

> We will support the officials just so long as they rightly represent the workers, but we will act independently immediately they misrepresent them. Being composed of delegates from every shop and untrammelled by obsolete rule or law, we claim to represent the true feeling of the workers. We can act immediately according to the merits of the case and the desire of the rank-and-file.
>
> (from an oft-quoted leaflet of the Clyde Workers' Committee published in November 1915, quoted in Saville and Briggs 1971, p. 164)

The shop stewards' movement came into being at this particular time, when capital was reliant on labour in an unprecedented way. However, rank-and-file militancy remained in place, and while the rank-and-file workers' movement was episodic throughout the following decades, it became central to the exercise of trade union power throughout the 1960s and 1970s.

Two sectors where rank-and-file militancy was evident in the 1960s and 1970s were the car industry and engineering. The power of these workers stemmed from the nature of the production line system, their level of inter-plant co-ordination, and the importance of these sectors to the British economy. In the car industry, there were nearly 1 million directly and indirectly employed workers in a small number of companies. These workers had very strong associational power, developed by shop stewards through the British Motor Company Combine Committee that had been formed in 1951 to link union organising and information-sharing across each of the motor companies. There was considerable variation in the level of earnings in and between companies, creating feelings of unfairness and resentment, which resulted in what became known as 'leap-frog' bargaining. Workers felt the formal collective bargaining machinery was not serving its purpose, so they turned to their shop stewards and unofficial action to engage in negotiation of 'piece rates' or job control at the hyper-local level to resolve these grievances. The nature of hyper-local bargaining inevitably led to substantial interest in and support for local shop stewards such that power was both created and exercised at this local level far away from regional or national officials of the unions. But what did this power look like, and what form did it take?

A lot of the conflict in the car plants in the 1960s and 1970s stemmed from disputes over the control of work, or as academics like to call it, the labour process. The 'frontier of control' – the ongoing struggle for control in the workplace, whereby managers try to secure new powers to organise and control workers, and where workers react by developing counter-strategies to win greater freedom from supervision – is an ongoing battle in many workplaces, and particularly in the UK car plants at this time. In Huw Beynon's (1973) in-depth ethnographic study of the Ford plant at Halewood in Liverpool, he explains how these battles were of crucial importance for the development of the power of the shop stewards' committees. The day-to-day victories of the union representatives in terms of job control helped to build and sustain the power of the union at the plant and sub-plant levels. Union activists of the time have reported how unofficial industrial action on these scales was in their view partly a consequence of the problems of cumbersome trade union structures (and conservative trade union officials) that made it difficult to sanction official union-sanctioned strike action against the employers (Thornett 1998). As a consequence, workers took industrial action into their own hands with the support of a network of shop stewards. In car factories, it's 'the line' that controls the pace of work, so this is a focus of discontent. The shell of a car travels along a moving production line, and workers add components as it passes by. To increase productivity, management requires the line to be speeded up. Following constant battles, including work stoppages and sabotage (by pulling the safety wire to stop the line), over what speed of work was reasonable, Beynon reports how shop stewards at Ford's at Halewood forced management to concede that a worker on each shift had the right to hold the key that locked the line. Management were coerced into accepting that the frontier of control – their power – was being pushed back by workers who had strong associational power with the determination to act collectively to shut down production if managers or foremen overstepped what workers deemed to be acceptable work practices. These workers were acutely aware of the structural power they held in being able to shut down the line and stop production. As Beynon explains:

> The extent and durability of job controls are subject to the market. Fluctuations in the sales of cars, in the rate of capital investment, soon reveal themselves in the social relations on the shop floor. It is in this sense that unionism and workplace organization can be seen as a direct consequence of economic forces. … It's got nothing to do with fairness. What it has to do with is economics and power.
>
> (1973, pp. 132–133)

THE POWER OF THE 'UNSKILLED': FORD MACHINISTS' STRIKE OF 1968

Another fine example of the use of structural power was the dispute by the women machinists at Ford Dagenham who took strike action in 1968 over a pay regrading exercise that saw them graded as 'unskilled labour'. Angry at the perceived injustice of being graded lower than 'unskilled' men they considered to be doing work that was less skilled, 187 women silenced their sewing machines and walked off the job. In an integrated factory system where each part of production is dependent on the one before it, it can be relatively easy for one section of the workforce to bring the whole production process to a halt. The women workers made car seats, and as one commentator at the time pointed out, 'no machinists meant no seats and no seats meant no cars'. The four weeks of strike action by the women resulted in the company laying off 9,000 workers and closing substantial parts of the production line. The dispute was immensely costly, particularly when it spread to the Halewood plant, where another 195 women joined the strike.

The company claimed to be losing £1 million a day in stopped production, and this threatened future exports:

> Ford's managing director Bill Batty indicated the sense of panic when he proclaimed the strike to be a 'critical problem for the British economy' and suggested that 40,000 men could lose their jobs as he sought assistance from prime minister Harold Wilson to bring a swift resolution to the dispute.
>
> (Moss 2015, p. 43)

The women had a partial win, in that they gained a 7 per cent increase in pay, but it was still 8 per cent below that of the men doing similarly valued work, and they didn't achieve the regrading that was at the heart of the dispute. So, while this was a win of sorts, so much more could have been achieved given the extent of the industrial power they held in their hands at the time they were on strike. They clearly had the whip hand with regard to their employer, as their structural power was rooted in point-of-production that gave them a strategic advantage, but union officials, eager to get the men back to work, urged the women to end the strike with the offer of an immediate increase in pay, a consideration of the regrading issue at a later date through a court of inquiry, and the promise of future equal pay legislation.[4] Later, the women expressed their profound disappointment, and felt they had been duped by their union officials into accepting a shoddy compromise – a view also confirmed by the Court of Inquiry into the dispute (Moss 2015). The inquiry criticised the union leadership's handling of the dispute and found that the union had 'rejected a deal to narrow the differentials between male and female wages at the factory two years earlier.' As one of the strikers said: 'although we did get more money, we did not gain the point [on the grade scale], we won a battle, but lost the war' (Moss 2015, pp. 43–44). One account of the union leaders' actions explained that the union had spent two years working with management to formulate a revised grading structure for all the workers (including the regrading downwards of the women workers). Management had included the unions in the process in an attempt to stem the militant tide of industrial action across Ford factories. Having agreed to be part of this process and reached agreement with the employer on the new grading structure, the union leadership was compromised and thus reluctant to support a regrading for the women as it would have likely reignited a new wave of industrial action over wage drift as other workers put forward claims for upgrading.

What is to be learnt about levers of power from this dispute? Firstly, it shows the extent to which the power balance in the employment relationship is constantly shifting and how different aspects of power come into play at various times. It's clear that the women strikers had considerable structural power – they brought Ford's assembly plants to a standstill. The associational power of the union – the support from the rest of the workers – could have been used to force the employer to compromise, but the union chose a different strategy that took away the power held by the women strikers. Ford's senior management described the dispute as 'the gravest labor situation [Ford] has ever faced in its long and sometimes turbulent history' (Friedman and Meredeen 1980, p. 171). As such, in an attempt to get the dispute resolved, the company turned to the government for assistance.

When capital feels under threat and hasn't got confidence in its own power, it will look for other sources wherever it can find them. A political commentator recently quipped, 'just as there are no atheists on a sinking ship, there are no free-marketeers in a pandemic' (Freedland 2020), which, although related to a very different situation, nevertheless makes the point that despite their routine cries for a smaller role for the state and a free economic market, employers will appeal to the state to come to their aid when they are in serious trouble. In 1968, Ford appealed to the prime minister and minister of labour to use their power and influence to bring about a resolution to the crisis. The message was that the dispute was of great significance not only for the company, but for the nation as well. The government response was to intervene to broker the dispute by suggesting an independent court of inquiry and promising to introduce the Equal Pay Act. This shows how employers, when in crisis, can, if the stakes are high, rely on institutional power through legal redress or appeals to government to come to their aid.

In this case, we find that the women had enormous *potential power* to win this dispute as they had brought the assembly plants to a standstill as a result of their strike, and were costing the employer around £1 million a day. But they lacked a willing union leadership or the strategic capacity to capitalise on their power resource to achieve the outcome they were seeking. This contrasts with another example that will now be considered – the Upper

Clyde Shipbuilders sit-in – where, objectively, the workers appeared to have little structural power when they took action over the proposed closure of their workplaces, but they did have strong strategic leadership that meant they were able to leverage other forms of power in a novel way to lead them to victory.

POWER AND LEADERSHIP:
THE SIT-IN BY THE UPPER CLYDE SHIPBUILDERS

The story of the factory occupation by the Upper Clyde Shipbuilders in the west of Scotland in 1971 shows the importance of leadership, strategy and tactics in the exercise of power (Thompson and Hart 1972). In July 1971, the company had gone into receivership as a result of serious cash flow problems caused by a deliberate withdrawal of support for the industry from government. Despite having full order books, a request to the government for a working capital loan to tide the company over was rejected because of the political ideology of free-market capitalism of the Conservative government of the time. The liquidation of the shipyards spelled disaster for the 8,500 workers employed at the four sites. The loss of so many jobs and the knock-on effect in the community (as many as 20,000 job losses in ancillary trades) was likely to be immense, resulting in mass unemployment and poverty for many families.

On hearing about the likely closure of the yards, the shop stewards and union members held a mass meeting of 800 to formulate their response. Initial plans were for a token strike and a mass demonstration. This initial strike went beyond the workplace – it involved an estimated 100,000 workers in Scotland, of whom 50,000 joined the demonstration in Glasgow. When the decision was taken to close the shipyards at the end of July 1971, the workers went into occupation. But they didn't *just* occupy the plants, they took control; they didn't strike, instead they carried on working without management in place – it was a 'work-in'. It was an industrial action strategy without precedence. On the face of it, the workers had little power: the yards were closing, they were all to be made redundant, the company was in receivership – it was, effectively, bankrupt. The decision to keep the yards operating was taken at workplace meetings. As one of the work-in union leaders explained:

71

We went through all the options and none of them fitted...If we went out on strike we would have had to leave the yard and they would have closed it. It was as simple as that. If we had a sit-in it would appear negative. So gradually the concept of the work-in evolved, a concept where we could demonstrate we were really fighting for the right to work. And what better way to do that than by continuing to work?

(Reid 1976, pp. 78–79)

Initial scepticism about the idea of a work-in gave way to figuring out practicalities – not least the issue of money and how the 'work-in' workers[5] would be paid. A co-ordinating committee made up of shop stewards made weekly payments to those who had been made redundant based upon their average earnings prior to dismissal. Workplace discipline was enforced because the shop stewards wanted to demonstrate the long-term viability of the yards and convey the message that workers were anything but 'work-shy' and should have the *right* to work.

However, this wasn't an attempt to create a workers' co-operative, this was industrial action to force the government to take action to save the yards – and an excellent example of the strategic capacity of union leadership and the use of alternative power resources to that of the strike to effect change. By the end of the year, the work-in had achieved its purpose: 'the planned rundown had been stopped dead in its tracks, and an unprecedented public opposition had been aroused to the idea of liquidation ... achievements possible only on the basis of the skilled leadership demonstrated by the stewards' (Thompson and Hart 1972, p. 84).

The industrial action taken by the workers was as much political as it was economic, and there are a number of lessons relating to power that can be drawn from this example. First, we can identify the importance of leadership and strategy in framing this dispute. It was evident to the shop stewards that the traditional method adopted by workers to defend their jobs – the strike – would be ineffective in these circumstances. Workers would have been left outside the gates, picketing while watching the shipyards being dismantled before their eyes. It took a level of class-consciousness and political leadership to convince the workers that the strategy of a work-in was viable. The key leaders of the dispute were politically astute, members of or associated with the Communist Party, with a level of discipline, political education, and an awareness of power structures and resources that allowed them to frame the industrial action in a way that resonated not only with their fellow workers, but with the wider community as well. As this quote from just after the lock-in explains:

> Their action, and the public campaign which sprang up around it, involved much more than a redundancy fight. It stemmed from a reaction to the rundown of industry and employment in Clydeside and Scotland. The stewards were not only battling against the liquidator who was now in charge. They had taken up arms against the Government and its policies. And they were receiving backing, to an extent never before given to an unofficial action, from every section of the Labour movement, from nearly every political party, and from many broader based sections of the community. Indeed, a whole town of 50,000 people practically put its entire services, from the municipal bank to the dust carts at the disposal of the shop stewards.
>
> (Buchan 1972, pp. 11–12)

There was a sophisticated framing of this dispute that drew upon various levers of power to win. Moral power – the notion of the 'right to work' – the Declaration of Human Rights concept that people have a human right to engage in productive employment and shouldn't be prevented from doing so, was utilised to great effect. It drew backing from Church leaders, among others, in the community to add legitimacy to the workers' cause. It also drew on discursive power – the framing of the worker's demands that were simply articulated as 'all four yards and the entire labour force'. This framing was a master statement in simplicity, one that not only the workers, but also the wider public could easily understand. Yet none of this could have been achieved without the associational power of the unions, not just from the solid support from workers themselves, but the way the dispute was widened to the broader union movement to help contribute to the fighting fund and draw solidarity from far and wide.

However, when thinking about the networks from which the workers in Glasgow were able to draw support – the clergy from different denominations in the local community, and the Communist Party's networks across the world – it's notable that today these very different but nonetheless at one time ubiquitous hubs of industrial communities are much weakened, if not entirely absent, and consequently they are less able to serve as reservoirs of power than they were in the past – an issue we will return to later.

By February 1972, the workers had talks with a company in the USA which was interested in taking over the shipyards, an agreement was reached with the company, and the government pledged to commit to devoting £14 million to cover capital developments and inherited losses. The workers had won, and in the words of the leader of the shops stewards, Jimmy Reid, 'not a drop of blood was spilled, not an arrest was made, no disturbances took place. The workers of Clydeside had fought for, and won, their right to work, in a bloodless industrial coup' (Reid 1976, p. 83).

THE 1970S: THE HIGHS AND LOW OF UNION POWER

Before concluding this chapter, let's recap on the extent of union power in the 1970s, and the manner in which it was exercised. It is often stated, by friends and enemies alike, that the UK union movement's power reached its pinnacle in the early 1970s, and ended that decade with the 'Winter of Discontent' in 1978–79 when there were widespread public-sector strikes across the country. Around 10.5 million strike days were lost in the early months of 1979[6] (1.5 million on the 22 January 1979 day of action) as mainly public-sector workers protested against the government's pay policy that had limited pay increases since 1975 in an attempt to control inflation (and in 1978 were limited by government policy to 5 per cent). But wage restraint wasn't successful, and workers had had enough of the value of their wages falling. Following the Ford workers' strike in September 1978 where they had pushed the employer to agreeing a 17 per cent wage increase, other workers decided to follow suit and challenge the pay restraint. Many were struggling to make ends meet as prices continued to rise, and inevitably unions demanded pay increases for their members. The result was chaos across the country as more and more public sector workers withdrew their labour. Many services came to a standstill, and the army were called in to undertake essential work in some areas where ambulance workers were on strike.

At this time, union membership had reached 13.5 million – over half of all workers were in unions, and in the public sector 70 per cent of workers were members. The unions at this time had immense associational power that some groups of workers were able to put to good use to achieve increases in pay and better working conditions. While the strikes of late 1978 early 1979 are often characterised as revolt by public-sector workers against government policy because of rising prices and chronic low pay, it was in the private sector that unions had greater success in achieving substantial settlements.

In January 1979, road haulage workers began unofficial strike action, later official, in response to a claim for a substantial increase in pay – way beyond the government's 5 per cent pay limit. These workers had the advantage of being the key node for food distribution across the country. With over 200,000 workers on strike and very little or no movement of food or commodities, this provided these workers with considerable structural power. The dispute was settled after a few weeks, resulting in above-inflation pay increases and a reduction in the working week (Smith 1999).

In terms of public-sector workers, while these formed the bulk of the industrial action in the Winter of Discontent, their successes were much more limited. The gravediggers, for example, settled on a 14 per cent pay increase, but despite almost solid strikes – other than workers who were providing essential emergency cover – most unions ended up settling for pay increases that were either at or below the level of inflation, meaning that in real terms there was no increase in the standard of living of workers, the key issue for which workers were fighting.

Clearly, there is a lot more that could be said about the intricacies and influence of this period – and this has already been done by many other writers (see, e.g., two recent books on this topic: Martin López 2014; Shepherd 2013) – but perhaps one element for consideration that is relevant to our discussion is the issue of power. Without doubt, public-sector workers were demonstrating their anger, but there is a sense that this was in fact expressed in the form of protest rather than as an exercise of structural power to effect change. Rethinking this period, perhaps it should be considered as a high point of union *protest* rather than being successful in terms of material gains for workers and a high point of trade union power. It was also a period in which the capitalist class were putting a lot of effort into formulating strategies to weaken the labour movement.

The structural power of unions had been increasing throughout the 1960s such that the Conservative government of the early years of that decade had proposed an inquiry into trade union activity with a view to limiting union power. When there was a change of government in 1964, the incoming Labour government also decided to instigate a Royal Commission on Trade

Unions and Employers' Associations (its findings known as the 'Donovan Report', named after the person who chaired the commission) to look into a solution to the problem of unofficial industrial action that was considered to be contributing to the UK's ongoing economic crisis caused by price rises and low growth rates. It was against this background that there was a growing demand for a reassessment, and perhaps overhaul, of the British system of industrial relations (Banks 1969) – an issue we will return to later. The Donovan Commission reported in 1968 with a number of key recommendations, one of which was to improve collective bargaining procedures, with recommendations on dismissal procedures and the establishment of the National Industrial Relations Court. The Labour Party produced a White Paper, *In Place of Strife* (Castle 1969), in response to Donovan which proposed a 28-day period of conciliation on unofficial strikes and the introduction of secret ballots before official strikes could be held. Barbara Castle, secretary for employment, also proposed statutory recognition of trade unions, in an attempt to win over the unions. It was, however, argued that this amounted to the replacement of voluntary collective bargaining with a formal system of industrial relations legislation, so there was considerable opposition to the proposal from trade unions and many Labour MPs.

A rank-and-file movement led by Communist Party members under the title the Liaison Committee for the Defence of Trade Unions (LCDTU), organised the opposition to *In Place of Strife*. The LCDTU was comprised of numerous trade union branches, trades councils, shop steward combines and district committees – it was a coming together of Left-led union bodies. It called for, and led, a number of political strikes in 1969 against the proposed legislation, in opposition to the official labour movement. John McIlroy and Alan Campbell (1999, p. 14) claim that it was the industrial action orchestrated by the LCDTU that played a role in the decision by the Labour government to drop the proposals for the legislation: 'The LCDTU was willing to urge independent action to stimulate the union leadership in the face of powerful opposition, and it garnered significant support' – demonstrating the political power of union activists when they are able to organise across unions.

Yet similar legislation was to return under the Conservative government by way of the Industrial Relations Act 1971. It was the use of this Act to constrain the behaviour of workers taking industrial action that led, in a number of cases, to further unrest among workers. Ralph Darlington and

Dave Lyddon's book *Glorious Summer: Class Struggle in Britain 1972* (2001) provides an exceptionally detailed account of the extent of the power of industrial action as it was building throughout this year, some cases of which have already been mentioned in Chapter 1. At the beginning of 1972, miners went on strike, which culminated in the legendary 'battle of Saltley Gate' when 15,000 pickets forced the closure of an essential coke distribution plant in Birmingham that cut the country's power supply by a quarter. The two authors quote Prime Minister Edward Heath's later reflections on how the government was caught off-guard by the tactics used by the miners: 'What we did not anticipate was the spasm of militancy from a union which had been relatively quiet for so long, and the tactics it was willing to adopt. The use of "flying pickets" ... took us unawares' (Darlington and Lyddon 2001, p. 211).

The tactic adopted by the miners was to ignore their own workplaces in terms of picketing. There was no need to be there, because they were all out on official action. Instead, their focus was on the real locus of power – the electricity stations and coking depots that used the coal from the mines. If the workers could prevent coal entering the power stations, they could essentially stop large sections of industry operating. This is what happened at Saltley Gate, when the flying pickets, aided and abetted by tens of thousands of engineering workers who struck to support them, stopped the movement of coal and coke. The shortage of fuel meant the government was forced to introduce a three-day week to conserve the nation's energy supplies.[7] The miners won with pay increases of between 15 and 31.6 per cent. In effect, the union movement discovered the vulnerabilities of supply chains, and used their strategic power to outwit the government.

A second demonstration of considerable power, also highlighted earlier, was the events surrounding the imprisonment of five dockers for contempt of court for ignoring an injunction instructing them to stop secondary picketing of a container base in London. The support they received from other workers was immense. The picket outside the prison where the men were held became the unofficial organising centre for solidarity action. Workers from here were sent out to garner support, and achieved that with solidarity from the print workers, who closed down the national newspapers. What these workers did was to think through and develop strategy and tactics that were able to harness as much collective power as possible to force the release of the workers:

the Pentonville mass picket caught the imagination of many trade unionist around the country. It has been estimated that at the very least 90,000 workers (including 40,000 dockers) were on indefinite strike by the time the five were released.

(Darlington and Lyddon 2001, p. 164)

In the same year, there were sit-ins by engineering workers and strikes by building workers, and this was followed by a second national strike by the miners in 1974, which eventually brought down the Conservative government – a momentous demonstration of the power of workers. It was impossible to live through this decade without an awareness of what seemed like a daily rolling succession of industrial action being reported in the media. Yet the signs of union power dissipating were already evident – there were some notable defeats from which the union movement failed to learn lessons, particularly in relation to strategy, tactics and the use of power, as well as a lack of attention to the counter-offensive being developed by those representing the capitalist class. As one commentator noted:

The very determination and breadth of the 1979 road haulage strike was a major factor precipitating the mobilization of the coercive power of the state during the 1980s to counter the power of militant trade-unionism and weakness of trade-unionism in Britain were simultaneously revealed.

(Smith 1999, p. 53)

Indeed, it wasn't just this strike that precipitated a change in the balance of power between unions and employers and the state. There had been a slow period of reflection and planning throughout this decade and beyond to ensure that the state and capital reasserted their control over workers and the unions. A few examples help to illustrate this point. In 1972, during the national building workers' strike, workers in the sector, many of whom were casualised, faced extremely hostile employers. Despite this, an all-out strike was won after 12 weeks when they succeeded in winning the highest ever pay rise in the history of the building industry.[8] But the employers were powerful, and they persuaded the government to investigate the workers for aggressive picketing after presenting the home secretary with a dossier of 'evidence' alleging intimidation and violence. As a consequence, 24 building workers were arrested and prosecuted for conspiracy to intimidate, affray and unlawful assembly. Six of the workers were imprisoned and sentenced to between nine months and three years. In March 2020, following a long campaign against the injustice these workers faced, the Criminal Cases Review Commission finally announced that it would refer the pickets' convictions to the Court of Appeal. The appeal was upheld on 23 March, and overturned the criminal convictions after concluding they were unsafe because original witness statements had been destroyed by the police – a fact that was withheld at the time from those convicted.

Not only were the arrests part of a concerted plan to intimidate the trade union movement, the employers worked with a right-wing free-enterprise organisation, the Economic League, to keep a 'black-list' of left-wing or militant trade unionists to ensure they never got jobs in the industry again. It's also likely that the so-called 'spy cops' were already active in this period. These were undercover police officers who were infiltrating left-wing organisations and campaigns with a view to gathering information, some of which was passed directly to the black-listers (Chamberlin and Smith 2015).

A final example here is that of the celebrated strike by a group of women workers at a small photo-processing factory in north London that began in August 1976 and only ended in July 1978. This strike, at Grunwick, was led by Asian women and became a *cause célèbre* in the union movement as the workers received support from all over the country – not least from the miners, who came down in their thousands to join the picket lines. There were many mass pickets and 550 arrests, yet despite this, the dispute over union recognition went down in defeat. The police and the state had learnt lessons from the mass picketing of the early 1970s, and used these to great effect in withstanding the pressure of the dispute.

Grunwick became a marathon, not a sprint, and mass pickets are very hard to maintain in the long term. Violence was used against the pickets by the deployment of what was termed a 'special patrol group' – in effect, a paramilitary police unit. And the employer, which showed immense hostility to unionisation, was supported and advised in its tactics by the right-wing libertarian organisation the National Association for Freedom, whose remit was to counter the power of trade unions. The organisation was described by one journalist as 'Thatcherism's extra-parliamentary advance guard against a fading Labour government and its union allies' (White 1989). The union movement had simply assumed that it could re-use and re-package tactics that had been successful in the past, but had little consciousness of the strategic counter-offensive designed to challenge its power that was already taking shape behind the scenes.

The incoming Conservative government in May 1979 had been planning its own power grab, and would over the next couple of decades implement a range of strategies to increase its political, economic and institutional and ideological power, and in doing so, do everything it could to constrain the union movements' associational power. To this end, it was spectacularly successful. David Marsh, in his book the *New Politics of British Trade Unionism* (1992), explores the Conservative counter-mobilisation designed to break the power of unions under the governments of Margaret Thatcher. The 'Ridley Report', which was written by a close confidant of Thatcher, Nicholas Ridley, set out a detailed long-term strategy to transform the way industrial relations were conducted in the UK by dismantling nationalised industries and fragmenting the power of unions to make them less effective. Contained within the report were detailed plans to equip the police to break strikes and to pick battles with unions to break the resolve of workers.

However, a similar level of forward planning and strategising wasn't taking place within trade unions, despite the changing nature of the economy and working-class consciousness. Eric Hobsbawm, whose words began Chapter 1 of this book, argued that the forward march of militant labour had already begun to falter before the 1970s, despite what he terms the 'economist militancy' of that decade. His point was that 'straight-forward economist trade union consciousness may at times actually set workers against each other rather than establish wider patterns of solidarity' (Hobsbawm 1978, p. 286). He also identified, ahead of many, that there were structural changes in the economy that would have an impact on traditional bases of union power. The Conservative Party were successful in capitalising on the growing divisions and inequalities within the working class through their superior ideological messaging (their 'right to buy' policy, which privatised council homes *en masse* was, for example, often popular among council tenants at the time) as well as managing the economy to benefit the free market, and creating a climate of fear among workers by allowing mass unemployment to become endemic. The labour and trade union movement was ill-prepared to counter any of this, which led, over time, to its massive decline and a decreasing ability to exercise power to any great effect since that time.

This chapter has considered a range of examples of where the power of workers lies – both in the workplace and in the community, as well as the power resources open to them to effect change in their working lives. The role of leadership and the inventiveness of workers have also been highlighted, showing how, at different times, unions have made great use of their associational power, and at the same time have been able to figure out how to get around the power of institutions, to manipulate the power of political leaders and to use discursive and moral power to frame their disputes to mobilise a wider constituency. The lesson that can be learnt from the examples in this chapter is that power cannot be divorced from strategy, and the capacity to put that strategy into action. Each dispute is contingent and requires an evaluation of what types of power can be utilised and in what particular circumstances. More often than not, single sources of power are not sufficient to win. The inventiveness of rank-and-file workers in devising their own strategies has demonstrated that they have the ability to take employers (and sometimes their own unions) by surprise to force them to meet their demands.

But what went wrong after 1979? Yes, it is well known that the Conservative governments from 1979 to 1997 were virulently anti-union, determined to roll back the welfare state and to impose greater state control. But as the previous chapters in this book have shown, economic and political climates for workers have been exceedingly difficult in the past, so what were the particular factors that caused unions and the working class to concede or lose so much of the power they had built since their formation? And why, despite concerted attempts in some quarters, has the UK union movement not been able to reverse the downward spiral of union power and membership? It is to this question that we now turn.

5

Structural Change and the Weakening of the Power of Workers

The tail end of the post-war boom, which extended into the 1960s and early 1970s, was arguably the height of union power in the UK. An almost inevitable consequence was that the state was mobilised extensively to curb union power in the following decades. As we will see, a whole range of hostile factors came into play in the last quarter of the twentieth century that were to have a significant impact on the way unions operate, but unfortunately, these were little met by a strategic response (or even a strategic re-evaluation) from the unions themselves. The influential 1968 Donovan Commission, whose remit was to consider the introduction of legal constraints on unions, and reform of the collective bargaining system (among other things) set the scene for the increasing codification of labour relations. Attempts by both the Wilson (Labour) and Heath (Conservative) governments to introduce these changes by consensus with employers and unions failed, and the 1979–97 Conservative governments, which became increasingly anti-union, brought in a raft of legislation designed to restrict the power of unions. At the same time, structural, economic and technological changes began to affect the labour market (e.g. the shift from manufacturing to service industry, the adoption of just-in-time production, privatisation and outsourcing, new technologies and the de-regulation of the financial markets) that would have an impact on the culture and effectiveness of trade unionism and eventually see greater 'flexibility' for employers and greater precariousness for employees.

Alongside this was the increasing introduction of individual employment rights, often emanating from the UK's membership of the European Union (although even these reforms were increasingly sidestepped by the creative use by employers of 'bogus' self-employment or zero-hours contracts). Yet the impact of these structural, cultural and legal changes has been little studied, either in unions themselves or in the academy, in the specific context of trade union organising and the rebuilding of union power. The aim of this chapter is to consider the individual and cumulative impact of these factors on the decline in union power, and why these factors should be re-evaluated when thinking about the lack of union power today. It will be argued later that the negative impact of these changes could perhaps have been reduced, or reversed, if the movement had adopted a more strategic and dynamic response to organising. The changing social, political, cultural and economic environments required a wholesale rethinking of strategy along with new tactics to meet the challenges, rather than continuing to use tools that worked when addressing different, and now largely histori-cal, challenges.

A RECONFIGURATION OF POLITICAL AND ECONOMIC STRUCTURES BEYOND THE NATION

The shifting of power dynamics at a geo-political level may appear to be unrelated to the smaller-scale power dynamics in the workplace, yet the two are inextricably linked. Major events like the First World War of 1914–18, the Russian Revolution of 1917, the Great Depression of the 1930s, the Second World War of 1939–45 and the Fall of the Berlin Wall in 1989, among others, were all pivotal events in world history that had a momentous impact on societies. They changed the actions and reactions of governments, the state, finance capital, workers, and society more broadly. Old certainties were rethought, and dominant ideologies changed, at times becoming more reactionary, and at others more progressive. Power potentialities shifted at macro, meso and micro levels in favour or against one class or another, and all of this has had a significant impact on workers and the labour movement. Unfortunately, the changing power balance in the last half-century has not, in the main, been favourable to the working class. The Donovan Report, published in 1968, is a useful anchor point to reflect on these changes and the ability of unions in the UK to gain substantial wins for workers in the recent period.

It was during the economic crisis in Britain of the 1960s that serious con-sideration was given to a review of industrial relations practice, and more precisely, a rethinking of how to manage collective bargaining and the rights of workers to withdraw their labour. But it's interesting to note that governments, employers and financiers, particularly those committed to free-market capitalism, are not averse to asking the state to intervene when crises develop and when they are forced to concede power to workers. Not only did the Labour government of 1964 propose the Royal Commission on Trade Unions and Employers' Associations that reported in 1968, but previous British governments had 'shown a remarkable attachment to the Royal Commission as a method of investigation and recommendation in the field of industrial relations' (Smith and Sloane 1969, p. 1). A Royal Commission on Labour was set up in 1891 to look into trade unions and labour relations (note this was in the period of 'new unionism' and the growth of the new general trade unions, which were just starting to flex their power). Another body was set up in 1917 during the war – the Whitley Committee – to report on industrial relations in the wake of the growing shop stewards' movement, and the widespread protest action against dilution.[1] At this time, there was an urgent need to ensure the smooth running of industry during the war to guarantee a continuation in essential supplies. This, it was believed, required good and harmonious industrial relations, so consultative committees made up of workers and employers were established to negotiate over pay and conditions, and where settlement couldn't be reached, these could be referred to arbitration.

Perhaps unsurprisingly, there was another state intervention in the form of legislation that was brought in immediately after the 1926 General Strike. The strike action began with mine workers who were facing longer hours with lower pay and who were locked out by the mine owners, and other workers feared the same would happen to them, hence the largest-ever industrial dispute in Britain. Following the strike – which ended in inglorious defeat when the Trades Union Congress withdrew its support – the Conservative government passed the Trade Disputes and Trade Unions Act in 1927. The Act banned political strikes that were designed to coerce the government as opposed to employers, sympathy strikes and mass picketing, and created a system whereby trade union members had to opt in to paying the political levy to the Labour Party.[2]

These examples show the extent to which political intervention and state mechanisms (institutional power) are used in an attempt to re-take the power captured by workers when they use their associational power to challenge governments and employers. But governments and the ruling class can also be cautious in their actions, recognising that they need to be able to correctly read the balance of class forces and choose when to go on the offensive to avoid fanning the flames of unrest. Infamously, the Conservative MP Quintin Hogg, conscious of the strikes during and following the 1914–18 war, warned of a similar situation arising again after the Second World War, saying: 'if you don't give the people social reform, they will give you social revolution'. There was an understanding, at least by the more sophisticated members of the establishment, that British capitalism faced a new reality at the end of the Second World War. There was a post-war consensus that society needed rebuilding, industry needed re-constructing, and the UK needed to rethink its empire. To do all this, there needed to be political co-operation from workers and their unions, the unemployed and the general public. This wasn't the time to go into battle with the working class, so social reforms were needed. Many of these reforms were at the heart of union demands: full employment, welfare provision for all, a national health service, social security, national insurance, and the nationalisation of industry and public utilities. A consequence was that for many politically engaged workers, this showed that concessions could be squeezed from employers and government. Poverty, low wages and poor working conditions were choices made by capital. During the 1950s and 1960s, the growing collective organisation of workers revealed how it was possible to challenge the balance of power between capital and labour through strikes and industrial action. A fairer distribution of wealth was attainable if workers were organised. We have already seen examples of how workers during the post-war period organised – the rediscovery of rank-and-file militancy as workers pushed their unions to be less cautious and accommodating, each win creating more and more confidence. But, unsurprisingly, capital and the ruling class were also planning ways to regain an ascendency of power.

REFORM OF THE UK'S VOLUNTARY SYSTEM OF INDUSTRIAL RELATIONS

A common refrain during the 1970s was that trade unions had too much power. This emanated from the Conservative Party, employers' bodies, political pundits and, of course, the media. But while this might be expected, it wasn't just the voices of capital expressing such views; influential figures within the Labour Party were also suggesting that some trade union activities needed to be curbed for the benefit of the country's economy. As already mentioned, it was the Labour government, as early as 1965, that established the Royal Commission on Trade Unions and Employers' Associations to 'conduct a searching examination of British industrial relations and to make recommendations for reform, including changes in labor law' (Banks 1969, p. 335). The 1964–70 Labour government was struggling with economic stagnation, a huge trade deficit, a decline in industrial competitiveness and an increase in prices as a result of expensive imports following the devaluation of the pound. On top of this, there were problematic labour relations, dwindling levels of investment and low productivity compared with other countries, making products more expensive. It was this industrial relations issue that was the focus for the Royal Commission. Its terms of reference 'implied that legal restrictions on unions would redress the balance of bargaining power in the labour market so increasing the efficiency and profitability of industry' (Marsh 1992, p. 6). While evidence and data were being gathered by the commission from both sides of industry, the Conservative Party was putting together separate proposals to deal with 'problematic' industrial relations. It published *Fair Deal at Work* (Conservative Political Centre 1968), which suggested the creation of an Industrial Relations Court to manage/determine disputes; the right of workers not to join a trade union (in opposition to the closed shop that operated at the time, and which often required workers at a union-recognised company to become union members); a move away from voluntarism, and the acceptance of legally binding collective bargaining agreements; that union immunities from prosecution for industrial action should be narrowed; and the establishment of a certification officer who would keep a register of unions and employer associations, and it would only be those registered that had legal rights.

The general election of 1970 saw the Conservatives returned to power, resulting in the implementation of many of their proposals in *Fair Deal at Work*, as well as others contained in the Donovan Commission report.[3] However, the Industrial Relations Act 1971 that enacted these proposals was ill-judged. Although the Conservatives fought the election with trade union reform as a central proposal, it was nevertheless extremely unpopular with trade unionists and little used by employers, who were concerned about the consequences of exacerbating union militancy. It seems that employers perhaps had a greater awareness of the possible consequences of using the Act to control workers than the government. The balance of power in the employment situation can shift quickly in either direction depending on the circumstances at any particular time, and the government hadn't quite recognised that enacting measures to control the unions is not the same as controlling union members and their workplace militancy. As one author remarked:

> The Act's authors presumed that unions were (or should be) business organizations in which executives gave orders to subordinates: hence the Act's main purpose was to force union leaders to control their members, especially shop stewards. But this ignored unions' dependence on the activity of unpaid officers and workers' representatives, whether or not union leaders were sympathetic to strong workplace organization. ... Also the economic situation during this period gave workplace leaders who had the backing of their members, as the dockers' shop stewards' committees had in the major ports, considerable power to defy union executives as well as their employers.
>
> (Lindop 1998, p. 66)

As we saw in Chapter 1, it was through the actions of the dockers' unofficial or rank-and-file movement that other workers were organised to take action in response to the imprisonment of the Pentonville Five, and it was this that defeated the Industrial Relations Act. David Marsh in his book *The New Politics of British Trade Unionism* (1992) on the decline of union power remarked that this particular legislation was a major failure for the Conservative government, but it did have a significant effect on future Conservative thinking, the results of which were to become painfully evident to unions from 1979 onward. However, by the mid-1970s the power of unions had begun to wane. Marsh argues that the Trades Union Congress worked closely with the 1974–79 Labour government, providing input into economic policy, sometimes achieving concessions, and at others accepting plans that were less favourable to workers than they would have liked. While it may have been the case that the union movement was consulted on a scale never seen before in peacetime by this Labour government, and although there were a range of individual workers' rights such as around redundancy and dismissal, this relationship with the Labour Party didn't result in an increase in power for the unions or their members – indeed, quite the opposite. David Coates makes this very point:

At critical periods in the Labour Government's history [1974–79], those consultations took the form of public negotiations with leading TUC members, to win support for government initiatives. All this served to sustain the popular mythology of trade union power. But publicity is never the most reliable index of influence. At best, it is an indication of importance, not of leverage.

(Coates 1983, p. 203)

The symbiosis between the political and industrial wings of the labour movement meant the two sides were, on occasion, dependent on each other for their power, but as in any relationship, one of the parties is likely to be more dominant at particular times. In this period, the government determined that its incomes policy (to keep wages down to prevent inflation) was essential, as were considerable cuts to public expenditure. The unions, while unhappy about the effect this would have on their members' jobs and pay, felt that with living standards falling and employment starting to rise, there was little they could (or should) do at this time. In essence, the unions helped to prop up an ailing Labour government. The point made here is that the weakening power of the union movement was already becoming evident at this time, and this was capitalised on by the incoming Conservative government in 1979. Union reform (or breaking the power of unions) was a central plank of the Conservative manifesto prior to the election, and it's worth quoting a section of this at length:

The crippling industrial disruption which hit Britain last winter had several causes: years with no growth in production; rigid pay control; high marginal rates of taxation; and the extension of trade union power and privileges. Between 1974 and 1976, Labour enacted a 'militants' charter' of trade union legislation. It tilted the balance of power in bargaining throughout industry away from responsible management and towards unions, sometimes towards unofficial groups of workers acting in defiance of their official leadership.

(quoted in *Times Guide to the House of Commons*,
1979, p. 285, cited in Marsh 1992, p. 23)

So, while the 1970s is often perceived to be the high point of UK trade unionism, the signs of its declining power, which have continued until today, were evident from the middle of the decade. To what extent were the unions aware of this at the time, and what were the responses in terms of strategy and tactics?

THE STEADY DECLINE IN UNION POWER
FROM THE MID-1970S ONWARD

Perhaps one of the early indications that the power of the unions was waning and the power of the employers and state increasing was in the, now infamous, dispute over union recognition at the small Grunwick photo-processing factory in north London 1976. The 500 workers at Grunwick were at first – given the prevailing stereotypes of the time – unlikely militants. It was a workplace of predominantly women from Asian and black Caribbean backgrounds, where films that were sent to the factory via the mail were processed, and pictures returned the same way. The factory was owned by a virulently anti-union employer, and the strike became centred on a demand for union recognition, but the initial issues were around a humiliating management, low wages, working conditions and a lack of grievance procedures. The militancy of the workers, combined with an economic climate where workers' wages were being held in check by the government's incomes policy, together with interference from the right-wing, well-funded pressure group the National Association for Freedom (NAFF), led to an explosive industrial dispute of national significance. Accounts from the workers reported that management at the factory was petty and vindictive; workers were expected to work overtime without any notice, and women had to raise their hands to male foremen if they wanted to use the rest rooms. The strike and the dispute that followed is well documented elsewhere (Anitha and Pearson 2018; Dromey and Taylor 1978; Phizacklea and Miles 1978; Rogaly 1977), but the aim here is to examine the power dynamic between the unions, the employer, the government and outside pressure groups like the National Association for Freedom, and the extent to which this influenced and reflected the weakening of power within the labour movement.

Lasting almost two years, the dispute at Grunwick had extraordinary support from national and local unions, trade councils, political organisations and some Labour MPs (including a Cabinet minister who appeared on the picket lines). At the start of the strike, the unions acted in an exemplary manner. The Association of Professional, Executive and Clerical and

Computer Staff (APEX) accepted the non-unionised strikers into the union, and within a matter of days had begun to pay strike pay. On the picket lines, where there were many violent confrontations between mass pickets and the police, the 137 strikers[4] were joined by postal workers, transport workers, bank workers and the Yorkshire miners. Given these factors, and following previous well-supported disputes, this appeared to many to be a strike that could be easily won despite the fact the factory had already replaced the strikers and continued to have a functioning workforce. More seriously, the unions were unaware of the anti-union counter-offensive that was being formulated to break the industrial power that had seen workers' wages and conditions generally improve in the previous couple of decades. This particular dispute wasn't one that could have been predicted to become the centre of the battleground over power in the industrial relations arena. It wasn't planned by union militants, the employer, the government, nor the NAFF, nevertheless it was opportunistically capitalised upon, and became a dispute that would have such far-reaching consequences for the future decline in power of the union movement. The dynamics in the Grunwick dispute were complex, but as one scholar has pointed out:

> It became a focal point for contested explanations and proposed remedies for that 'disease' [chaotic and adversarial industrial relations]. Grunwick became a test case of ideological binary oppositions: 'individual freedom' versus 'solidarity'; 'over-mighty unions' versus 'over-mighty bosses'; 'voluntarism' in industrial relations versus 'the rule of law'; 'us' versus 'them'.
> (McGowan 2008, p. 384)

This is a neat summary of what was taking place during this battle of opposing forces, and it was one that was most definitely about ideology, power and control. It also exposed, although few recognised it at the time, the redundancy of previously successful union tactics faced with an altogether more strategic opposition which changed the 'rules' of industrial relations and drew upon hitherto unused and unexpected power resources.

The initial response from the workers' union (and then the union movement) was to set up picket lines (a) to persuade other workers to join the small number that first walked out on strike, and (b) to prevent the factory from operating by blocking exit and entry of goods. Seven weeks after the dispute began, the TUC asked other unions to show solidarity action. The Union of Post Office Workers refused to handle Grunwick's mail, which effectively meant the factory could not operate as its business was mail-order photo-processing. In normal circumstances, this action would have been enough to force any recalcitrant employer to eventually back down, but these weren't normal circumstances. In the background supporting the employer was the National Association for Freedom. This was a right-wing libertarian pressure group that was virulently opposed to trade unions, and particularly their power to effect change. It was formed in 1975 by 50 prominent figures from politics, business, the Church and the armed forces with the aim of supporting individual freedom and promoting small government (Freedom Association 2020). Founding members included supporters of General Pinochet, the Chilean dictator who assumed power following a United States-backed coup d'état in 1973, and those on the right of the Conservative Party. We are informed that:

> The Association's ideological contributors included Sir Robert Thompson, who advised Nixon on his policy in Vietnam, and Brian Crozier, former director of a press agency part-funded by the CIA. Crozier shared an admiration for General Pinochet with NAFF's Director ... Robert Moss. Moss concurred with Crozier's judgement of Pinochet's Chile as 'one of the most interesting economic and constitutional experiments in the world today'.
>
> (McGowan 2008, p. 393)

This gives some indication of the type of organisation that threw its weight behind the employer at Grunwick, and this would become even more relevant later when Prime Minister Thatcher came to power in 1979. This 'interesting' experiment was in fact the birth of what has come to be known as neoliberalism. The brutal dictatorship of Pinochet drowned Chile's democracy in blood and then set about redistributing wealth from the poor to the already rich. Wholesale privatisation was just one of the many experiments, a model that was already being promoted by elements within and without the Conservative Party. Thatcher was impressed by the success of Chile's neoliberal economic programme and Pinochet's violent opposition to communism in Latin America (Moore 2013). In the mid-1970s, Thatcher was publicly advocating for an offensive against the power of the trade unions and for a shift to a smaller state and monetarist economics (Marsh 1992).

Behind the scenes, the ideological right were putting such plans into action. The NAFF was a useful 'front' to intervene to organise a massive blow to trade union power, and the organisation was to demonstrate its superior strategy and tactics in this dispute. As McGowan (2008) noted, the NAFF was 'litigious to the point of vexation'. The organisation was behind the legal action to force the courts to declare secondary action by the postal workers unlawful, and the union was ordered by the courts to call off the action. And when postal workers organised a second unofficial blocking of the post, the NAFF organised its members to enter the factory in the middle of the night and remove 100,000 items of mail that had been waiting to go out and get them into the wider postal system without the unions noticing. Both of these events had an impact on the effectiveness of the industrial action, weakening union power.

In November 1976, the union APEX referred the dispute to the Advisory, Conciliation and Arbitration Service (ACAS), a Crown non-departmental public body of government, on the advice of the secretary of state for employment, in the hope that it would rule in favour of the worker's demands for union recognition. ACAS did finally make this ruling in March 1977, but the employer refused to comply, and ACAS didn't have the enforcement powers to make it do so. The response from the union side was to begin mass picketing in June 1997, through to a final mass picket in November that year. These were often violent confrontations with aggressive policing that resulted in many injuries and arrests – more than 550 during the course of the dispute. The unions drew upon the same tactics that had been used during the miners' strikes of 1972 and 1974. Indeed, the miners came *en masse* from the Yorkshire coalfields to lend their support to the strikers, and at one point there were 20,000 people joining the picket lines in the narrow streets of north London.

Yet preparations by the government were in hand to ensure the power of workers would not be realised in this way again. The police were not only acting as paramilitaries on the street, they were operating behind the scenes with undercover police embedded within unions and left-wing groups,[5] and had been given the green light by the home secretary for 'adopting a more proactive response to the demonstrations and pickets, mindful of the "danger of bringing the government down"' (Anitha and Pearson 2018, p. 127). The strikers' union, APEX, came under pressure from the Labour government to pull back on the mass picketing, which it agreed to do. Once that occurred, what little power the workers had at this stage (it was clear the mass picketing was not effective) dissipated, along with the solidarity action from other unions and the TUC. While the women continued to fight without this support for the last few months, they eventually conceded defeat in July 1978 without having won any of their demands, including reinstatement.

Jack McGowan, in his insightful paper "'Dispute", "battle", "siege", "farce"? – Grunwick 30 years on' (2008), talks about how this strike came to be about class warfare – a battle for power – that neither side could afford to lose. It was, he reports, 'a crucial early triumph for "Thatcherism" *en route* to hegemony over economic and industrial policy' (McGowan 2008, p. 386). In terms of strategy and tactics, the unions had relied on methods that had served them well in the past, but as we learned in Chapter 2, power is a relationship, and the dynamics of that relationship are in constant change, which means protagonists who fail to constantly re-evaluate what is needed to win in the specific circumstances of a particular struggle are likely to pass the advantage to the other side. The employers and ruling class do not give up without a fight, and the ideological ground was shifting from that post-war consensus to an early form of neoliberalism. In terms of Grunwick, the unions were no longer on the offensive; instead they were, in McGowan's term, consigned to 'reactive antagonism' – they were forced to engage on the terms dictated by a more strategic opposition, rather than setting their own agenda– and in this sense, they were caught unaware. Perhaps this was not a surprise: the concerted response of the employer, government and NAFF was novel, but it set the tone for the future, and decades later, the trade union movement has yet to catch up.

Future plans to curb the power of the unions became evident in May 1978 when a report was leaked to *The Economist*, the Ridley Report,[6] setting out contingency plans to defeat any challenges from the unions. With a particular focus on the miners – perhaps unsurprisingly given the events of 1972 and 1974 – the report included plans to build up coal stocks to ensure no shortage of supply if there was a future strike, to make plans for the import of coal in case any strike was lengthy, to arrange for the recruitment of non-union lorry drivers to move coal where necessary and, to weaken the union fundamentally, to move away from coal to nuclear power. But the Ridley Plan went further than ensuring power supplies were stable; the intention was to emasculate the National Union of Miners, and thus send a message to the rest of the labour movement. Other tactics were to include 'cutting off the money supply to strikers and make the union finance them', but also to directly challenge union members picketing their workplaces. The report stated:

> it is also vital to our policy that on a future occasion we defeat violence in breach of the law on picketing. The only way to do this is to have a large, mobile squad of police who are equipped and prepared to uphold the law against the likes of the Saltley Coke-works mob.[7]
>
> (Ridley 1977, p. 25)

The report also stated:

> We might try and provoke a battle in a non-vulnerable industry, where we can win. This is what happened when we won against the postal workers in 1971. We could win in industries like the railways, B.L.M.C., the civil service and steel. Victory on ground of our choosing would discourage an attack on more vulnerable ground.
>
> (Ridley 1977, p. 24)

The strategy set out in this plan was based on the view that it was necessary to check union power, which was seen as interfering with market forces. Free-market neoliberalism was embraced by the Conservative government of 1979, and as a consequence, power needed to be taken away from the labour movement. Gradually, a well-thought out strategy was building to do just this, and it began almost immediately the Conservatives were elected in 1979 with the introduction of anti-trade union legislation. In 1980, the Employment Act was brought in to curb the power of unions, and this was reinforced, with even tighter restrictions on union activities, by a second Employment Act in 1982. This was just the start of the implementation of a raft of anti-union legislation that was introduced 'salami-style' every few years, and was done in this way because there was fear that the unions were, in the early 1980s, still strong enough to defeat a full-scale legal assault.

STRUCTURAL CHANGES LEADING TO THE REPEATED DEFEAT OF UNIONS IN INDUSTRIAL STRUGGLE

One of the many factors mentioned at the start of this chapter contributing to structural change in the workplace was the introduction of new technologies. This was particularly evident in the print industry, where computers came to replace the manual imputing of type (among other things). The print industry was heavily unionised with a number of unions, the National Graphical Association (NGA), Society of Graphical and Allied Trades and National Union of Journalists (NUJ), representing different job types in the sector. Print unions had operated a very tight closed shop (until it was made unlawful in 1990), restricting entry into the industry and operating strict demarcation lines, and workers were particularly highly paid compared to other sectors. Unions had, from the start, fought hard against new technologies that threatened to displace workers from their jobs. Nevertheless, despite this resistance, changes were being introduced, and it's reported that there were around 63,000 job losses in the industry between 1969 and 1976 (McIlroy 1988). The collective strength of the print unions meant that workers were, initially, able to stave off the introduction of some of the new technology. There were notable wins in 1976 at the *Daily Mirror* newspaper, and in 1979 at Times Newspapers. In the first case, the employer wanted to switch to photo-composition, which would reduce the need for compositors, and in the second, an attempt to introduce new equipment led to a year-long lock out, but ended in defeat for the employer. As one writer has noted: 'Advanced technological change has provoked the most extended and vital resistance in the printing industry because of its radical, far-reaching effects on trade unions' (McIlroy 1988, p. 120).

Indeed, the unions were acutely aware of the potential detrimental impact of new technology on their conditions of employment, the control over the labour process, and the likely reduction in the number of jobs needed. While the benefits of speed, productivity and control are important factors in the introduction of new technology, the saving of labour costs was/is also a significant consideration for employers. A dispute that exemplified this, and one that illustrated that the unions were unprepared for the changing power dynamics of industrial relations that had started to take place, was at the Messenger Group – a small provincial newspaper group in the northwest of England – in 1983. On the face of it, this was a strike over a closed-shop agreement, but in reality, what was at stake was the power of the union's role in the printing industry. Historically, through its control of work practices the NGA was effectively in control of hiring and firing workers due to the pre-entry closed-shop agreements with the employers. This was a uniquely powerful position which the union did not wish to lose. Failing to reach an understanding with the employer over the issue, six NGA union members withdrew their labour in July 1983, followed by 14 NUJ members who came out in support. The details of the dispute are too lengthy to recount here; suffice to say that the strike became protracted and the two sides entrenched. Once again mass pickets took place (estimates say 4,000-strong) and the paramilitary tactics experienced at Grunwick were once again in evidence. In a debate on the strike in the House of Lords, one speaker, Lord Harris of Greenwich, said:

> I believe that what has happened in Warrington this week has shocked public opinion in this country. It has been one of the worst episodes of industrial violence which we have witnessed in this country for several years.

> (Hansard 1983)

While this referred to alleged violence from the pickets, there were also contemporary reports that the violence from union members was a response to attacks from police who used baton charges to disperse many hundreds of pickets. Media reports talked about 'military style operations from the police. The employer, Eddie Shah, appeared to revel in the dispute when he stated it would take '3–4 armoured cars, a battalion of paratroopers and a couple of American Jolly Green Giants with machine guns on top' to stop him keeping his presses running (British Universities Film & Video Council 1983). Yet the weapon that was most effective as the employer armour was the use of a number of court injunctions against the union to stop the secondary action, and to force it to refrain from asking advertisers and suppliers to refuse to supply goods and from inducing customers from breaking commercial contracts with the company. This was a multi-pronged challenge to the union's power. As a result of non-compliance with the injunctions, £125,000 of the union's funds were initially sequestrated, but continuing non-compliance led to fines of up to £535,000 (approximately £1.8 million at today's prices). The balance of power the print workers had held over the industry was beginning to crack. In previous disputes across the sector there was widespread solidarity action that swiftly brought employers back to the bargaining table, but with the dispute dragging on for 11 months, power was ebbing away from the unions. The union was reliant on industrial dispute tactics from the past that had provided print workers with good industrial wages and comparatively good terms and conditions. Print workers were fully aware that newspapers are worthless if they are not produced on time, and in the past just the threat of strike action was enough to achieve con-cessions. A time-limited product like a newspaper can provide workers with considerable leverage and power in relation to their employer. However, in this dispute the unions had lost the discipline of their wider membership, which meant calls for solidarity action were not always heeded. Despite some valiant support from Fleet Street union members (always considered to the most militant and effective group of print workers) for a weekend of solidarity strike action in late November 1983, a significant number of chapels (union branches) at national newspapers broke the line and did not strike. Again, court injunctions and the sequestration of union funds were used by employers to restrict the activities of unions which supported the action. The dispute ended in defeat after 11 months of industrial action. John Gennard's article on the implications of this dispute for future indus-trial relations practice in the UK revealed some important elements in the dispute that contributed to the loss of union power:

> The NGA pursued this dispute against a non-traditional employer in the way that it pursued traditional employers for many years past. The Employment Acts perhaps impinge on the behaviour of the NGA more than any other union and in the Messenger dispute their fears in this respect proved to be well founded. The Acts present a severe dilemma to it since compliance with them means acting contrary to their own rules. For example, the NGA rule book requires its members not to supply work to non-unionists or to assist an antagonistic employer.
>
> (Gennard 1984, p. 12)

It was the use of the Employment Acts 1980 and 1982 that tied up the unions in litigation. First, regarding the closed shop, the Act introduced workplace ballots whereby at least 80 per cent of the workers in a particular establishment need to vote in favour. In this dispute, the non-union workers who had been brought in by the employer had a majority and voted against the closed shop. This meant the union was immediately on the back foot as it didn't have the support of most of the workers for its industrial action. Secondly, the Employment Act restricted picketing to only those who were actually party to the dispute, and further pickets were only allowed at the premises of their own employer. Breaching the Act, or continuing with the actions after injunctions were issued, not only meant huge fines, but also the sequestration of union funds, making it difficult for the union to function. What this means for the unions is that their power is essentially constrained. The in-union solidarity action that the print unions had drawn upon so successfully in the past had become not only unlawful, but also, more importantly in this dispute, largely undelivered. The use of this legislation, which had been enacted by the Conservatives under the leadership of Margaret Thatcher, who was virulently anti-union, demonstrated how the Acts were able to 'substantially curtail the degree to which unions can lawfully ask other trade unionists to take sympathetic action, and how the boundaries of lawful action have been successfully redrawn in favour of the employer' (Gennard 1984, p. 19). Gennard also notes that a further conclusion that can be drawn from the dispute is that 'the police now appear more efficient than previously in handling mass picketing and ensuring the employers receive essential production supplies' in order that they can continue with their business: they had, he said, 'learnt the lesson of the 1972 mass picket at Saltley' (1984, p. 15). Unfortunately, few in the labour and trade union movement recognised this decisive shift in power which made a previously unfailing strategy – calling for secondary action and mass picketing – largely undeliverable and ineffective.

It's clear that the state and the employers were both learning the lessons from past defeats, and the mechanisms for restricting the power of unions were being put into place to prevent future industrial action from being successful. There are two further events that illustrate how there was a divisive shift in power and control by capital being meticulously orchestrated from the 1970s onwards. It also quickly became evident that the labour movement did not have the same strategic planning or understanding of how the power dynamic was changing such that a complete rethinking of tactics was needed. Past tried-and-tested forms of industrial action were becoming increasingly less effective in this period of structural change.

THE 1984-85 MINERS' STRIKE AND THE 1986 BATTLE OF WAPPING: TWO SET-PIECE POWER STRUGGLES

It is not the intention here to provide a detailed analysis of the ins and outs of these two particular disputes, but merely to highlight the extent to which these events – unlike the Grunwick and Messenger strikes – were pre-planned clashes with a particular intention of undermining union power and deliberately weakening the union movement as a whole (Howell 1987; Towers 1985; Winterton and Winterton 1989). The government understood that a pit closure programme would likely precipitate a strike, and it was this 'tactical provocation' (Towers 1985) that set the wheels in motion for the defeat of the NUM in the 1984–85 strike. The manoeuvres set out in the Ridley Plan were all in place – almost to the letter – when the government announced the closure of Cortonwood Colliery in South Yorkshire, one of the regional strongholds of the union. As Brian Towers (1985, p. 16) noted, the government had 'all the physical and financial resources of the state at its disposal' and it had the determination to see through a lengthy strike – which it did. The strike lasted almost a year from March 1984.

The NUM's tactics were to use mass pickets, as it had done in 1972 and 1974. 'Flying pickets' were also used to spread the strike to other regions, but this time the police were well prepared. Not only had the state placed a spy[8] in the union's HQ so they were aware of the union's plans, they had developed paramilitary tactics learned from Northern Ireland and mainland street riots in the 1970s and early 1980s (Joyce and Wain 2014). There was a set-piece battle at a 5,000-strong mass picket in June 1984 at the Orgreave Colliery, where miners in shorts and T-shirts were violently attacked by police on horseback and in riot gear. Six thousand police officers were deployed, and 95 miners were charged with riot, unlawful assembly and violent disorder, and while the all trials collapsed some two years later when it was shown that the police had systematically falsified evidence, the damage was done. Recalling the events of the day 20 years later, historian and journalist Tristram Hunt (2006) remarked:

> What is not in dispute is that the battle for the Orgreave coking plant was one of the great set-piece confrontations of the miners' struggle. Almost medieval in its choreography, it was at various stages a siege, a battle, a chase, a rout and, finally, a brutal example of legalised state violence.

The NUM was outflanked on all sides in this dispute – legally, ideologically, economically and tactically – and in the end the union simply didn't have the power resources to win. Despite the heroism of the miners, their families and the wider community that provided financial assistance, the power resources of the state were stacked against them from the start of the strike. The tactic of the mass picket just wasn't enough to win this time. The secondary action and solidarity that unions had been able to draw upon in the past had also vastly diminished. Unions were now fearful of having their funds sequestrated, having witnessed this happen to the print unions just a few years earlier. In addition, some groups of miners were also doubtful about their chances of success and either didn't join the strike, or did, but were reluctant to do so. Furthermore, the Conservatives had also taken control of the narrative: unions were too powerful, they contributed to inflation and low productivity, exacerbating Britain's ongoing economic difficulties, they were undemocratic and had too much control, they were run by militants who wanted to take control of the country, etc. A large percentage of the general public – which, of course, also includes trade union members – came to believe these views. Tara Martin López reports in her book on the Winter of Discontent the way the Conservatives began using the media to leverage Thatcher's policy advisors' communication plan ('Stepping Stones'; Hoskyns and Strauss 1977) to create negative views of trade unions (Martin López 2014). A few quotes from the 69-page policy document show the intention – which was put into practice extensively during the 1984–85 miners' strike – to use the power of ideological control to shift the working class from the view that Labour and the unions had their interests at heart: 'Skilfully handled, however, the rising tide of public feeling could transform the unions from Labour's secret weapon into its major electoral liability, and fear of union-Tory conflict could be laid to rest.' It went on to say that a principal objective of the communication strategy was to persuade the electorate to reject socialism and its continued promotion by the trade union leadership. To do this, the Conservatives needed to make Labour voters feel 'a deep aversion to the Labour–trade union leadership link and its result – the "Sick Society". (Disappointment with material results is not enough.)'

These factors outside the union, and divisions within, contributed to the weakening of the NUM's power, but also trade unionism itself. It's often been said that the defeat of the miners affected the very soul of the labour movement, and in a way, it was a blow from which it has never recovered. The Conservative governments, over their period of 18 years in power, further demoralised millions of union members, and their monetarist economic policies resulted in privatisation and mass unemployment which stripped unions of one their major strengths – their memberships –

while also weakening the propensity of trade union members to take action through a genuine and realistic fear of unemployment.

Before considering the larger questions that arise from the decline in union power from the 1970s to the 1980s, it's important to consider another set-piece challenge to the union movement, but this time from the perspective of a hostile employer. Again, it is not the intention here to consider the detail of what happened in the News International dispute in Wapping, London in 1986 – the year after the miners' strike ended – but to further consider how structural, economic and ideological changes in the labour market and society, along with ever more restrictive legislation governing the affairs of trade unions, contributed to the weakening of the power of workers and the decline in trade union membership.

The Trade Union Act 1984, the third piece of anti-trade union legislation introduced since 1979, required trade unions to hold a secret ballot before calling industrial action.[9] The strike at the Rupert Murdoch-owned enterprise News International erupted at new premises producing national newspapers, but with new technology that would have resulted in massive job losses. In a heavily unionised industry where the unions were used to controlling the labour supply, this was a direct challenge to their power. Immediately following the walk-out, the 6,000 staff were dismissed and replaced with around 700 (all that were needed to produce the same work with the new technology). Anticipating the reaction from the unions, Murdoch had been in secret negotiations with the Electrical, Electronic, Telecommunications and Plumbing Union to recruit replacement workers. This was a union known for its 'sweetheart deals' with employers who wanted to undermine trade union power, and it was subsequently expelled from the TUC as a direct consequence. Combined, the new legislation was extremely useful to employers. Mass picketing and secondary action – traditional trade union tactics – were now unlawful as they were undertaken without a ballot, meaning the union could be fined and its funds could be sequestrated. News International initiated a whole range of legal actions against the unions. As John McIlroy explained:

Its [the Society of Graphical and Allied Trades'] assets were sequestrated and it was fined for contempt. It now did something a union had never done before: it quickly took steps to purge its contempt and gave the courts assurances that, in the future, it would operate within the law. The unions were, henceforth, severely impeded by the existence of the legislation in effectively running the dispute.

(1988, p. 91)

The unions attempted to mass picket the newspaper plant, but were met with the same paramilitary tactics seen the year before in the miners' strike. The scenes of violence resembled riots, with cavalries of mounted police charging down Wapping High Street into lines of pickets and fully tooled-up officers attacking the unions' speaking platform and vehicles. Hundreds of pickets and police were injured, with more than 1,200 people arrested. Again, the extent of the resources deployed by the state to protect the plant and the replacement labour allowed the employer to break the power of unionised labour. The strike went on for a year, but it eventually ground to a halt as it became obvious to everyone that the pickets were not succeeding in causing economic damage to News International.

THE PRICE OF DEFEAT

The much more aggressive style of management witnessed in the examples in this chapter didn't end when the disputes concluded, and those who retained their jobs in either the mines, the press, Grunwick or elsewhere, found a new and controlling management approach emerging. This developed as 'human resource management' throughout the 1980s, and in order to work, it required compliant or non-existent unions. The ideology of neo-liberalism adopted by the Thatcher governments required the markets to operate freely, and this meant driving down labour and increasing the share of income going to capital. But, as we have seen, free-marketeers are not averse to assisting the needs of capital by implementing legislation which provides it with an additional lever of power to challenge any threat from workers to profits. Unions are the very antipathy of free-market capitalism, thus their potential for power – membership and collective action – had to be destroyed, or at least severely limited.

Undoubtedly, the period covered in this chapter was a time of fundamental change, not just in terms of politics and the economy, but culturally and socially as well. The impact on the union movement was transformative, but not in a positive way. The decline from a high of over half of all workers in the UK as members of trade unions at the start of the 1980s to just under a quarter in 2020 shows the extent to which the aim of the Conservatives to reduce union membership was successful. The combined challenges of technological development, the decline in manufacturing and monetarist economic policies led to slack labour markets with high levels of unemployment during Conservative rule – none of which is helpful to trade union membership or trade union power.

In terms of strategies to undermine the strength of trade unionism, the right had spent considerable time planning the approaches it would take. Considerable thought had gone into the power resources upon which it could draw. Institutional power, in terms of control over the legislative process, was one of the strongest levers the government had. The effect of legal sanctions on union power was evident in the cases outlined in this chapter, constraining the ability of unions to draw upon their main sources of power – the associational or collective power of union members in withdrawing their labour. The power of the state in terms of secret information-gathering by infiltration of unions, providing a paramilitary force to protect employers, and the intimidation and creation of fear among striking workers and their supporters was also utilised to great effect. Perhaps more insidious, but no less effective, was the sophisticated use of the media to create an ideological narrative that portrayed unions as outdated, too-powerful,[10] politically motivated, self-serving bodies only concerned with their own sectional interests.

In terms of the power resources available to labour, this chapter has shown how different forms of traditional power were slipping away from unions. While trade union membership was at its peak during this time, the ability to utilise this collectively was hampered by emerging structural changes in the economy, fear of the law, violence and lack of confidence in the ability to win when others had failed so spectacularly. It is perhaps easy with hindsight to speculate why unions appeared to be so unprepared for the attacks they were to face from the mid-1970s onward, when the right had not tried to hide just how well it was preparing. However, hindsight does gives us the opportunity to reflect on whether or not the union movement could have responded differently to the onslaught it faced or why it responded in the way it did.

As more traditional levers of power were diminished, were new and emerging sources of potential power left untapped despite the scale and the extent of the some of the defeats recalled here? Why did unions rely on tried-and-tested tactics that were no longer effective, and why did new tactics not emerge? There is, perhaps, a whole book to be written on this topic, but a contributing factor may be that the over-reliance on the closed shop for membership meant that unions didn't place a premium on the organising and recruitment of members. When the closed shop was made unlawful, there wasn't a culture or practice of shop stewards undertaking organising activity at the capacity that was needed. Similarly, the decline of the shop stewards' movement and the increasing dependency on union full-time officer staff meant that decision-making increasingly moved away from the workplace and the members themselves. As workers were afforded increasing numbers of minimum statutory rights and with a lack of industrial power, a more servicing approach of unionism was adopted whereby the union became to be seen more as an insurance policy if there was a problem at work, rather than a collective endeavour to improve working conditions for all. Thirdly, there was little focus on the organising of new workplaces, or in emerging sections of the labour market or where part-time workers, women or migrant workers were located. Eric Hobsbawm considered this point in his essay 'The forward march of labour halted' (1978). He said 'there are people in persistently low-paid occupations virtually beyond the range of effective trade unions'. But there was no strategy to organise these into the unions, creating a gap between the poorest sections of the labour market and limiting the extent to which they could benefit from collective organisation:

> A hundred years ago the labour movement recommended its forms of struggle and organisation to everybody – trade unions, co-ops, etc. But it was then not *accessible* to everybody, but only to the favoured strata of workers. Let us ask ourselves whether there isn't a similar complacency among some sections of the movement today.
>
> (Hobsbawm 1978, p. 284)

By 1986, the gauntlet had not only been thrown down, but two of the great armies of the trade union movement, the print workers and the miners, had suffered previously unimaginable defeats. That other force once believed unconquerable, the dockers, soon experienced their own defeat as the National Dock Labour Scheme, which had eliminated casual labour from the docks, was abolished in 1989. The old ways were no longer working, and bravery and a militant mindset were no substitute for a strategy to meet the new challenges and rebuild trade union power. As we shall see in the next chapter, the trade union movement adopted a strategy of 'new realism', but unfortunately it wasn't designed to regain power, but rather to accommodate to the loss of power that the unions had eventually recognised.

6

Union Responses to Decline
and Loss of Power

This chapter considers the response of the UK's trade union movement to decline and its progressive loss of power from the mid-1970s onwards. Over half of all employees were union members in 1979 when the Conservative government was elected, and by the time Labour entered government in 1997, that figure was down to only one third – a loss of approximately 5.5 million members (Department for Business Innovation and Skills 2014). What was the response from unions to this ongoing decline? In particular, what were their approaches to defending the terms and conditions of many of their members at a time when pensions, pay, jobs, and even the status of employment, were under sustained and systematic attack? Similarly, what was the response to the loss of union influence over policy-making at national level?

The cumulative effect of the defeats on the unions that were explored in the last chapter were immense, but these were also compounded by the deep recessions of the early 1980s and 1990s. From 1979 to 1984, unemployment rose from 5.3 per cent to 11.9 per cent, and inflation was 18 per cent at the start of the 1980s. In 1990, there was another five-quarter recession which saw unemployment rise from 6.9 per cent to 10.7 per cent in 1993.[1] Research shows that unemployment and recessions generally have a negative impact on trade union membership as union members lose their jobs and other workers become fearful that they might (Carruth and Disney 1988; Gallie et al. 1996; Mason and Bain 1993). Structural changes in the labour market (e.g. from manufacturing to servicing, and the increase in part-time working), the ideological promotion of the 'new individualism' in society as opposed to the 'old' ideology of collectivism (epitomised by Thatcher's famous assertion: 'there is no such thing as society'), the reduced bargaining power of unions and hostility from employers were all reasons that contributed to the drastic fall in union membership (Waddington 1992). These factors, of course, created a considerable challenge to the labour movement, but the impact of declining power seemed to have led to an (albeit unconscious) existential crisis for trade unions.

Before this period of decline, unions were generally clear about their purpose: the reason for their very existence was to improve/defend the working conditions of their members, but this was becoming increasingly difficult. Without the power to gain formal recognition from employers, without the ability to effectively collectively bargain, without securing material gains, why would people join trade unions or retain their membership – what was the point of trade unionism? The union movement needed to consider these questions and develop strategies to either rebuild power or ensure its continued existence without it. But before we consider these questions, we need to step back a little to consider one important point that might inform our understanding of the future directions taken by the TUC and its affiliated unions.

THE CONTINUING INFLUENCE OF THE DONOVAN REPORT ON INDUSTRIAL RELATIONS THINKING AND THE DECLINE OF UNION POWER

The previous chapter discussed how the inquiry into collective labour law and industrial relations practice (the Donovan Commission), set up by the Labour government in 1965 and reporting in 1968, contained proposals to reform the process of collective bargaining. The importance of the report cannot be overstated as it 'marked the start of a series of attempts to alter the nature of British collective bargaining; attempts which different governments have continued through varied policies to the present day' (Palmer 1986, p. 267). It is useful to revisit one particular concern of the report – informal workplace bargaining by local shop stewards – because this perhaps provides an insight into the diminishing power of unions in later decades and the response to declining union membership.

It should be noted that the Donovan Commission was comprised of both employer (four members) and trade union representatives (two members) – along with industrial relations and labour law academics (three members) and three independent members, including the chair. George Woodcock, general secretary of the TUC, and Harold Collinson, who was president of the TUC in 1965, were both members representing the political power of the trade union movement. There was a consensus from the members that unofficial strikes and restrictive practices were in need of reform, but it would seem that there was also a 'broad pluralist common ground', and while 'several members of the Commission were simply looking for tougher legal controls to punish unofficial and unconstitutional strike action', within the group as a whole, 'no one doubted the central role of unions and collective bargaining' (Ackers 2014, pp. 71 and 75). While there were differing views on solutions to the perceived problem of informality of the British industrial relations system, the consensus within the commission appears to have been that the state's role should be that of encouraging employers and unions to work together voluntarily to bring about reform and promote best industrial relations practice.

The Donovan Report was critical of the unofficial and unconstitutional strikes over local issues not covered by the formal industry-wide agreements.[2] It said that the key locus of collective bargaining had, over time, shifted from the industry level (by national union officials) to the factory level, where negotiations were in the hands of local shop stewards. In the inter-war period, when there was high unemployment, the formal system of industrial relations led by national unions and their counterparts in industry had been perceived as working particularly effectively. But after 1945, when there was full employment, it was felt that this formal system began to break down as it was no longer regulating wages and conditions (Ackers 2014). A consequence was that workers took matters into their own hands, and power became devolved to the workplace between workers and local managers rather than between national employers' associations and trade union general secretaries. This informal workplace bargaining was considered haphazard and disruptive, and often resulted in disorderly pay structures that had a knock-on effect across industrial sectors with 'leapfrog' bargaining pushing up wages and inflation. As the report noted, this changed the balance of power *within* unions between local shop stewards and full-time officers employed by the unions. Unions thus had much less control over their members:

> Management acceptance of local bargaining, together with full employment, has inflated the power of industrial work groups. Work group solidarity also has enhanced the position of the shop steward in the plant ... it is not so much that unions have lost power as there has been a

downward shift of authority within them. In this regard, the multi-union character of the British labour movement has strengthened work group independence in the plant in several ways … however, as a result of their extra-constitutional status, these committees are not easily made responsible to formal trade union structure outside the factory.

(Banks 1969, p. 339)

The issue of workplace power controlled by shop stewards raised in the quote above was an issue that was at the heart of the proposed reforms that came about after the Donovan Report. The informality of workplace bargaining, and how this was changed following Donovan, may also provide some understanding of the measures taken by the TUC and unions to address their declining membership, and their apparent inability to rebuild the labour movement and regain the power it once had. Prior to the 1980s, local shop stewards had far more control over the labour process and bargaining over pay, hours of work, the distribution of overtime, recruitment and redundancy than is the case today. The industry-wide agreements of the past laid down minimum standards which the local shop stewards generally exceeded in their local negotiations with their own employers. Another concern was that as shop stewards' committees were often multi-union, it meant that they were not accountable to individual trade unions. Operating outside formal union structures meant that full-time officers, or national unions, had little influence over what happened at local levels. Inevitably, this left negotiating power in the hands of the lay worker representatives who controlled these committees.

While the government and employers were keen to have a more streamlined and accountable formal collective bargaining system, unions also bought into the idea that reform could redistribute power in a way that encouraged responsibility on each side of the employment relationship. Importantly, given it was a Labour government that instigated the Donovan Commission and was pushing for reform because of the perceived impact of poor industrial relations on the state of the economy, the informal bargaining system, which was out of the control of national unions, made tripartite[3] incomes policy impossible to manage. On the one hand, the Labour government needed the unions to control their members if it was to manage the economy, and on the other hand, the unions wanted a seat at the table to secure better terms and conditions for their members. Institutional power through legislation and policy-making, rather than collective power through strike action and disruption, was their preferred means of conducting collective bargaining, as was evident in their participation in and contribution to the commission. This approach to negotiations, being carried out by union officials (lay and staff) and general secretaries, not *ad hoc* members at shop floor level, would, the commission (and some trade unions) believed, more likely be orderly and controllable. Donovan's proposal was to redistribute power more evenly within unions by assigning more formal and clear roles to shop stewards in union rulebooks and within the multi-level collective bargaining structures, with the aim of formalising their role and tying it more tightly to union structures.

The report also recommended that the state's role should be to encourage voluntary reform and best practice – the idea of the model employer – but also that management should professionalise employment relations by regaining control over working practices and wages through productivity bargaining. This represented a fundamental shift from distributive bargaining – where unions argue for an increase in the share of profits – to integrative bargaining, where unions agree to increased productivity in exchange for an increase in pay, which contributed significantly to the transfer of power toward the employers. The recommendation in the Donovan Report was for 'partnership through adversarial bargaining' (Ackers 2014, p. 82), and this is where the seeds of the TUC's 1990s partnership approach to union renewal were planted – an issue to which we will return later in this chapter.

In summary, emerging from the Donovan Report was a consensus that trade unions represented a legitimate interest and that there needed to be a fair process of bargaining between labour and capital, but that this process needed to be formalised and professionalised. There needed to be an end to the endemic wildcat strikes that were seen by the commission as inefficient and disruptive – although presumably they were perceived differently by those workers who participated in them and won concessions through them. A belief in this largely mythical 'fair and balanced' approach to industrial relations promoted by the Donovan Report led the leadership of the trade union movement to adopt policies and practices based on false assumptions that were to be unhelpful in rebuilding the union movement. The first assumption, that unions were legitimate 'partners', intellectually disarmed unions before the approaching onslaught from Thatcher and neoliberalism. The key leadership thinking was that if unions played a more responsible role, their future would be assured – this was the basis of 'new realism' proposed by the TUC's general secretary, Len Murray, at the annual congress in 1983. The second proposition, that unions should police their members and put an end to the 'disruptive' influence of rank-and-file militancy, effectively demobilised their capacity to use structural power through collective action when their influence at 'top table' negotiations proved insufficient. It would, however, take a number of years for this tragedy to fully unfold.

AN IDEOLOGY OF 'NEW REALISM' IS PROMOTED BY THE TUC IN THE EARLY 1980S

The acceptance (albeit sometimes reluctant) for much of the twentieth century of the incorporation of trade unions into the machinery of government and decision-making, and the belief that unions were a legitimate tripartite partner along with employer organisations, changed fundamentally with the election of the Conservative government in 1979. The move away from tripartism during the 1980s, and the unwillingness of the Thatcher governments to countenance any role for unions as a social partner, raised some important questions about the future role of British unionism: it created a period of reflection on the structure, form and internal relations of unions, and importantly, the role of the TUC itself. In essence, what had changed at this time was the shift in power between unions, the state and employers, which meant the unions were rapidly losing the power they once held. It has been argued by Joe England and Brian Weeks that the former strength of British trade unionism lay in the fact that it was able to exercise power at three different levels: the workplace through shop steward activity, via industry-wide negotiations through full-time officers, and at the level of the TUC and its relationship with the state (in particular when the Labour Party was in government). Yet this strength was weakened because:

> Divisions between national leader and shop stewards, between the leaders of different unions, between shop stewards and rank-and-file members, and between the workers in different factories have been successfully exploited by employers and governments in recent years.
>
> (England and Weeks 1981, p. 426)

111

Not only fully aware that there were deep-seated challenges to its power from government and employers, the trade union movement was also experiencing its own crisis in how to manage power within its own structures and between its own constituents. While unions have never been homogenous in their political or industrial strategies – they are often categorised as left- or right-leaning or moderate or militant – significant divisions and ideological changes within the union movement began to open up in the early 1980s in terms of future strategy. These were exploited by employers and governments and would further undermine union power over the next few decades.

The Electrical, Electronic, Telecommunications and Plumbing Union was one of the first to make clear its ideological break with the militancy of the 1960s and 1970s and to demonstrate a new approach of moderation, co-operation and partnership with employers when, in 1981, it signed a single-union binding pendulum arbitration[4] deal with manufacturing company Toshiba (Kelly 1996). This pre-empted the TUC's adoption of what was termed 'new realism' – a recognition that after the re-election of the Conservatives in 1983, there was unlikely to be a return to a co-operative relationship between unions and government – so, instead of confrontation, unions should adopt a more conciliatory approach. After 1979, the initial union response to declining membership was to 'wait for Labour' in the hope that the Conservatives would be voted out after one term in office. Indeed, there was a belief by union leaders that there would be a natural correction of the anti-union rhetoric of the right-wing of the Tory party by the more liberal Conservative MPs. Robert Taylor quotes from Len Murray, TUC general secretary, who said:

> we simply did not believe what she said she would do and we didn't believe most Conservatives did either ... we simply misread history ... believing she was a passing breeze which would blow itself out .... [The TUC] delayed far too long in making some changes that were patently necessary and got stuck in a rut of opposition.
>
> (Taylor 2000, p. 246)

However, with the landslide victory[5] of the Tories in the 1983 general election, it became evident that the Conservative right were not going away, and it would likely be many years before Labour was back in government (although the unions probably did not expect it would actually be another 14 years). The labour movement knew from Conservative policy documents and manifesto commitments that it faced increasing attacks and legislative restrictions on its use of collective action to challenge the power of employers. It was only a year after the promotion of new realism that the labour movement realised that conciliation wasn't the approach the Conservatives wished to take. This was forcefully demonstrated when the government provocatively banned trade unions at the Government Communications Headquarters, the central communication intelligence and security organisation, and then provoked the miners' strike in 1984.

In a 1993 'think piece' for the Fabian Society on the future of trade unions, two authors closely associated with the union movement[6] discussed the different strategic approaches adopted by unions from the mid-1980s onwards to counter union decline (Bassett and Cave 1993). In summary, there were five main ideas that were promoted in this document:

- to increase recruitment where unions were already recognised by the employer for collective bargaining;
- to build membership in new non-organised workplaces;
- to expand a range of legal and financial services that weren't traditionally associated with trade unionism;
- to consolidate by merging with other unions;
- more controversially, to make unions more appealing to employers through 'partnerships' by making concessions such as single-union recognition, and no-strike agreements.

The authors' conclusion to their report was that unions needed to accept that their role should change to one of greater provision of individual services becoming 'insurance-based' organisations that dealt more with workers as individuals rather than as a collective. This thinking, a decade on, was a reiteration of the re-visioning of the trade union movement that was promoted by the TUC at its annual congress in 1983, when unions approved the so-called 'new realism' strategy put forward by the general secretary Len Murray. The rationale was that if unions adopted a more moderate approach, then the Conservatives' legislative programme could perhaps be lessened through dialogue and partnership working with employers. While it is understandable, given the drastic fall in membership, that unions needed to try new approaches to rebuilding, it's difficult to comprehend how partnership would build power. There had been a definite shift to more hard-line anti-union stances by employers since the early 1980s, and an accompanying re-establishment of managerial prerogative through the use of human resource management practice, so it is puzzling why this was considered a realistic way forward. However, let's take a look at what impact the adoption of the five different approaches to rebuilding had on the union movement.

THE NEW UNION AGENDA OF PARTNERSHIP WORKING WITH EMPLOYERS

In 1984, the TUC put forward its strategy document advocating the need for greater collaboration with government and employers. Its vision of a less adversarial employment relations style was aimed at expanding union membership into sectors of the economy where membership and density were low. Part of this approach, particularly promoted by the TUC and the more moderate unions, was to accept single-union deals (favoured by employers as the union was easier to manage), no-strike clauses in union recognition agreements, more flexible working practices, and increased individualist employee policies like performance-related pay. The positioning document *A New Agenda: Bargaining for Prosperity in the 1990s* (General, Municipal, Boilermakers and Allied Trades Union 1991) laid out a set of bargaining issues based on benefits to the individual worker, including training, equal opportunities, job satisfaction and job security. These very much accepted the Thatcher ideology of individualism – that workers were now only concerned about what benefited them as individuals. John Edmonds, author of the report and general secretary of the General, Municipal, Boilermakers and Allied Trades Union (GMBATU, usually shortened to GMB), explained that this was a 'top-down' strategy from the unions, and originated from the need to 're-market' trade unions as modern organisations that could provide a service to individuals, because it was perceived that workers wanted an answer to the question ,'What can you do for me?' He said:

The British system is too conflict-based to allow sensible handling of the wider agenda at the moment [dealing with those issues mentioned above].

The present institutions actually create conflict – almost out of anything. The British industrial relations system is lousy, it's awful. It doesn't work.

(John Edmonds, in Storey et al. 1993, p. 69)

This was also the view from the leadership within the TUC. John Monks became general secretary in 1993 and was, in his own words, an enthusiastic advocate of partnership working. In an article in the *Independent* newspaper in April 1999, he said:

we [the TUC] wanted to make partnerships with employers the goal, seeking relationships to gain trust, and using that basis to change quickly and smoothly without disputes and disruption. We have started to evangelise this kind of trade union.

(Monks 1999)

This strategy was approved by the TUC Congress in 1999, and resulted in the establishment of the Partnership Institute in January 2001:

The General Council have continued to promote partnership at work as an important approach to industrial relations, which will deliver improvements to members' jobs and economic benefits for employers. The aim is to encourage unions and employers to develop effective working relationships. The intent is to extend union influence at a corporate level over an organisation's policy and strategy, and increase reps' and members' involvement at a local level in the implementation of business decisions.

(TUC 1999, Chapter 5, 'Partnership Institute')

Unions were in this period very much on the back foot; membership was declining year on year, and they had lost much of their influence in effecting change. Partnership was a defensive strategy, but it was believed by some of the movement's leadership to be *the* way forward if unions were to survive. While examples were provided of progressive employers who were prepared to do partnership deals (Samuels and Bacon 2010; Wills 2004), there were also critics who argued that there were likely to be negligible gains for workers, or trade unions, as workers only made gains where unions were strong and where companies were performing well (Jenkins 2007; Kelly 1999). Monks himself admitted that 'many companies still don't respond positively to the partnership message', but there was hope that by demonstrating moderation and assisting in making business more productive, more employers would consider unions to be of benefit. The TUC general secretary explained that unions were now operating in a changed era and that they needed to adapt to a 'new realism' – whereby the political influence unions once had was no more. Now unions needed to find a new way to operate:

> The future of trade unions will be shaped by a mixture of factors, including the economic context, the structure of the labour market, the political situation and prevailing social attitudes. It will also be shaped by our own competence and the way we operate … labour looked almost exclusively to the national government – in terms of either winning political power or securing corporatist influence – as the best means to obtain some or all of its desired ends.
>
> (Monks 1993, p. 230)

It is perhaps understandable, given the political and economic circumstances that had weakened the power of unions to the extent they had, that the main focus of union leaders was on survival – keeping unions in place until there was a possibility of recovery. Remaining in the workplace and being recognised by employers – however limited the influence of the union – was perhaps considered a better alternative to de-recognition and having no seat at the table. Yet the idea that social partnership could replace class conflict with a new era of understanding between employers and unions was misguided given the social, political and economic environment. Twenty years after the partnership approach was first mooted, evidence in 2003 reported that union gains were limited, and that employers were less than enthusiastic in engaging with unions in this way: 'From trade union and employee perspectives, however, the implications of such pragmatic acceptance are less positive, since the evidence of any corresponding union strengthening appears at best ambivalent and that of employee benefit negative or non-existent' (Terry 2003, p. 504). Other analysis of the union partnership model also finds that the actual number of partnership agreements have been relatively modest and their content limited. Peter Samuels and Nick Bacon note that this is unsurprising given the imbalance in power between employers and workers:

It appears that voluntary partnership agreements are weak instruments for extending fairness at work in the low-trust industrial relations contexts of liberal market economies, such as Britain. Despite the partnership rhetoric of New Labour's Third Way since 1997–2010, it seems that in the absence of stronger statutory and institutional supports for employee participation and gain sharing, voluntary partnership agreements in Britain express only modest aims of limited ambition.

(2010, p. 446)

From the vast body of research evidence into partnership at work,[7] there is little that shows this approach from unions had any significant impact on union membership and density – and even less that demonstrates an increase in union power (Danford et al. 2002; Heery 2002; Kelly and Badigannavar 2011). The one exception is the case of the Union of Shop, Distributive and Allied Workers (USDAW), which has transformed itself into being based primarily on partnership working with four big retail companies. Retail is a high-turnover sector, and the union consequently reportedly loses around a third of its membership each year. USDAW describes itself as an 'organising union', having set up its own organising academy along similar lines to that of the TUC's Organising Academy. Its aim is 'for workplaces to be self-sufficient with little need to call on an Usdaw official' (Parker and Rees 2013, p. 525). Its partnership approach has allowed it to significantly increase its membership and density in the four companies (when in most other unions it has been declining), including through agreements for shop stewards to have 'stand-down' time to recruit and represent members. It became, in many ways, the type of union recommended by the Donovan Report: it had a consensual and co-operative relationship with employers, there was a role for the union in promoting the interests of its members, shop stewards were trained to deal with grievances themselves while leaving collective bargaining to the full-time officers, and there were effective consultation mechanisms over changes to working practices. While all this was beneficial to the finances and continued existence of the union, what was missing was any attempt to build power so that in negotiations, the employer might – using the measure articulated by Martin Luther King – be forced to say 'yes' when they wanted to say 'no'. While USDAW members get a visible union and trained reps to support them over individual matters, there is little ability within the partnership agreements to either challenge the employer's right to manage, or redistribute wealth through winning higher wages.[8]

UNIONS MERGING: WHERE IS THE POWER IN THIS APPROACH?

A second strategic approach taken by unions to counter decline was to rationalise their organisations in an attempt to minimise costs by avoiding duplication. Following a business model strategy, there was a belief that merger into larger unions would result in economies of scale, and perhaps growth and expansion. It was argued that this restructuring of the bound-. aries of unions would produce more effective and efficient unions and contribute to union revival (Undy 1993). In terms of revitalisation strategy, it was theorised that larger unions would lead to increased bargaining power with employers. Some unions thought that merger would result in greater consolidation of members in particular sectors or occupations, and perhaps the ability to expand into new areas. Yet 'there was little evidence of the recruitment of significant number of non-unionists in new territories following transfers' (Undy 2008, p. 232). Further, it was shown in Roger Undy's book *Trade Union Merger Strategies: Purpose, Process and Performance* (2008), that the leading merger unions all recorded very significant losses,[9] rather than gains, of membership, indicating these were defensive moves at a time of generally falling membership. Without doubt the 'mega-mergers' into super-unions (Unison and Unite) created the *potential* to wield political power, with almost 4 million members between them. As significant funders of the Labour Party (to the tune of millions of pounds annually, topped up further at times of elections), it might be expected that this connection – along with reserved union seats on the party's national executive committee – would result in substantial political influence and increased bargaining power. Yet, as Labour prime minister Tony Blair said when elected in 1997, unions could expect fairness, but not favours:

> you run the unions. We run the government. We will never confuse the two again. For the first time in 20 years, trade union leaders came into Downing Street; they are consulted, they are listened to, just as the CBI [Confederation of British Industry] are. No favours, but fairness.
>
> (Tony Blair, speech to TUC Congress, 15 September 1999)

It was evident from this time, and throughout the New Labour governments that followed, that the political power unions were once able to draw upon as a result of their relationship with the Labour Party had largely dissipated. Some in the union movement questioned whether that organic relationship between the two wings of the labour movement was at an end. Indeed, the Fire Brigades Union (FBU), and the Rail, Maritime and Transport union (RMT) – a founder of the Labour Party – decided this was the case and severed their links. RMT delegates at its annual conference in 2004 attacked the Labour government for failing to support working people and union policies, and the same year, the FBU argued that Labour was no longer a party of the working class when it withdrew its funding and affiliation. The significance here is that while unions believed that an increase in size would lead to an increase in political influence (through bargaining power), as Undy (2008, p. 121) commented in his book, unions had tended to 'confuse increased bargaining power with increased bargaining coverage' in the industrial arena. Moreover, what was happening in practice in the political sphere was that unions were simply not seen as relevant to the New Labour 'third way'[10] project, and as such, some (albeit smaller) unions and their members believed this former potential power was gone, so they began to look elsewhere for the means to regain their structural power. Even where unions had the potential to enhance their political power through merger, the external political environment in which they operated at that time tended to nullify such gains (Gennard 2009).

Other critical reviews of union mergers point out the extent to which the process of merger – often lasting years – created a distracting focus on internal re-organisation where political wrangling and factionalism, rather than member organising, was the main activity of union staff and committees (Terry 2000). This didn't, as was envisaged at the start of merger process, result in more effective organisations. Instead, there was increased bureaucratisation, particularly in the 'super-unions', where full-time officers had hundreds of committees to service and senior shop stewards spent time attending more and more meetings as they navigated the different committees at workplace, local, sector, regional and national levels within the bureaucracy. Michels's 'iron law of oligarchy' has often been quoted in relation to the problem of trade union bureaucracy stifling democracy. His theory is that the leadership in unions are able to centralise their power with little accountability because most members have little engagement with the running of their union. While the 'iron law' isn't an inevitable process, with larger organisations it is likely that more bureaucracy is needed for them to function effectively. As a result, tasks and decisions are centralised, and when this occurs, the tendency is that power will end up in the hands of a few. In trade unions, this means that there is a widening gap between union leaders and the members in the workplace and the decision-making processes. But, as has been pointed out, there is 'no iron law, just behavioural tendencies to stick to the status quo' (McGaughey 2017), but the consequence of this is that unions become either slow or resistant to change and innovation as people within the organisations strive to protect their own jobs or their bases of power.

INFILLING ALREADY (PART-)UNIONISED WORKPLACES, AND SERVICING OF MEMBERS

A third response to reversing union decline focused on recruitment activity, in the main concentrating on increasing the membership in already unionised workplaces, although there was targeted 'greenfield' recruitment in some non-unionised sectors, particularly after the formation of the TUC's Organising Academy in 1998. Following the abolition of the closed shop, prior to which unions could rely on high union density by compulsion, workplace density declined either through membership drop-off or by 'never members' not wanting, or not feeling the need, to join the recognised union at their place of work. The approach of targeting the 'low-hanging fruit' of potential members in already unionised workplaces was considered less troublesome or time-consuming than attempting to organise in new places were there weren't any members. The former, at least in theory, could be undertaken by shop stewards in their own sections, speaking to colleagues and persuading them to join, and was the approach adopted by many unions. The latter needs greater resource and more often relies on full-time officers or committed activists agreeing to put the time and effort into finding ways to build up a core of new members who are able to get their fellow workers to become union members.

An early example of a concerted and strategic targeted recruitment campaign (called 'Link Up') was devised by the Transport and General Workers' Union (TGWU) in 1987 after the union had lost just over one third (700,000) of its membership since 1979. Its aim was to convince officers and members that recruitment was a priority, and there were quarterly targets to meet. Full-time paid officers were tasked with ensuring these were met, yet there were two responses: one was that there was resistance since staff reported they didn't have time to add this to their current workload of negotiating and servicing members, and secondly, there was a lukewarm response from some about recruiting part-time and temporary workers who were being targeted alongside those in recognised workplaces. Part-timers and temporary workers were seen as difficult to organise and not cost-effective given the support they needed (Snape 1994). Despite some limited success in recruitment (14,000), six years after the Link Up recruitment campaign began, the union had seen a loss of 90,000 members. A major stumbling block reported by TGWU officers was that it was difficult to gain recognition in new workplaces because of employer opposition. As one officer explained:

> I don't find any difficulty in recruiting in this area .... The union's problem is that the employers, following what I consider to be the government's line, are resisting trade union organisation. (How do you resolve recognition disputes?) You don't. ACAS has no statutory procedures now. The workforce, because it's frightened, invariably won't take industrial action to force the issue, so you lose out. You don't get the union organisation, and so the membership drifts away.
>
> (quoted in Snape 1994, pp. 229–230)

Snape's review of the campaign suggested that the TGWU's past militancy 'which served it well in attracting employees during the 1970s might become something of a liability in winning recognition when employers have the upper hand' (1994, p. 231). A consequence of this, and this was similar in other unions, was that the TGWU's campaign switched to focusing on retention – attempting to maintain membership levels in currently recognised workplaces – and, as a fourth response, rolling out services to members in the form of finance, legal advice and cheap insurance deals. This model of serviced-focused unionism was promoted by the TUC in the 1980s and picked up by many unions. The idea was that by offering these add-ons, union membership would become more attractive. However, there was scarce evidence that this was the case. In Jeremy Waddington's research into the reasons why people joined unions, financial services were low down the list. His survey research showed that there was little support from members for an individual servicing approach, and that mutual support at the workplace was the central reason for joining: 'the key issue is thus to ensure that unions are available to potential members and are able to support members in the workplaces' (Waddington and Whitston 1997, p. 538).

This led to an unresolved debate between servicing and organising in terms of what the balance should be between individual representation for members, and building the union by actively organising workplaces such that members are able to represent and negotiate for their own constituents (Fairbrother 2000). A servicing model of unionism is one where members rely primarily on professional staff – simply described, it is where things are done *for* the membership (reliance), in contrast to the organising model of unionism where members are encouraged to find solutions *by themselves* (self-reliance). In the former, membership is relatively individualised and passive, depending on union staff to negotiate on their behalf, and in the latter, members act collectively to resolve their own grievances through workplace organisation and, if necessary, through militancy. Clearly, these are simple heuristic characterisations of union form, and no union would neatly 'fit' into one or other of these models. More likely, individual unions, if represented by a Venn diagram, would show one particular model dominating (to a varying degree). But given this caveat, if we were to characterise the British union movement in the post-1979 period of retrenchment, then arguably servicing would be the dominant trajectory adopted by the majority of unions at this time.

Ed Heery and John Kelly (1994, p. 1) have described the 1960s and 1970s as the period of 'participative unionism' – 'marked by an activist conception of union membership and facilitating a role of union officialdom', which they contrast with the period following (1980s–1990s) as 'managerial unionism' – 'a view of union members as reactive consumers whose needs must be continually tracked and responded to by unions drawing on the techniques of strategic management.' A perhaps unintended consequence of this managerial approach is that if a union's focus is reactive, then it is unlikely to be actively shaping the needs of members or acting strategically. The two approaches have different locuses of power. In servicing, it is a top-down, centralised form of unionism where there is a reduced role for shop stewards in terms of engagement with members and in negotiations with employers. As we saw from earlier chapters, in the more participative/

organised form of unionism, union representatives are able to draw upon the collective power of their colleagues to challenge management prerogative and win concessions themselves. But union leaders became wary of shop floor militancy: in some unions, full-time officers became managers of dissent, using procedure and bureaucracy to dampen down the attempts of activists to mobilise their members (Darlington and Upchurch 2012). In effect, the result was to draw power in their organisations to the centre, and away from the members.

The practice of managerial unionism parallels the changes taking place within the workplace at the same time. The Donovan Report was critical about the extent to which managers had the necessary skills to negotiate and manage their relationships with unions. At the time of the report, many firms had no personnel function, and in others it had a relatively lowly status in the management hierarchy. The recommendation was that there needed to be greater emphasis on management involvement in and responsibility for industrial relations (Banks 1969, p. 346). While not necessarily related to the Donovan Report, the 1980s saw the beginning of a shift from the personnel management function within firms to the new human resource management (HRM) approach. The personnel management role was transactional, tending to focus on administrative tasks (recruitment, contracts, pensions, wages etc.) as well as industrial relations issues, but didn't have a strategic role in the management of employees. HRM, however, is operational and strategic, linked to ensuring the 'fit' of employees with business goals, corporate culture and developing shared vision. Here, the focus is on individual performance and improvement, where pay is determined at appraisal, and employees are encouraged to see themselves as part of a team adding value to the company.

In practice, what happened was a decentralisation of personnel policy, and a shift from negotiating with unions toward human resource management practice, where the attention was on the individual – not the collective. It has been argued that HRM – in combination with all the macro-economic and labour market changes and the social and political climate – was perhaps another contributor to union decline and subsequent loss of union power. The HRM/substitution explanation for union decline was that the increased adoption of HRM practices provided the basis for a new mutual-gains relationship between workers and managers so that there was less perceived need or role for unions, or they become to be seen as holding back individual advancement. However, research evidence could find little evidence this was the case (Machin and Wood 2005), yet unions considered the adoption of HRM a deliberate attempt to minimise their voice in the workplace and that its purpose was to create a union-free environment. Essentially, the concern was that HRM developments, particularly employee participation, could undermine union organisation and weaken collective bargaining. This was the view of the general secretary of the TGWU in 1989:

> A new era of crafty Rambo managers has come into existence which seek to ignore or deliberately disrupt union organisation and collective bargaining procedures, by bringing in their own schemes based on fake committees and centred on the individual worker, not the organised workers, with the aim of undermining established working practices and bargaining methods.
>
> (quoted in Martínez Lucio and Weston 1992, p. 85)

Whatever one's viewpoint about the pros and cons of HRM, the adoption of sophisticated management techniques is likely to have an influence on the power dynamic in the employment relationship. With the greater focus on the individual, it is more likely that the collective voice of the union is less important or marginalised. When this becomes the dominant practice in the workplace, workers may perceive the union to be of marginal benefit, leading to falling membership. Instead of HRM being a specific strategy of union substitution, the failing may lie more in the inability of unions to respond to the change and demonstrate the material value of union membership.

A STRATEGY FOR ORGANISING: THE ESTABLISHMENT OF THE TUC ORGANISING ACADEMY

The fifth strategy put forward for revitalising the union movement was the establishment by the TUC of an Organising Academy (OA) in 1998. The aim was to build an 'organising' culture inside the union movement by training a new cadre of (mainly) young people, many from outside the union movement, to be sent into non-unionised workplaces to build membership (Heery 1998; Heery et al. 2000a; Simms et al. 2013). More precisely, the OA was preparing the ground for unions to take advantage of the statutory recognition procedure that was to be enacted in the Employment Relations Act 1999.

When John Monks was elected as general secretary of the TUC in 1994, he said that the time was right for a resurgence of trade unionism in Britain. It was beginning to become clear that the Conservative government was on the wane and that there was a possibility the Labour Party might win the next general election. Monks wanted to reposition the trade union movement to be able to respond to what was hoped would be a more favourable political climate for workers. As a response, the TUC re-launched in 1994, and the 'New Unionism' campaign was born in 1996. At the heart of both was a strategy for membership recruitment and possibilities of union renewal. This more positive environment was what unions had been waiting for, but the Labour Party made clear that it would not assist unions in increasing their structural power in the labour market. There was a commitment to introduce the National Minimum Wage in 1998 and to encourage employers to enter into partnership, but where there was resistance, employees should, where the majority agreed, be able to have their union recognised through a statutory procedure. The New Labour 1997 general election manifesto stated that there would be no repealing of the anti-trade union legislation, however:

> In industrial relations, we make it clear that there will be no return to flying pickets, secondary action, strikes with no ballots or the trade union law of the 1970s. There will instead be basic minimum rights for the individual at the workplace, where our aim is partnership not conflict between employers and employees.
>
> (Labour Party 1997)

The training of specialist organisers through the TUC's academy provided sponsoring unions with the opportunity to target particular sectors and employers, especially those where they had encountered resistance. The print unions, which had encountered much hostility, including de-recognition, after the strikes at the Warrington Messenger and at News International at Wapping in London, were particularly keen to take advantage of the new statutory recognition procedure. But the OA's aims went beyond organising in these areas; they also included infill recruitment at already-recognised workplaces, as well as promoting a specific approach to trade unionism that was, at least in the way it was articulated, based upon member involvement and participation – it was an attempt to change the culture of unions from being reactive to being proactive. It was, however, never intended to recreate the shop floor militancy of the 1970s: the 'member-led' activity was designed to be orchestrated and led by full-time organising staff.

There was a great deal of proactivity in the early years of the Organising Academy. Prior to the statutory recognition procedure, the number of cases of unions attempting recognition was low (27–76 per year in the late 1980s and early 1990s), and affected small numbers of members (approximately 5,000–9,000 over the same period) (Gall 2003, p. 11). In the six years following the Employment Relations Act 1999, there were 2,461 cases of recognition covering 728,000 workers (Gall 2006, p. 15). The vast majority of these were voluntary recognition deals – only 38 went through the full statutory procedure. This suggests that the places targeted by unions were, by and large, those where employers were less hostile to unions or where they accepted that union membership was above the threshold so there was no point in fighting the issue through the courts. However, the number of cases dropped drastically after this time, suggesting that unions had picked the low-hanging fruit of willing membership and now faced more difficulties from intransigent employers. Analysis of the 'turn to organising' in the UK union movement has been extensively covered in the academic and practitioner literature, and to summarise in a sentence, in a non-nuanced way: the picture was mixed in terms of success. There were many examples of successful campaigns in terms of recognition and membership gain, and it is the case that some unions would have been much worse off if they hadn't devoted resources to rebuilding their membership, but overall, when judged against a range of measures the unions set themselves, the conclusion was that 'the UK union movement is judged to be at least no stronger – and probably weaker – than it was in 1997 despite the changes in the institutional and political context' (Simms et al. 2013, p. 171).

It is interesting to note that, other than mentioning collective bargaining coverage and strength – which, by the way, have continued to fall – the analysis of the Organising Academy has had little to say about power in its many different forms, as discussed in Chapter 2. The traditional proxies used for union power – membership and union density, which are both crude measures – tell us very little about actual bargaining power that has provided real benefits for workers. What we do know, however, is that the gap between the profit share going to capital and the profit share going to labour has increased massively over the last 50 years as union power has diminished (Stockhammer 2013).

WHERE WAS THE CONSIDERATION OF POWER?

The aim of this chapter was to consider the responses from unions to the loss of union influence over policy-making at national level, the decline in membership, and the ability to defend the terms and conditions of members in the period when governments and employers were increasingly hostile to trade unionism. The loss of structural power was particularly evident. Undoubtedly, as Eric Hobsbawm (1978) had recognised, the labour market was changing, and this was to have a considerable impact on the loss of union members. The traditional bedrock of trade unionism had been largely the manual working class, in mining, shipbuilding, engineering and manufacturing, but the economy was being repositioned to become more orientated toward a growing service sector where there was less of a tradition of union militancy. Yet the approach of unions seeking to force employers to make concessions over pay and conditions meant they initially behaved as if nothing had changed. While the power of workers to withdraw their labour is one of the strongest sources of workers' power, tactics need to be refined and reconsidered in order to respond to different points of leverage in changed circumstances.

The previous chapters have demonstrated that using the same approach to industrial action doesn't always result in a similar outcome. Eventually, unions lowered their expectations and made fewer demands on employers, but they still failed to reconsider how to rebuild power. Further, the union movement as a whole was ill-equipped to re-focus on previously under-unionised new constituents, such as women, part-time workers, immigrants, casualised and contracted out workers, and those employed in the non-unionised sectors, and this was the growing, and soon to be largest, group within the labour market. While unions understood that the labour market was changing and that this was likely to affect their members – and those workers who came to the labour market after them – there appeared to be little strategic thinking about how unions might adapt or change organisationally and strategically in order to win power on behalf of workers in these new and emerging sectors of the economy.

The responses to decline discussed in this chapter seem to implicitly accept some of the findings in the Donovan Report that suggested that unions should become more orderly, more formalised, more professional and more legalistic, and that their decision-making should be more centralised. Re-reading the Donovan Report in the light of what unions have done since the commission reported, we can see that four of the responses taken by unions to counter decline that are discussed in this chapter are to be found in the report's recommendations. Initially, unions adopted a 'wait for Labour' position, expecting that Margaret Thatcher's unpopularity would see a Labour government back in after one term. The Falklands War reversed that unpopularity, and when Thatcher was re-elected with a landslide, it became evident that the Conservatives would be in power for quite some time, and the union movement was initially at a loss as to how to respond. The measures adopted were largely piecemeal and ineffective. There was resignation that industrial action was unpopular, too difficult, and that structural power was gone, at least in this period.

It is evident from the strategy papers produced by union leaders and the TUC during the 1980s and 1990s that unions felt that they would be unable to achieve much in terms of gains for workers in this period. So it became a period of retrenchment. Partnership at least meant that the unions were still in the workplace, where, at least nominally, they still had a seat at the collective bargaining table, but in reality, they appear to have mistaken workplace voice for workplace power, or perhaps believed it was equivalent to, or at least a substitute for, collective power. The approach taken by unions with regard to shop stewards was, as suggested by the Donovan Report, to professionalise their role by providing training and managing them to deal with increasingly complex individual disciplinaries and grievances in the workplace. Negotiation over many of the substantive issues of collective bargaining (e.g. pay and redundancy) largely became the preserve of full-time staff in many unions – leading to a consequential loss of potential power at the level of the workplace. Members, of course, soon recognised that what happened locally had limited impact on their terms and conditions, and most union branches rapidly became irrelevant, and in some cases, mere shells.

By the mid-1990s, when there was again an expectation of a Labour government, the TUC began preparing for the new opportunities a Labour government would bring – the minimum wage, statutory union recognition and much-heralded new labour rights that were emanating from Europe at the time as a consequence of signing the EU Social Chapter. The expectation from unions was that legislation would provide a floor of employment rights and that employers could be held to account through laws and regulations. This reliance on structural power appeared to negate the effective use of associational power, except in terms of protest – hence the increasing use of what were often token one-day strikes.

Perhaps one ray of hope for trade union renewal was the development of the TUC Organising Academy. Unfortunately, the model adopted became largely instrumentalist. The primary objective became recruitment designed to increase membership as a way to legitimise the status of, and the positions advanced by, union negotiators. Of course, recruitment was also a way to ensure the financial stability of the union. However, neither of these approaches were specifically designed to build collective power. In terms of the role of shop stewards, the focus was largely on casework, representing members in disciplinaries and grievances, and acting as a conduit for information between the full-time officers and the branch. Meanwhile, the role of members was increasingly passive and transactional – the only interaction between most members and their unions occurs if they found themselves needing individual representation. In short, the function of membership was not to organise or to act as a power resource if and when the union was in conflict with local managers, but their contribution to union density was felt to be useful in the process of the integrative bargaining of the union.

In conclusion, the measures taken by unions and the TUC were, in the main, largely superficial and lacking a strategic response when considering the social, political, cultural and economic circumstances – which were largely hostile to labour unions. As one commentator on union organising has noted:

> What is missing in these measures is an adequate appreciation of the changing terrain of trade unionism. Effectively, the locus of power both within and between trade unions has shifted so that the basis for past relationships and practices no longer exists.
>
> (Fairbrother 2000, p. 12)

The mantra of the 'need to organise the unorganised' led to only cosmetic change, without unions making any fundamental change to the way they are structured or organised. As a result, *transformative* organising has been little understood and largely interpreted as a toolbox of tactics – or a separate department designed to increase membership – but without any understanding of building power at the same time (McAlevey 2016). Increased membership, or at least an arrest of membership decline, has been assumed to be equivalent to an increase in power, or at least a reduction in its loss. A large membership was seen as a way to legitimise the aspirations advanced by union negotiators, rather than as an indication of the union's potential power should it call on members to stop work. But union power is dependent not on numbers alone, but on the extent to which members develop the capacity and willingness to act collectively, something that is occasionally paid lip-service to in organising theory, and as we will see in the next chapter, almost totally ignored in organising practice.

7

Organising in Theory:
Recruitment in Practice?

The establishment of the TUC's Organising Academy in 1998 initiated what became known as the 'turn to organising' for a number of UK unions. A number of union leaders had been sufficiently alarmed by the sight of Australian union official, Michael Crosby's 'scary graph', which provided a stark visualisation of the financial implications of declining membership, that they accepted something needed to be done to bring in new members. Crosby showed that if membership continued to decline as it had been doing, it would only be a matter of time – perhaps only a few years – before the resulting loss in income would mean that unions could not cover expenditure, and if nothing changed, they would likely become bankrupt. Michael Crosby has been a long-time union officer, and was the director of the Australian Congress of Trade Unions Organising Centre from 1995 to 2005. He became well known as an adviser to unions facing catastrophic decline and loss of power, and in particular, his use of 'scary graphs' demonstrated clearly to union leaders they needed to act, and to act quickly (Crosby 2005).

His advice was that unions needed to motivate their membership to act in their own interest, that they needed to educate non-members about the advantage of unions, and that unions 'must have the capacity to demonstrate to the employer that it is commercially irrational for them to resist the wishes of employees for collective representation' (Crosby 2005, p. 105). To do this, he argued, a cadre of specialist organisers was needed to build new networks of members and activists – these were staff who would spend 100 per cent of their time on this work. The 'servicing' of members by undertaking grievance talks and negotiations with employers was to be left to negotiating officers and union reps, who should be taught to do this work themselves. But overall, Crosby's message was that there was a sense of urgency – unions needed a particular 'organising model'. This included a forward-thinking union leadership, a commitment to change, the invest-

131

ment of resources, and strategic planning – in essence, what was needed was top-to-bottom change within unions. It was this vision of organising, primarily as a tool to offset imminent financial decline, that was sold to constituent unions by the TUC when it set up an Organising Academy in 1998.

The TUC Organising Academy was similar to the one set up by Australian Congress of Trade Unions' 'Organizing Works' and the American Federation of Labor-Congress of Industrial Organizations' (AFL-CIO) 'Organizing Institute'. There were however, some fundamental differences in the approaches adopted. In the USA, the industrial relations system of collective bargaining requires unions to be recognised by the employer, and when unions secure a 'contract' to do so, this covers all workers in that particular bargaining unit. Importantly, and unlike the UK and Australia, once a contract is in place, unions have been allowed to collect fees from non-members in the same workplace through the collective bargaining agreement.[1] There has therefore been a real financial incentive for US unions to gain recognition, which is why large teams of staff organisers are often allocated to organising campaigns to ensure sufficient members are recruited to win the contract. These contracts often have important benefits for workers, not least employer-paid health insurance, but also better terms and conditions, employee protection and generally a significant wage premium. Workers are thus aware of the material differences between 'union jobs' and 'non-union jobs'. Statistics show that unionised workers in the US have, on average, around 20 per cent higher wages that workers who are not in unions – in some occupations, it is considerably higher (US Department of Labour 2020). Union membership dues in the US labour movement are generally considerably higher than those in the UK, which goes some way to explaining why unions in the US are much more financially sound than their UK counterparts – and have less concern about investing a considerable percentage of their income in organising initiatives. As others have explained:

> This structure of trade union membership and collective bargaining informs a clear logic of organizing at the workplace level. Within this context, organizing activity largely focused on prerecognition work, that is, persuading workers that a union could effectively represent their interests if they collectivized.
>
> (Simms et al. 2013, p. 41)

The point being made here is that throwing union resources – in terms of paid outside organisers – at a unionisation campaign is likely to have significant pay-off for US unions if they are successful in securing a contract: once the collective bargaining contract is achieved, the organisers and union activists can 'stand down' while negotiation over the details can be left to a full-time union officer who can 'service' the contract. There is, of course, a huge debate to be had about the power of workers in this type of relationship and the form of unionism adopted, and this is an issue to which we will return later in this chapter.

Another fundamental difference between the US labour movement's adoption of 'the organising model' and the UK's relates to the political nature of the different approaches. In the US, the turn to organising had, for a while, a more ideological political agenda that came about after the first contested election for leadership of the AFL-CIO in 1995. John Sweeney's election as president signalled that the radical organising tactics adopted by his union, the Service Employees International Union (SEIU), would be pushed forward by the AFL-CIO, encouraging affiliated unions to adopt a similar approach. The new leadership was the beginning of a break with the 'business unionism' of the past. Instead of economic interests being privileged over political reform, and union activity conducted by bureaucrats rather than the rank and file, a form of 'social unionism' began to be promoted as the future direction of the labour movement. Again, debates can be had about the extent of the radicalism adopted, but it did nevertheless represent a significant narrative shift in a leftwards direction for what had a been a fairly conservative union body. Simms et al (2013) note that:

> While the practices associated with organizing transferred to the UK, many of the political ideas that can be identified within US approaches to organizing were absent ... some senior TUC figures were highly aware of the political underpinnings of ideas about organizing but saw that the way to encourage adoption of organizing polities was to discuss practices and tactics rather than the broader political agenda.
>
> (pp. 41–42)

Also crucial for the consideration of power are the organising tactics adopted by US unions. The SEIU in particular, focused on figuring out how its campaign to organise contracted-out janitors could force company building owners to negotiate with the union. To do this, it undertook power analyses to understand how and where the companies were weak, and thus vulnerable. For a period of time, the union changed the rules of the game by taking actions that were off the employers' risk registers. Guerrilla street actions by rank-and-file union members, strategic intelligence, the building of coalitions with other social justice groups and utilisation of political capital were all measures used to confront intransigent employers (Waldinger et al. 1998). The key power resources deployed were moral, associational and political – tapping into these was important because it was felt that the workers, who were employed by various companies down a sub-contracting chain, didn't have sufficient structural power from traditional strike action and collective organisation in their specific workplaces. Although strikes were undertaken, and in the end were vital in securing a deal, it was the analysis of different power resources available and how these were used during the campaigns that resulted in the win for this particular group of workers.

In the UK, the transfer of the 'organising model' adopted in the US took a different form. From the start, nowhere near the financial resources were committed to organising as were in American unions, some of which were spending 25–30 per cent of their income on organising drives. In contrast, unions in the UK made relatively minor financial commitments to pursuing an organising agenda. In most cases, this involved sponsoring one, two or three organisers per year through the TUC's Organising Academy, and once trained, these people were told they were the 'agents of change' within their unions – an expectation that was both unrealistic and unfair (albeit unintentionally) on the individuals concerned. The newly recruited organisers were, in the main, young and inexperienced. Some had no history or prior involvement in the union movement, and they entered their unions as relatively junior staff (Heery et al. 2003). As such, they had little influence and tended to operate in self-contained teams where they were unable to draw upon other resources or obtain support from influential mentors. These new organisers also had to deal with 'active opposition to organising from groups within unions whose interests are threatened by the switch in priorities' (Heery and Simms 2008, p. 25). Heery and Simms, who studied the Organising Academy intently over many years, found that passive resistance, or in some cases overt opposition, came from:

paid officers, whose bargaining and representation skills are ill-matched to an organising strategy, [and] elected leaders whose office is placed in jeopardy by the recruitment of a fresh electorate or union activists resistant to the heavy demands of participation in organising campaigns.

(2008, p. 25)

In such circumstances, these 'specialist organisers' were in junior roles, and many of them found they had little management support or were given unrealistic targets and workloads. Some reported that they felt they were expected to reverse union decline on their own, and in reality, their role was to recruit, or 'bring the members in', rather than to organise workers to enable them to realise, create and use their own power (Simms et al. 2013, p. 97).

The ideological commitment to the new organising agenda from union leaders was also relatively muted – indeed, some have suggested that perhaps rhetoric outstripped genuine commitment (Heery and Simms 2008). While some general secretaries and other senior officials espoused the idea of the need to organise and there was strong support from some for the TUC's Organising Academy, this wasn't accompanied by the necessary internal organisational change to have a significant impact on membership growth and activity, nor did many unions have the strategic capacity to drive this forward. Besides the positive overtones about the 'organising model', there was also considerable scepticism in the UK about the 'cultural fit' of the organising model's tactics as deployed in the US (Heery et al. 2001). Nevertheless, a number of unions committed to sponsoring a number of Organising Academy trainees over several years, and some set up specialist organising teams. There has been much research into the effectiveness of the various campaigns undertaken and the impact that taking an organising approach has had upon unions, but little consideration in most of this research of the issue of power (Alberti 2016b; Gall 2006; Heery et al. 2003; 2000a; Holgate and Simms 2008; Simms 2003; Simms and Holgate 2010a; Simms et al. 2018; Turnbull 2005; Waddington and Kerr 2000).

The remainder of this chapter will therefore dig deeper into specific campaigns by individual unions to illustrate how and why the 'organising model' tactics adopted did not deliver transformative change, or increase the power of workers. In doing so, the role of members, the role of leadership and the structure and politics of the unions themselves will be considered. Taking a cue from internal union and TUC documents that set out the aims of the turn to organising, we will consider how these were met. The general aim was broad – to increase union membership – but more specifically, it included organising in new sectors ('greenfield organising'), organising under-represented constituents (migrants, women and young workers) and (re)engagement with 'community' by organising beyond the workplace. How successful was this turn to organising, and to what extent was the power of workers increased in these areas, and in what form was it utilised?

ORGANISING IN RETAIL: A LOOK AT USDAW'S APPROACH

USDAW is a private-sector union operating in retail and distribution, and was an early adopter of the organising approach. USDAW sponsored 17 organising trainees over five years through the TUC's Organising Academy, and following that, it established its own academy in 2002, but adopted a different approach by recruiting lay USDAW members whose employers had agreed to their secondment to the union for a period of six months. I began researching USDAW's organising campaigns in 2001, spending 18 months talking to union leaders, full-time officers, organisers and local reps.

Shortly after 1998, when the TUC's Organising Academy was established, USDAW produced material for activists to explain the 'journey to becoming an organising union' and the 'revolution in the way we go about recruiting and organising'. This was spelt out in the union's organising manual *Sustainable Organising: Power to Usdaw Reps* (USDAW 2002), which introduced union shop stewards to the techniques associated with the 'organising model', such as mapping the workplace and identifying issues of concern to workers. The material was clearly aimed at workplaces where the union has already achieved recognition, and its emphasis was on consolidating USDAW's presence in workplaces such as food retail, where 70 per cent of the union's membership was to be found.[2] As a consequence, particularly bearing in mind the high staff turnover in retail (the union estimates it loses around 30 per cent of its membership each year), the main emphasis was on ensuring recruitment became a regular and systematic activity. However, the union cautioned against a purely recruitment-based approach:

This isn't just an exercise in recruitment. If it is seen as simply an attempt to get numbers into the union, people will not warm to it. You have to be seen to be tuned into and dealing with the issues in the workplace as you go about your mapping.

(USDAW 2002, p. 11)

This indicates that there was at least a superficial recognition that recruitment couldn't be successful as a stand-alone activity. Despite this view, some USDAW officials who were interviewed at the time weren't convinced that the message had been understood at all levels of the union. As one official explained:

USDAW is probably one of the unions, from the TUC's point of view, that you would most readily associate with the organising agenda because we've been very completely on board with it. We have been seen to embrace it. We've put in an enormous amount of investment into it. We've taken on a significant number of [TUC Organising Academy] trainees and we've got our own organising academy now. But my personal view is that I think we're seeing organising as recruitment and I don't think we've fully embraced the ideology of organising. I don't think we've fully got to grips with the ways in which it is different, and particularly, issues around like-recruiting-like. There is still this idea that if you are good at recruiting you can either recruit, or you can't ... and it's really unhelpful.

(national official, 2002)

A number of the USDAW members and officials interviewed weren't convinced that the union could easily make the transition from servicing to organising. Despite statements to the contrary, they felt the emphasis remained on recruitment, and others were sceptical whether organising was an appropriate form of activity within particular sectors of the union:

I think we're definitely coming on board with the rhetoric, but generally I think our investment is in organising in terms of numbers of academy trainees we've got and all the rest of it hasn't really hit home at base level ... fundamentally we are still a servicing union.

(national official, 2002)

organisers [Organising Academy trainees] are really glorified recruiters. They have a lot of good knowledge but are not able to share it. We talk about organising, but it is really recruiting.

(area organiser, 2003)

Ideally it would be nice to get into an organising culture …. [But] the organising culture will not work within the retail sector because of the type of people we have got … any union in this sector would struggle because retail mentality is different from industrial. In the industrial sector, you have stronger characters … people who believe in that unity togetherness, but in retail you have a type of people … that is difficult to bring together. The way forward is the organising model but it has to be a different model in retail from the one adopted by the TUC.

(senior regional official, 2003)

These comments illustrate the real tensions between recruiting and organising, and USDAW initially struggled to make the transition from one to the other. The requirement to replenish the membership, or to 'fill the leaky bucket', is still of constant concern to USDAW, and this is no easy task for a union with such a high membership turnover. In 2006, an internal review of organising took place, and the revised approach was to focus on infill recruitment in the four retail giants with which the union had recognition (or partnership) agreements. Two former officers within the union have written in detail about the union's organising model, so it's interesting to explore their analysis of the union's organising through these internal eyes (Parker and Rees 2013). First, the authors acknowledged that USDAW's organising model was based on employer co-operation and that it 'shied away from antagonistic industrial relations'. As mentioned in the previous chapter, USDAW has tended toward a partnership approach with employers, believing that with low density across the sector, it has little structural power, thus its ability to use industrial action as a means to securing concessions is perceived as almost non-existent:

With such low densities Usdaw's power to influence has not been strong. It has relied on strong argument and persuasiveness rather than more industrial responses and, as such, the power of Usdaw has been more 'legitimate' power than 'coercive' power.

(Parker and Rees 2013, p. 523)

USDAW's adoption of its own version of the organising model has been life-saving for the union, helping to create financial stability and consolidating its membership in its key areas. However, as well as the increased employee protection as a result of more workplace reps who are able to take on disciplinaries and grievances (issues that are not insignificant), it's also important to consider the benefits for workers in terms of collective bargaining (increases in pay or improvements in terms and conditions) emanating from this particular organising approach. There is no evidence that there was an increase in the union's power to gain concessions from the employers. Members were recruited, but largely remained unorganised – this was not designed as a strategy to increase associational power. Neither did the increase in membership result in an increase in any of the other forms of power that were discussed in Chapter 2.

TRANSPORT AND GENERAL WORKERS' UNION: A CASE STUDY OF ORGANISING MIGRANT WORKERS

As part of the move toward a (new) organising agenda, the TGWU (now Unite) published an action plan, *Organising for Change: Recruitment and Organisation* (TGWU 1998), which stressed that 'in a changing labour market, cognisance has to be given to the way in which trade union organisation matches up to that labour market'. Having reached the conclusion that the union needed to understand the turn to organising in the context of the labour market, the report went on to say:

> The question of recruitment and involvement of currently under-represented groups needs to be considered separately, not because organisation should be separate, but because particular circumstances apply and must be taken into account .... Recruitment teams must reflect the diversity of the targeted membership .... A planned programme of recruitment in areas of high ethnic minority density ... should be supported by material in relevant languages.

From this action plan, a national framework was established for implementing a new organising agenda. This included the employment of dedicated organisers 'capable of recruiting under-represented groups'. The TGWU seconded a member of staff to the first intake of the TUC's Organising

Academy, but it took a number of years before the union decided on a more strategic organising agenda that comprised a specialist organising unit of 100 dedicated organisers. Prior to this, regions of the union were tasked with developing their own strategies, and the intention here is to focus on a particular organising campaign studied at the same time as the USDAW initiative mentioned above. It is chosen as an example because one of the aims of the 'turn to organising' was specifically to increase organising among black, minority ethnic and migrant workers, and to address the lack of collective bargaining power in the sectors of the labour market where many of these workers were located.

The campaign was based on an industrial estate in north-west London in a food factory where nearly all 500 workers were new migrants from minority ethnic groups (Holgate 2005). While this is obviously only one campaign, and therefore not necessarily representative of what was happening across the union as a whole, it does demonstrate how the turn to organising was operationalised in this region of the union at that time – the region with the highest number of minority ethnic, and migrant workers. The union's organising strategy has changed and been refined a number of times since this study (2001–2003), but it's useful to reflect on the approach to organising under-represented constituents – in this case, migrant workers – to think through where the consideration of power was in the campaign strategy adopted at this time. What was the role of members, the organisers and union full-timers?

Workers were clear about the reasons why they, rather than white people, were working in the factory, and this point was repeated by many of the workers interviewed:

> actually the problem is the money, which is why the white people don't come in this place. Most of the people who work here are foreigners. The money is very low, very low, that is why the white people don't work here …. Because the work is very hard, it is a heavy job, very heavy job and the money is very bad. That is why all the people are foreign, Asian or black [in the factory].
>
> (union member, 2003)

One worker described how his manager was constantly saying, 'If you don't like this job, go and get another one, we don't care about you, you can easily be replaced.' Sadly, that appeared to be true. On one visit to the factory, the company was holding a recruitment day and a queue of over 200, mainly Sri Lankan, men hoping to find work was witnessed. Many felt they had little choice but to work there, despite the low pay and difficult working conditions. A lot of the workers had second jobs in order to earn enough to survive, and they were clear that the level of exploitation was greater for black and minority ethnic workers than for white workers in the company's other factory in the north of England. At the start of the union's campaign to gain formal recognition, a shop steward was recruited. He explained what he and other workers felt the reasons for the different terms and conditions were between the two factories:

> There is a serious, serious difference between the London and Yorkshire factories. The pay, the treatment and the behaviour of managers is very, very, different. Here, the pay is very, very low and it is more expensive to live in London .... So, for example, you can check the difference between a team leader's pay here in London and compare with Yorkshire ... there's a lot of difference. And there [in Yorkshire], because the workforce is mainly white, the treatment of staff and the style of management is very different.
>
> (shop steward, 2003)

This view was repeated many times in the interviews, and there was particular concern from everyone about the way they were treated and the lack of respect afforded to black and minority ethnic workers. Many workers had joined the TGWU because they were desperate for the union to help to make their working lives more bearable. One, who had worked at the factory for four years, explained:

> the situation is very, very sad between management and staff. They don't respect people. They are always abusing the staff. It is like we are not human. The managers in this factory don't respect us and that is why we don't get a pay rise. Because we are different, we are strangers. That is why the British people treat us bad. That is why we want the union to fight for us.
>
> (union member, 2003)

It is noteworthy that this member said 'we want the union to fight for us', which is perhaps an indication of the understanding the workers had of unionisation. Instead of 'we need to organise a union in order to build our power to effect change', there appeared to be an expectation that their issues would be resolved by paying a membership fee. Whether this was a result of misunderstanding by the member (or members) or whether this was the (inadvertent) message from the union organisers, we do not know, but it clearly has an impact on the behaviour of members within a union campaign.

The union's strategy in organising this factory was to secure enough membership to apply for statutory recognition as set out in the Employment Relations Act 1999. A young Asian woman, Gita, was the union's staff organiser allocated to the campaign alongside a much older white male negotiating officer, Harry. The campaign at the sandwich factory began in March 2001, when it was allocated as a target for the union's Organising Support Unit. The union had knowledge of the factory since 1999 as it already had a few members on site, but no organising activity was taking place. The union was aware that all other company sites in the UK, with the exception of the London factory, had secured union recognition agreements, and in view of this, union staff felt there would be little difficulty organising this factory. With a few members already in place, the union, not unreasonably, thought it had a good basis from which to start the campaign.

However, when the organising campaign began, it was still seen by the TGWU as an extension of the unionisation of the other factories that belonged to the parent company. Thus, little thought was given to the particular demographics of the workforce and how this might be addressed. Gita, the union organiser, explained why she thought that this was problematic:

> the difference between west London and the other sites is quite major, not least because we are talking about a significant migrant population in this area and it is a completely different kettle of fish.

By this, she meant that the campaign needed to recognise the specific issues facing migrant workers in this workplace, and the difference in organising a multi-ethnic workforce.

The employer had recognition agreements at its other factories, so it made a concession to the union that it could hold regular recruitment sessions in the staff canteen, but was clear that it wouldn't agree to a contract without the union demonstrating majority membership. However, it was often difficult for the union officials to engage with workers on site as many didn't speak English. Although some workers went to Gita for advice about problems, she was limited in what she could do to resolve them, as the role of servicing was the responsibility of the regional official Harry, or the local shop stewards. While it was perhaps understandable that the TGWU thought the company wouldn't be hostile to the union given its attitude at its other UK factories, this presumption may have resulted in the slow start to the campaign, as there was little attempt to actively involve the workers from the beginning – effectively, it was a top-down recruitment campaign. There was no attempt to build associational power by organising around the issues that were of greatest concern to the workers – clearly, low pay was important, but the ill-treatment of workers as result of their ethnicity and migrant status – a key concern – was never a focus of the campaign. The young Asian organiser and the white full-time negotiating officer had opposing views on this issue, and Gita, as a junior member of staff, felt unable to organise around this without the support of Harry, although she felt it was fundamental to what was going on in the factory:

> There is the point that the company has given recognition to every other factory, but the London factory. I am very clear about why that is ... but Harry does not see it like that. I take a very racial perspective on it, but Harry doesn't.
>
> (Gita, union organiser, 2003)

Harry didn't consider issues in the factory, nor the position of the migrant workers in the labour market, to have a 'racial' element. He took a very economistic line, explaining that the reason the company employed almost no white workers was purely a matter of supply and demand. It was, he believed, the fact that they were cheap labour, rather than the fact that they were cheap *and* from black and minority ethnic groups, that allowed the company to exploit these workers. Yet this wasn't how it was perceived by many of the workers in the factory, who were much more conscious of the way the labour market reinforced the racialisation of migrant workers. In the end, the campaign petered out as the union was unable to secure or sustain enough members in order to gain statutory recognition.

What was evident from the campaign for organising in this factory was the way it didn't follow the 'organising cycle' model – issues–organisation–education–action – that was promoted by the union as the best approach to building associational power. The question is why, given the fact that both union officials were cognisant of the new organising model adopted by the union, it wasn't applied in this case. The research suggested there are three key reasons.

The first relates to the identification of issues around which to mobilise the workforce. It was clear from comments from many of the workers that racism was the key issue. They reported racist practices from the company management, such as abuse, victimisation, refusal to allow shop floor workers to use the car park, and the fingerprint clocking-in system that was introduced instead of identity cards (because managers claimed they couldn't distinguish who staff were). But there was, in effect, a 'race-blindness' in the approach taken by the union in these matters. The organiser was concerned about the senior officer's refusal to acknowledge the racialised nature of many of the company's employment practices. Gita felt strongly that the company needed to be challenged on its racism, but was not prepared to overstep Harry on this matter. Thus, the opportunity was lost to organise around those issues the workers felt passionately about, and the failure to acknowledge the racialised nature of the employment practices at the factory did nothing to build trust and respect in the union – thus weakening any chance to build associational power of the union.

The second key finding concerns the different roles of union officials within the structure of the union and the practical effect this has on the operationalisation of the organising model adopted. In this case, the role of specialist organiser was a relatively new position within the union. Organisers were few in numbers, and although they had a specific brief to target new workplaces for organising, their relationship with other officials in the union, and the cross-over of responsibilities, were not clearly defined. It was evident from the research that Gita and Harry felt constrained by their respective roles. The perceptions of both union officials of what 'belonged' to each of them restricted what they did and what they were prepared to do. It was not clear to what extent these were self-imposed constraints or whether they were merely unwritten rules or the established culture of the union. Whatever the cause, the demarcation of roles appeared to hamper the development of unionisation at the factory. Harry, in particular, talked about how he did not have the time to devote to the Food-to-Go workplace. As he repeatedly said, this factory was only one of many others he had responsibility for, and it became just one day a month in his already busy schedule. He very much saw his job as that of a servicing official – the traditional role of a union official. Harry was content in this position and had no real desire to get more involved in the organising side of unionisation. This he felt was a 'specialist' role, requiring officials who were dedicated to this work. On the other hand, Gita felt unable to carry out her work effectively as she did not have the authority or the resources to run the campaign in a way that fitted with the unions organising model. The research highlighted that seeing organising as an 'add-on' to an otherwise business-as-usual approach was counterproductive. It simply does not work to tack organising onto existing structures of the union. Instead, it needs to become the mainstream union work and be allocated at least the same status as negotiating.

The third key finding relates to the impact of identity. Although the union recognised the importance identity can play in union organising and was fully aware of the theory that a like-recruits-like approach can be utilised to build trust, the campaign surfaced a number of important questions of identity that were never resolved. Gita was a young Asian organiser who felt that she was allocated the factory campaign because of her identity. However, her profile couldn't have been more different to that of the workers she was trying to recruit. She was female, British-born, university-educated, and didn't speak any of the community languages spoken by the workers. Gita was not the stereotypical old, white, male trade union official, but her language, culture and lived experience were very different to nearly all of the workers in the factory.

Gita also argued that unions needed to broaden their appeal if they were to be successful in organising the type of workers in this particular factory. Many workers were migrants who had all sorts of difficult issues in their lives to deal with, so she said, 'in a way the things that happen at work are sort of minor'. In saying this, she wasn't underestimating the distress working conditions created for these workers, but recognising that they also had much bigger issues like immigration, housing, racism and basic survival to deal with as well. Finding a way to provide support in trade unions for these non-work-based problems is an approach for widening the appeal of unions as well as opening up new channels of organising opportunities. Many of the workers in this factory would have appreciated the opportunity to turn to the union to assist them with some of these problems, but this would have required a fairly fundamental shift in the union's sense of identity. Effectively, the union needed to, at some point, demonstrate it had the power to improve the lives of these workers. However, at no point in this campaign was the power of workers, or their union, demonstrated or articulated in any form, or in a way that convinced enough of the workers of the benefits of collectivisation, which is why, in the end, it failed.

ORGANISING IN THE COMMUNITY: THE GMB'S
UNIONISATION OF ASIAN WORKERS IN WEST LONDON

A very different approach to identity was adopted by the GMB in a contemporaneous campaign to that in the example above. In August 1998, the general union the GMB secured a 'voluntary' recognition agreement with a large food factory in Southall, west London, following a long and difficult battle with an anti-union employer. The predominantly female south Asian workforce campaigned for over a year for the right to have their trade union recognised, and more importantly for some, the right to be treated with dignity and respect at work. The campaign generated immense publicity in the locality and received widespread support from the wider Asian community; people signed petitions in their thousands and came out onto the streets to support the workers when they organised a march through Southall.

It was this event, in conjunction with the adoption of an organising form of trade unionism in the London region of the GMB, that became the catalyst for membership growth of Asian workers in Southall. There was a growing sense that collective power could win. Union organisers learned to use networks in this community to develop a new scale of organisation around a geographical community containing different ethnic groups. While the workplace remained the focus for securing improvements in terms and conditions, the normal geographical boundary of unionisation campaigns – the workplace – was extended to include public and private spaces outside the place of employment, and in a radical departure from tradition, this encompassed community space as well. Thus, with a focus on new membership constituencies – again, a specific aim of the TUC's turn to organising – a new organising culture, largely instigated by local union activists, was created in this region of the union in the early years of this century, and this led to a widened spatial framework for union organising. The organising approach adopted engendered a degree of trust in trade unionism among Asian workers in this area which had not previously existed to any great extent. The GMB is a union with strong regional autonomy, and my research into the organising approach adopted by the London region took place in 2001–2004.

In the London region, the union's overall organising philosophy was summarised in a document detailing its regional organising plan for 2001–2005, where it was stated: 'The GMB is a campaign for economic and social justice in the workplace as opposed to an institution providing services to members in return for a fee.' This was a significant departure from the servicing model of unionism, and it was a move toward a form of organising unionism where the members were expected to play their part. As one organising official explained:

> The way we see it is that there is a deal. We say to them what are you prepared to do? We set out what the options are and say to people, if you are not up for it, then we are not up for it…We don't take the view that members are due a service because they pay £8 per month. We take the view that the £8 per month is a solidarity payment to the union and if they ask for help then we will ask for something in return.
>
> (lead organiser, 2001)

Through the involvement of groups or individuals from outside the workplace, the London region of the GMB began to build community alliances. This assisted in the unionisation of greenfield sites that had contingent, or marginalised, workforces. This was an important development in the way UK union campaigns were approached at that time, and reflected similar developments that had taken place in Canada and the USA (Milkman 2000). It suggested a move toward a 'social movement' unionism, which sees trade unions as part of a much broader social project (Fairbrother 2008). The regional GMB recognised that this philosophy required a different approach from traditional trade union organising strategies and it was at the heart of the change in direction:

> The days of short 'recruitment drives', factory gate leafleting and 'here today gone tomorrow' recruitment stalls should end. Most of our strategic

plans will involve considerable commitment of time and resources. There are no quick fixes. To achieve permanent membership growth we need to make a long-term commitment to workers in our target workplaces.

(lead organiser, 2001)

As part of its approach, the GMB London region established an organising team of 13 officials dedicated solely to recruitment and organisation, which was a considerable investment of resources for the regional body of the union. These staff represented a third of the union's officials, an increase of 25 per cent. Two of the staff were south Asian and were recruited in 1998 following the recognition campaign mentioned above, and spent their time organising in workplaces where the workforce was comprised mainly of Asian workers. It was the work of these two organisers that was instrumental in bringing a new social movement model of organising into the region that drew on collective and associational power. In effect, these staff brought culturally specific assumptions about organising with them, and were provided with the freedom to organise in the way they felt was most suitable to the groups of workers they were organising. They were allowed the time and space to develop campaigns without being restricted by the normal work patterns expected from a union official. In addition, their success at recruitment and organisation brought issues of identity and culture into much clearer focus within the London region of the GMB. One (white) senior organiser stressed how important it was to the GMB's organising success that the union was rooted in the geographical and cultural space of the local community:

The two Asian organisers both live in Southall. Zaheer will sometimes disappear for a couple of months and come back with 200 membership forms in his hand from some firm that we have never heard of. When you ask him how did it go – he said it was all done in front rooms, which is a different way of organising. We would never really dream of knocking on people's doors. That is what is important – he understands the culture and the gender politics. He knows the way in. We can never intervene on this level.

(senior organiser, 2001)

This recognition that ethnic and cultural difference played an important role in organising was an important lesson for the GMB. As this senior organiser pointed out, the fact that most officials of the union were white meant they were often unable to gain access to minority ethnic workforces. While being aware of their limitations in recruiting and organising among minority ethnic workers, it was only after the employment of Aasim and Zaheer that the GMB began to fully understand what effect these officials could have in unionising the south Asian community. The realisation that the workplace was not the only place where the union could organise was important. The fact that some workers were likely to identify their lived space and their community as a safer space to organise than the workplace was important for the way the campaigns in the south Asian community were carried out.

In order to build wider support, the campaign at the food factory extended beyond the workplace onto the streets of Southall, where new union activists set up street stalls, and organised marches and social events. The union organisers held several social events: on one occasion, they took members on a trip to France, and on others, they organised parties during festivals such as Diwali and Christmas where it was clear these were union events, with recruitment materials urging everyone to join. It was these community events that encouraged the families and friends of workers to get involved, and at the same time helped to build the profile of the union. So instead of organising one workplace at a time, the family of each union member was a link to other potential workplaces that might be ripe for organising. But there was an added dimension: the organisers aimed to portray the union as more than just a workplace support network. It was important that the union was seen as having a wider social conscience in order to attract a wider base of support:

> The people realised that the union was not only there for the workplace, we are out of the workplace as well. We need to do these sorts of things .... In one of the workplaces there are 300 people working there. These 300 people belong to 300 families. In one family, we could count three or four people, or maybe a husband or wife. So it means that the message could go to another 300 or 600 or 900 people. So when they hear a good thing [about the union] they will be passing that message on to the other people in the family.
>
> (Aasim, organiser, 2002)

Aasim and Zaheer, the two organisers, viewed the union as a social justice organisation, which meant their role extended beyond that of the traditional trade union official. Their approach was that in order to win the trust of all sections of the south Asian communities, it was essential that they were able to assist with issues outside the work environment at times when people needed help:

> The reason why I use these techniques is that people respect the community and respect the cultural differences. They listen very carefully and, when you speak their own language ... they understand more about what you are talking about. When you involve [yourself] not only the workplace, but their social life as well, for example, if they have difficulties like mortgage problems, immigration problems, you can help sort out their problems as well. That is an important factor. We try to sort out these problems through the union. You say to the people, 'If you need me on Sunday or on Saturday night, then call me.'
>
> (Zaheer, organiser, 2002)

While this conflicted with the general perspective of unions aiming to deal with issues collectively – and can be a weakness in attempting to build power if it isn't converted from advocacy into self-organisation of workers – the two organisers recognised that they needed to assist people on a personal level as well in order to win their trust and support. It was the appeal to the community, and the support received in the food factory campaign, which eventually persuaded the factory management to recognise the union. One of the organisers recounted how the resultant support from the community was overwhelming:

> I went to the community and had a stall in the Southall Broadway to get the community to sign the petition. We got 40,000 people to sign the petition in two days. Because [food factory] was in Southall, we asked the community to support us. I took that petition along with the MP for Southall to the Prime Minister. That was at the beginning of 1998. The Prime Minister promised that there would be legislation.
>
> (Aasim, organiser, 2002)

A recognition agreement was finally signed between the union and the company in August 1998, just a year prior to the statutory provision for trade union recognition being introduced by the Employment Relations Act 1999. Throughout the year-long campaign, the pressure on the company was intense, but the campaign was also a great challenge for the union, which had not previously been involved in this form of community campaigning. The lessons learned from the food factory campaign helped to further crystallise the GMB London region's development of an organising culture among its members and its officials, to the extent that within five years around 10,000 new Asian members were recruited into the membership, and 20 workplaces in the area were organised and gained recognition. Thus, the dynamic of the campaign at the food factory began a cycle of events which led to subsequent workforces becoming unionised. In turn, this changed the GMB London region's perspective on organising among minority ethnic workers. Issues of culture and identity arose in many of the campaigns which forced the union to rethink its traditional organising methods by expanding into the community.

Throughout its organising campaigns, the union attempted to collectivise issues rather than dealing with individual grievances (other than those carried out in the community or on a personal level – e.g. immigration or mortgage advice). The research showed that in the case of many of the campaigns in Asian workplaces, this was done around the issue of dignity and respect at work. This appears to have resonated among many of the south Asian workers in these factories, who were acutely aware that because of their personal circumstances, opportunities for more gainful employment were virtually non-existent. Whether the GMB London region consciously set out to challenge the racialised nature of this particular labour market in west London is unclear, but what its organising approach demonstrated was that by organising these workplaces, by creating a strong sense of collective power, unions can undermine the extent to which companies are able to exploit their workforces on account of their ethnicity. Clearly, challenging structural racism at this scale is much more effective than dealing with problems on an individual grievance level.

A key finding from the research was the extent to which the use of community spaces, networks and contacts played a vital role in many of the organising campaigns in the area. The use of community spaces to hold stalls, marches, meetings and social events allowed the union to move beyond the boundaries of workplaces to integrate itself more closely into the lived and social spaces of its members. The contacts that developed through these social and spatial networks meant that the union was not only able to pick up new leads for organising, but was also able to draw on members from workplaces already organised to build up relationships of trust that otherwise might have taken longer to establish. The development of the organising strategy at this particular scale meant it was able to focus more closely on the shared identity and lived experience of the participants in the campaign.

However, despite building the potential for both strong collective power as a result of high union density and associational power through community connections which were able to force employers to grant voluntary (and sometime statutory) recognition, the union often wasn't able to realise its structural power through industrial action, when employers refused to make concessions through the collective bargaining procedures. In one particular campaign, despite winning statutory recognition in a two-year campaign with a very hostile employer, when 76 per cent of workers voted and 87 per cent of these voted for the union, the members never secured any material benefit for its actions. In effect, despite the widespread support for unionisation, demonstrated by membership numbers, and the vote for recognition, the union had failed to educate and organise the members so that they were prepared to act if the employer refused to negotiate and reach a deal. The union didn't teach the workers that it was only by their own actions and a show of power through industrial action that they could force the employer to concede to their demands. The expectation of members was perhaps that they had fulfilled their side of the bargaining by paying their dues and voting in favour of the union, and now it was up to the union officials to deliver through negotiating. This is a fundamental misunderstanding (or abdication) of power in the employment relationship – yet one that unions need to teach in hostile circumstances where the employer won't concede to polite requests. Perhaps unions are tempted to avoid the difficult question, 'Are you going to put up with this, or are you going to take effective action to change it?' It's understandably easier to recruit new members on the basis that once they and their colleagues have paid their union dues the negotiators will take over and deal with the employer than it is to have a difficult conversation about how workers will have to build power for themselves and learn how to exercise it. However, failing to have this discussion early on in organising campaigns amounts to 'mis-selling' what unions are and how they can effect change.

RECRUITMENT IN PRACTICE: ORGANISING IN THEORY

The above are just three examples of organising campaigns that were researched in depth in the early days of the turn to organising and the adoption of the 'organising model' by a number of UK unions. I was embedded in these campaigns over a number of years and spent lots of time with organisers, union officials and members in order to gain an understanding of the approach that was being adopted and the impact it was having in terms of union power. These case studies resonate with a number of other studies of union organising campaigns since 1998 which suggest – particularly in the early years of the introduction of the statutory recognition legislation – that the focus of unions was on membership recruitment to pass the threshold to be granted recognition by the employer (for a number of detailed case studies of organising campaigns, see Gall 2003; 2006). But this didn't necessarily mean the workplaces were organised in such a way as to be able to exercise power – in effect, to be strong enough to get the employers to say 'yes' when they would rather say 'no'.

For example, Gregor Gall (2006) reports on the recognition campaigns by the National Union of Journalists in the provincial newspaper industry. As was noted in Chapter 5, the print unions were severely weakened by the job losses as a result of new technology, the power of the union's role in the printing industry was decimated by events at the Warrington and Wapping trade disputes, and the unions were eager to regain their former union presence with employers. In this respect, the NUJ had some significant success, mainly as a result of the determination of 'an activist milieu that had maintained union organisation throughout the lean years' (Gall 2006, p. 129). Yet an analysis of collective bargaining outcomes in around 40 workplaces immediately following the regaining of recognition shows that the 'gains' for workers were minimal – despite strike action in a number of cases. The inability to realise structural power in this way led the union to explore whether it could draw on political power and institutional power through friendly MPs sponsoring early day motions in parliament, or by putting pressure on the political elite in an attempt to influence the companies. But as Gall (2006, p. 131) concluded, 'this had very limited efficacy'. In effect, despite an increase in members, the union didn't sufficiently focus on what was needed to organise for its members to exercise their latent power.

Similarly, Melanie Simms, who also conducted many years' research into organising campaigns, found that, surprisingly, measures of organising success often ended at the recruitment and recognition phase of a unionisation campaign rather than assessment of bargaining outcomes. In her call centre organising study with the Communications Workers Union, she found that the measures of success were achieving recognition, developing diverse membership workplace activism, and small, but important, improvements in the lives of members. As part of the recognition agreement, the union agreed to binding arbitration, perhaps acknowledging that its power in terms of strike action was likely to be weak. And as a sombre postscript, Simms (2006) warned:

> if these tactics [in the organising model toolbox] leave activists ill-prepared for this transition [from recognition to representation], there is evidence that activism can fall away and representative structures can repeat patterns and problems seen in much more established union branches.
>
> (p. 180)

This message was further reiterated in a five-union study of organising campaigns over a seven-year period which concluded that gaining recognition was of little value if unions were unable to sustain representation and influence, as 'membership tends to ebb away if unions are unable to show their effectiveness ... and sustainable organizing is essential to any hope of wider union renewal because it relates directly to issues of union power' (Simms 2015, p. 418). Union officials often claim that post-recognition, union members expect too much of the union, but those high expectations have often been seen as an asset during the recruitment and recognition phase in terms of pulling new members into the union, and few unions are prepared to temper those expectations as they focus on gaining recognition.

Overall, the findings in the USDAW, TGWU and GMB case studies were similar to that of Simms et al. (2013) and others who have closely observed organising initiatives since the start of new unionism and the formation of the TUC's Organising Academy. The overall consensus from the vast amount of literature on this topic has been that the impact of the 'turn to organising' was mixed, so the hope that it would lead to widespread renewal was somewhat over-optimistic. This was, argued Simms et al. (2013), 'a consequence of the dominant focus of organizing practice targeted at membership development and, occasionally, securing recognition for collective bargaining *rather than the wider and more political objective of promoting worker self-organisation or social movement unionism'* (p. 171; emphasis added) – in essence, the very elements that are essential in building the power of workers to improve their terms and conditions of employment were at best secondary to recruitment and playing 'the numbers game' – where signing up more than 50 per cent of the workforce was often seen as an automatic gateway to union recognition, and the end game in organising.

In many ways, the organising practice adopted by UK unions reflects the way in which organising ideas transferred into the UK. The fact that the TUC played down the broader political agenda of the 'turn to organising' meant that, in practice, the organising models adopted were largely a 'toolbox' of tactics that different unions applied in different contexts to different ends. Individual unions developed models that reflected their own particular contexts, histories, backgrounds and politics. Underlying these approaches are very different ideas about the *purpose* of organising. 'What are we organising for?' is a question that many unions have neither considered nor explicitly articulated (Simms and Holgate 2010a). Membership growth, industrial and bargaining strength, cultural change and worker self-organisation all feature at different times and in different contexts, sometimes with different, and often competing, degrees of emphasis within the same unions. There has also often been a difference between the narrative and practice of unions. In general, the 'organising' approaches adopted were informed more by the objective of increasing membership in the erroneous belief that this would automatically lead to an increase in bargaining strength, rather than being driven by more radical ideas about workers gaining power through building a level of workplace organisation capable of exercising sufficient power that their employer would agree to the union's position even when it didn't want to do so.

Seldom since the turn to organising has the issue of power been at the heart of most discussions and debate on this topic, even though, without the ability to win in the ongoing battles with employers over terms and conditions of employment, the belief in union effectiveness will inevitably wane and membership will continue to decline. For those workers who have no previous knowledge of trade unions, this flawed model of organising – utilising as it does a narrative of workers winning – can lead to an initial sense of trust, but when the model is unable to deliver, that trust can be irreparably damaged. After nearly a generation since the 'turn to organising', why have unions not learnt the lessons of these early mistakes? What is it that prevents unions becoming effective at recruiting and then taking the next step to organise members into a powerful force capable of winning in the workplace? The next chapter will move forward to discuss the concept of strategic capacity of unions and the importance of leadership in instigating or restraining organisational change.

8
Leadership, Strategic Choice and Union Power in the Turn to Organising

Understanding the power dynamics *within* unions is as important as understanding the way power is navigated in the employment relationship. Unions are, in many ways, complex organisations. They are civil society bodies whose purpose is to maintain or improve the conditions of the lives of their members.[1] They are democratic membership organisations where decisions to set direction, policy and practice are made through the collective voices of those who participate. Yet, as democratic membership organisations, leaders within unions – if they want to retain their positions and power – are dependent on securing the support of at least a majority of those members who vote at election time. This can have an impact on the balance between long-term strategy and a focus on immediate concerns, especially a forthcoming ballot of members to elect or re-elect leaders. In the latter case, holding on to a position can become the primary objective of day-to-day work, with the development of strategic capacity for transformative change being postponed to a mythical 'sometime in the future'. At the same time, unions are bureaucracies – often highly structured, they are accountable in law, and are also themselves employers which have responsibility to their employees. On the one hand, they are expected to be responsive organisations – reacting to events in the labour market, employer proposals or government actions that affect the lives of workers – yet at the same time, the pace of organisational change in unions is often slow and cumbersome. Unions are also, largely, voluntary organisations, and while there are paid full-time officers and administrative support, they rely on the activity and commitment of their members if they are to function effectively as a bulwark against employer power.

These factors affect the capabilities, decision-making and strategic choices within unions, and are, at all levels, infused with power relations. The various actors (and leaders) within unions may have different and conflicting aspirations, as well as different ways of acting on them. For example, shop stewards may want the freedom and autonomy to act immediately on their members' interests (maybe taking industrial action at shop floor level), whereas negotiating staff, who feel they have a wider perspective, will consider it their role to speak to employers to seek to resolve issues through negotiation. General secretaries will be concerned about managing the relationship between elected committees and professional servicing staff, while at the same time protecting the organisation by ensuring that it functions within the limits of the law, and that its work programme and future direction are in line with democratic decisions made by conferences and committees. Each of these and many other inter-related processes will have an impact on the strategic capacity of unions to deliver organisational change. We will consider the impact of this inertia on the ability of unions to develop an organising agenda, and ultimately, to build union power. Central to all of this is the importance of strategic leadership, which is needed to transform organisations from (sometimes) sclerotic bureaucracies that are unable to respond effectively to externally changing circumstances, into organisations that develop the capacity of their members to respond strategically through exerting power to improve their pay and working conditions, or other, much broader, political or social justice demands.

Christian Lévesque and Gregor Murray (2010) have written about the importance of not only having an understanding of the power resources available to unions, but crucially having the *strategic capacity* to use them to best advantage in any renewal strategy. The role of leadership is essential in being able to capitalise on and direct these power resources to create transformational change within an organisation. A key power resource of unions is that of strong internal solidarity, because a collective identity contributes toward membership cohesion. The stronger that collective identification is, the more likely members are to participate in the life of the union (e.g. voting, industrial action ballots, organising and recruiting in the workplace, strike action etc.), this is what the authors call 'deliberative vitality'. A union with weak deliberative vitality cannot claim to be an organising union as it isn't involving its members in the functioning and direction of the organisation. A second power resource that helps to build strategic capacity in unions is that of 'narrative', which comprises 'values, shared understandings, stories and ideologies that aggregate identities and interests and translate and inform motives' (Lévesque and Murray 2010, p. 339). This narrative resource creates the opportunity to interpret and frame actions (and organisational change) in a way that mobilises members, and creates a sense of shared identity and confidence in collective action. In addition to these, infrastructural resources (material and human resources) and 'networked embeddedness' (the extent of internal and external links that can provide solidarity) are also essential in increasing the power resource of unions. Yet these become ineffective if there is little or no capability to use them to effect necessary change.

A key role of leadership is to create the space and opportunities for the strategic capabilities of members, activists and staff to grow and develop. One of these is the ability of leaders to arbitrate between conflicting demands within unions, and to provide a direction and vision that create a narrative of collective interest. A second was briefly mentioned in Chapter 2: the ability of unions to develop organisational learning (political education) to assist in the process of transformative change. This provides legitimacy, confidence and the tools to understand what actions are necessary for change to occur. As Lévesque and Murray (2010, p. 344) so neatly articulate, if a union does not have learning capacity 'it will remain a prisoner of its own history, caught in a path dependency of its repertoires and identities: it is likely to follow a trajectory that will not challenge its projects, values and traditions'. It is important, therefore, to consider the inter-relationships between leadership, strategic choice, the capability of various actors, and forms of union power in the turn to organising.

WHAT TYPE OF UNION LEADERSHIP BUILDS POWER?

The concept of leadership in terms of power relations is, surprisingly, wholly under-theorised in much of the union renaissance literature (an exception is the work of Lévesque and Murray 2010), although it is covered extensively elsewhere, particularly in relation to gender (Kirton and Healy 2012; Ledwith and Hansen 2013). Yet different ideological and practical approaches to leadership and the navigation of power relations within unions will lead to different outcomes, irrespective of the nominal strategic plans adopted or articulated. While it's important that leadership at the top is able to communicate a vision for the union and manage its direction, this doesn't happen in a vacuum: effective organisations need to gain the support of the different layers of leadership and power bases throughout the organisation from the bottom to the top. There must be buy-in (or at least acceptance) from union staff and lay activists of the leadership's vision, if strategic organising plans are to gain traction. It is here that the wholly under-utilised role of political education in transformative thinking, and the development of critical assessment are missing from many of the approaches adopted by unions in their organising strategies. Without widespread ownership of and engagement with the rationale for change and the positive benefits it might bring, the response to a 'turn to organising' is likely to be passivity, resistance or even sabotage. It's necessary, therefore, to consider to what extent unions have been failing at organising for power because their leadership has been constrained by archaic structures and oligarchic tendencies (Voss and Sherman 2000).

Robert Michels's (1915) theory of the 'iron law of oligarchy' asserts that there is a tendency (arguably not actually an iron law) for nominally democratic organisations to become controlled by self-interested elites who have their own (distinct) interests within the organisations. When organisations grow in size and their structures become more complex and divided into separate, specialised sections, there is an increase in rules and formal processes controlled by these elites. In trade unions, the word 'elite' is probably unhelpful, but power is distributed unevenly, lying in the hands of dominant cultures or those who control key committees or occupy certain roles. In some unions, this can limit the ability of rank-and-file members to challenge recommendations or decisions, or to overturn them. In such circumstances, this leads to an increase in the control (but not necessarily leadership) by those who occupy positions associated with power, and greater passivity among members.

Positional leaders – those whose status is based on the position of authority they hold – are, of course, only one form of leader, but they are often the predominant actors within unions. In terms of leadership hierarchy (in simplified form), the shop stewards or workplace representatives are at the bottom, followed by convenors on shop stewards' committees and other senior lay officers. In between are full-time officer staff (negotiators/organisers), who in many cases have a degree of power – if only through their control of information – over lay representatives. Above this are senior lay reps elected to national executive committees, and the most senior elected posts, the assistant general secretaries and the general secretary. All of these leadership roles are important in understanding the power dynamics within unions – and the ability to develop strategic capacity to effect change – but a focus on the most senior position, the general secretary, is important in terms of understanding the strategic choices made by unions when deciding to adopt an organising approach. This is because without strong leadership from the top, any vision of strategic renewal and transformational change is almost always going to stall (Kotter 1996).

It's important to acknowledge that leadership is not a one-way process. For organisations to function well, shared leadership via team working has been shown to be more effective than 'vertical' leadership pronouncing top-down instructions (Sanders 2014). Good general secretary leadership qualities include the ability to demonstrate vision, hope, confidence, inspiration, trust, fairness, empathy, consistency and respect. In addition, being a good listener, open-minded and having patience are required to get a feel of what is going on within the organisation. To carry through a transformative vision (e.g. becoming an 'organising union') requires organisational change, and effective leaders need to find like-minded thinkers and allies (who are also leaders) at every level of the organisation to overcome inertia and resistance, and to effect cultural change. But general secretaries may have very different visions of what leadership entails.

Clearly, there are different leadership styles – authoritarian, bureaucratic, consultative, democratic, participative, hands-off, exploitative, to name a few, and these will influence the direction and practices within the organisation, but the role is often misunderstood. There is a significant difference, for example, between a general secretary carrying out a managerial function and a general secretary carrying out a leadership function, yet these are often conflated when talking about positional leaders (Kotter 1996). Being able to manage personnel, finances and the function of the organisation effectively is what is expected of a leader in any organisation, but management is not leadership in and of itself. Leadership isn't about relying on positional authority to force things to happen (this seldom works well); instead, true leadership is about practices that are embedded in the relationships of actors at different layers within an organisation. Marshall Ganz, a long-time union organiser and academic, sums this up when he says:

> Leadership is accepting the responsibility to create conditions that enable others to achieve shared purpose in the face of uncertainty. Leaders accept responsibility not only for their individual 'part' of the work, but also for

the collected 'whole'. Leaders can create conditions interpersonally, structurally, and/or procedurally.

(2008, p. 527)

Yet in trade unions, there are many complicating factors that can restrict leaders looking to implement change, particularly if this is radical transformative change, as this will almost certainly be met with resistance in some, if not many, quarters. Navigating this resistance can be problematic. Unions, as democratic (supposedly) member-led organisations, are full of different structures where decision-making power is created. The various committees and sections within unions are filled with mechanisms of power and self-interested leadership, where factions – both within the membership and among staff – vie for resources, are cautious about change, and concerned about how a turn to organising might affect their own positions or interests.

It is evident from much of the research into organising in UK unions that there has often been hostility, indifference or suspicion between full-time officials and organisers who have been brought in to deliver the new organising agenda (Simms et al. 2013). Similarly, the turn to organising has led to resistance from long-time staff members who don't want to, or are unable to, take on new and unfamiliar tasks. It has been challenging for some officers who are comfortable in negotiating with management, but feel out of their comfort zone when asked to organise and recruit members. In some cases, it creates a feeling of loss of power and status, and perhaps even the fear of losing their jobs, particularly when recruitment targets are part of performance metrics.

In terms of union members, there has been opposition to the allocation of union resources to organising; the argument sometimes put is that union funds should be spent on supporting existing members. Workplace reps have often argued that they have too much casework to be able to engage in plans drawn up in head office that are, at least nominally, designed to build power in their workplace, and in some cases they have resisted organising on the basis that new members may threaten their position (particularly those on paid facility time).

Union leaders looking to create transformative change need to be able to persuade, manage or defeat these competing nodes of power, where often self-replicating cultures among groups can make transformative change appear as an existential crisis. Navigating the competing and oppositional demands within their unions has not been easy for many general secretaries, such that day-to-day functioning has been the key focus, leaving little time or resources for instigating the change to transform unions from servicing members to organising members.

To effect transformational change, leaders need a credible vision, a diverse base of support among both the bureaucracy and the membership, to be able to influence relationships to make that vision a reality – as well as having the strategic capacity and personnel capability to carry this out while taking sufficient numbers of people with them. A positional leadership approach that is not visionary, participatory and hands-on hinders the ability of unions to deal with the complex and dynamic situations that inevitably arise when attempting to adopt an organising form of unionism. This applies in all circumstances, in all unions, but it must also be noted that a union's identity, form and purpose will have a strong directional pull on the type of transformational change that is possible.

UNION IDENTITY, FORM AND PURPOSE, AND WHAT DOES THIS MEAN FOR POWER?

Richard Hyman's (2001) writing on the form and identity of unions is a helpful framework when thinking through the different approaches that unions have adopted in terms of an organising agenda. He explains how it is useful to imagine a union's identity being a point within a triangle where each side represents either an orientation toward class, market or society. In terms of class, this represents the struggle between employers and workers – the heart of antagonism in the employment relationship. The more radical unions have a greater predilection toward asserting their power though strikes and other forms of industrial action to achieve their demands. On another side of the triangle, the market represents a form of business unionism where the central concern is to regulate wage labour relations – where union staff manage the employment relationship through bargaining and compromise in a top-down rather than bottom-up way. In this form, there is less of a role for union activists (other than to recruit colleagues into membership, or to deal with members' grievances), and the union is largely run as a business or service on behalf of the members. Instead of organising power in the workplace, members are reliant on staff to advocate for them, but when the employer says 'no', the union has little power to make them say 'yes'. The final side of the triangle is society, which represents unions working alongside other civil society organisations in campaigns for social justice – the model of social movement unionism mentioned in the last chapter.

Hyman's theorisation is a useful way to conceptualise a union's identity, and while it isn't suggested that any union would be a perfect 'fit' into just one these categories, we can perhaps pinpoint a particular place within this imaginary triangle that would fit a union's identity depending on its particular ideology, culture, activism and politics. This 'identity' will help us contextualise the observable leadership approach, the power relations within the union, and the way it considers how to deal with issues of power to effect change within the employment relationship of its members. We can use this as a descriptive framework to assist in thinking about how a union's identity affects its attitude to organising its members – it helps in considering which way a union is likely to behave and how power resources are utilised in campaigns or in industrial action – does it, for example see members as a power resource, or does it consider that other sources of power are better deployed? Or, put more simply: what is the union organising for? However, it's important when considering these questions that union identity is not seen as something immutable – we have already seen how unions are changed by external and internal forces, particularly when the power of workers is either unleashed or defeated in the process of struggle and during times of political adjustment. As such, a union's identity and its ability to act according to that identity is contingent – external, more powerful forces may prevent, for example, a militant class-based union from taking effective industrial action, and similarly, a moderate business-type union may surprise itself by acting militant at times, when circumstances change. Hyman (2001, p. 5) noted that, 'in times of change and challenge for union movements, a reorientation can occur: with the third, hitherto largely neglected, dimension in the geometry of trade unionism perhaps exerting greater influence'.

We can build on this way of thinking about unions and the way they utilise power by understanding more about the type of *relationships* unions have with their members. Ed Heery and John Kelly (1994) provide a conceptual framework that allows us to do just this. The crux of the argument these authors put forward in the mid-1990s was that there has been a notable change in the form and operationalisation of unionism since the 1940s. They identify these phases as 'professionalism, participative and managerialism'. In each of these, we can see how the dynamic of power shifts within unions as leaders within the organisations reconfigure their relationship with their members. The different forms of unionism – as with Hyman's model – are not absolute, but they may be helpful in understanding some of the factors that contribute to, or prevent, transformational organisational change taking place within unions. In particular, this approach may assist in understanding how the current leadership practices and structures of unions are perhaps one element preventing unions from rebuilding power and organising for union renaissance.

Heery and Kelly present a view that the relationships of unions with their members have passed through three discernible stages. The first, which emerged during and after the Second World War, they term *professional unionism*, and it's where there is a 'reliance on a cadre of professional representatives to service a largely passive membership, principally through the medium of collective bargaining ... [which led to a] concentration of decision-making power in the hands of the professional negotiator' (Heery and Kelly 1994, p. 3). It should be remembered that in the post-war period there was considerable sectoral collective bargaining across industries that had employer and state support, as it was largely accepted that sectoral bargaining provided incentives to companies to compete based on greater productivity rather than lower pay. In this form of unionism, the professional staff (negotiators and researchers) played a really important role in delivering significant gains for members, but at the same time it created a degree of passivity and powerlessness at the local level.

However, during the 1960s, when the economy was strong with low unemployment and many workers felt greater prosperity because of the rise in living standards, shop stewards became leaders who were adept at bargaining with their employers at the local level. We have seen from earlier chapters that this was a period associated with shop steward militancy and wins. As such, there was a move away from professional unionism to a more *participative unionism*. This form arose as a 'challenge from below ... as steward-led bargaining in the workplace eroded their [professional officers] negotiating prerogatives' (Heery and Kelly 1994, p. 4), and in doing so, redirected structural power to the shop stewards' committees. As Heery and Kelly noted: 'The membership came to be seen in activist terms, capable of formulating and prosecuting its own interests, while the full-time officers were viewed as facilitators, assisting members in the task of self-organisation' (1994, p. 4).

This focus on activism also impacted on the role of professional staff. Increasingly, full-time officers began to be recruited from within unions. Activists earned their 'stripes' as workplace reps, and then worked their way up through the ranks of the union to become paid members of staff. As might be expected, this created a different culture and set of practices within unions, one of which was increased support for workplace activists, including through the provision of training courses and, importantly, political education: 'The principal change in union power relationships which resulted from the spread of participative unionism was a strengthening of the position of lay representatives vis-à-vis full-time officers' (Heery and Kelly 1994, p. 6).

Now, decision-making was more in the hands of activists, and professional officers 'serviced' the lay decision-making committees. It was this transfer of power to the shop floor as a result of the shift toward single-employer bargaining, piece rate negotiations and the rise in wildcat strikes that were outside of the control of the regional and national unions that was of concern to employers and government. This was raised as a serious problem for the 'troublesome state' of UK industrial relations, and was central to the recommendations in the 1968 Donovan Report discussed in Chapter 6. The report said that there needed to be more full-time officials responsible for bargaining, and that the role of shop steward should be professionalised, with time off for training in collective bargaining and negotiating, and undertaking day-to-day duties. Further, what might seem like a fairly innocuous proposal was that union dues should, as far as possible, be collected by 'check off' through the employer's payment system. In practice, though, this meant less direct contact between stewards, who were responsible for manually collecting dues, and their members. In effect, both of these measures served to create greater distance between shop stewards and their members, leading to what has been referred to as the 'bureaucratisation of the rank-and-file' (for a discussion of this, see Darlington and Upchurch 2012; Hyman 1979).

Then we come to the late 1970s and early 1980s, when unions were on the defensive and union membership and density began to fall drastically. We have already noted in Chapter 6 how unions often felt that they needed to respond to the changing social and political environment with partnership agreements, new member services and recruitment drives. Heery and Kelly refer to this phase of union form as *managerial unionism*. The assumption was that union members should be thought of as consumers who needed to be attracted by the provision of individual services. This view arose because of the reversal of trade union power experienced at that time, and the individualistic ideology promoted by the Thatcher governments which said that there was no such thing as society (i.e. collectivism) and that people should look after themselves first. This notion of individualism was taken up by trade unions in their re-focusing on individual member services.

Heery and Kelly argue that the emergence of managerial unionism was 'associated with a critique of both professionalism and activism as methods for pursuing members' interests' (1994, p. 8). One of the key components of this form of union was the shift in power relationships whereby there was a 'strengthening of the decision-making role of union specialists and consultants'. In this phase, the role of shop stewards has tended to become primarily that of servicing increasingly complex individual case work, rather than bargaining or organising members – and, as a consequence, their leadership role is much reduced. In essence, managerial unionism 'represents a swing back to officer dominance and member passivity after a period of member mobilisation' (Heery and Kelly 1994, p. 16), but with the added dimension of the infusion of human resource management practices within the union itself, and a greater focus on members as individual 'consumers' who are entitled to a service, rather than dealing with them as a group with collective interests. This emerging form of trade unionism inevitably re-ordered power relationships within unions that has led to nodes of internal power becoming centres of resistance to change in general, and the organising agenda in particular, making the implementation of change difficult. While general secretaries, as the top positional leaders, might espouse a particular strategy and direction for their unions – for example, a turn to organising – the implementation of the plan is dependent on the willingness and co-operation, or if necessary, coercion of sufficient power bases within the union.

While Heery and Kelly's paper was written in 1994, before the turn to organising really began to be developed, the relationship between unions and their members has perhaps not changed fundamentally from this managerialist approach over the intervening period. This is, however, not universal. There are some clear exceptions, with a number of unions taking a different, more radical and activist-based approach. But if we consider the movement overall, membership passivity is still high, and, in the main, full-time officers keep tight control over the more militant union branches. Individual servicing is the primary relationship most members have with their union, and effective collective bargaining has been greatly reduced. Instead of members being able to direct officers' activities for their benefit, as was the case in the past, it is still largely the case that unions (and the direction of unions) are run by officers rather than workplace reps. All of this has important implications for the roles of union leaders, full-time officers and members in implementing any strategic change – including the operationalisation of an organising agenda, where cascading decision-making and control to lower levels of the organisation is a key element in the process of building union power.

THE ORGANISING AGENDA AND LEADING CHANGE IN UNIONS

Many of the TUC-affiliated unions accepted in the early 1990s that there needed to be proactive recruitment and organising activity if membership decline was to be stemmed. In some cases, unions simply wanted membership growth without actually organising or reconfiguring the organisation's culture to build the strength of their base – in some unions, the 'organising strategy' could be characterised as recruitment masquerading as organising. Again, there are exceptions, but if we were to consider the movement as a whole, it could generally be characterised in this way. Unions took different approaches to how organising was implemented. Some set up specialist organising units within the union with new staff (often these were young people from other social justice movements who had little experience of traditional workplaces or of trade union structures, culture or practice), some reallocated the responsibilities of negotiating officers to organising and recruitment, while others focused on re-educating lay activists to take on greater responsibility for recruitment in their own workplaces.

When unions started to prioritise recruitment, targets were often set and monitored by senior managers, yet progress was slow, and at times resistance was met. Many full-time officers were accustomed to autonomous working, and there was resentment in some quarters at having to incorporate recruitment into their many other duties (negotiation and servicing of members), and particularly to having this work scrutinised by senior managers. Recruitment was low down on the list of priorities for most full-time officers. Research from the mid-1990s (Snape 1995) suggested that union leaderships were not, on the whole, successful in influencing full-time officers to shift toward a recruitment and organising culture. In part, it is suggested that this was because 'some union leaders were using the language of "culture change" in a manner reminiscent of senior managers in commercial and public-sector organisations' (Snape 1995, p. 566), making officers feel resentful at having their work scrutinised and having to meet quotas.

There emerged from this an extensive and possibly unhelpful debate in the academic literature, contrasting the needs of 'servicing' and 'organising', which contributed to a rethink in some unions and saw a reallocating of recruitment and organising work to specialist organisers, in some cases within newly formed organising departments (Simms et al. 2013). But to what extent were union leaders able to contribute to or direct organisational change to move their unions toward an organising culture? Indeed, to what extent did they understand what organising really involved or was meant to achieve (other than perhaps addressing the ever-falling membership) and the fundamental culture change that would be necessary if they were to successfully re-orientate their unions from a form of managerial unionism to a participatory, member-led renaissance?

Most of the major unions responded to the call to organise after the formation of the TUC's 'new unionism' project, but did so in very different ways. In the early days (between 1998 and 2004), only modest resources were apportioned to organising. An extensive survey showed that 'heavily resourced campaigns' – defined as more than five staff per union – were a rarity, which indicates just how little resource was allocated in this initial turn to organising. As a comparison, US labour unions can have teams of up to 20 working on a single campaign, and hundreds across a whole union. Furthermore, one of the key aspirations was that union activists would be key actors in campaigns, in their own and in new, non-unionised, workplaces. Yet the research by Ed Heery and Melanie Simms (2011, p. 28) reported that 'lay involvement is lacking in a fifth of campaigns and in more than two-thirds there are fewer than five activists taking part ... and that the limited supply of active members can impose a constraint on organizing'. In the 140 campaigns that were studied for their research, the messaging or framing of organising shied away from linking membership to any need for union militancy in order to achieve employer concessions. Instead, the stress was on 'the need for collective organization and the risk to workers if they failed to create a collective counterweight to management' (Heery and Simms 2011, p. 33).

It is noteworthy that power was missing from much of the discourse around organising. While the messaging articulated was that increased membership leads to increased bargaining power, there is no indication of *what* power resources would be needed, or *how* they would be deployed in order to secure improvements to pay and conditions. Heery and Simms (2011) found that in only 6 per cent of the campaigns studied was there messaging about how unions could use industrial action to raise pay and conditions. Again, this suggests that despite much of the 'radical' rhetoric associated with the UK 'organising model' approach to trade unionism, the role of member activism in creating power was, in some unions, continually played down – instead, members were 'sold' a form of unionism that still saw them as consumers in largely passive roles.

STRATEGY, LEADERSHIP AND ORGANISING OUTCOMES IN UK UNIONS

Having identified these broader concerns, it is important to consider the strategies adopted by unions, what objectives were set, and how success was measured (in their own terms) in the turn to organising – and crucially, what this means in terms of union power. In some cases, unions were very clear in articulating their leadership strategies, in others, the picture was more obscure. As already mentioned, the retail and distribution union USDAW was an early adopter of the turn to organising, but took a while to develop its own very distinct approach, which only came into being in 2006. When the union put together its strategic organising plan, this was led from the top of the union, with processes in place to measure effectiveness. The union's leadership identified that the 'bolt-on' approach to organising wasn't working. Instead, an organising culture needed to be 'mainstreamed' throughout the organisations, and this would need to be managed effectively. The overall target was 'infill' recruitment in the big four employers where it had partnership agreements, and where most of its membership was located.

USDAW's deputy general secretary was the lead on the project, demonstrating commitment from the top. Lay reps, rather than employed organisers, were the drivers of change. They were 'stood down' from their jobs (receiving full pay that was reimbursed from the union to their employer) while they undertook six months of training and recruitment activity in the union's own Organising Academy which was formed in 2002. In 2012, after ten years of intake, almost 450 reps has been through this process, and 35 ended up working as 'area organisers'[2] for the union – amounting to one third of the union's general full-time officer positions. Alongside the Organising Academy, USDAW also negotiated release for union reps who had been spotted as having an 'aptitude for recruitment'. The union paid the employer for these workers' time, which was spent in workplaces other than their own, bringing in new members. Combined, it is claimed that these two groups of activists brought in around 134,000 new members over the ten-year period (Parker and Rees 2013). The deputy general secretary succeeded in transforming the role of full-time officer (in some cases reluctantly) from 'servicing' to one which identified and coached lay reps to become leaders in their own workplace. Each officer was given a work plan and was responsible for meeting the targets set by their line manager. Under-performers were provided with advice and guidance and even more regular reviews. While this managerialist approach to its own staff had been considered anathema in unions, it was understood that where unions had merely appealed to (or instructed) staff to recruit and organise, they had tended to fail. Instead, the leadership in USDAW recognised that:

> Delivering its strategy meant that divisions and ultimately individual FTOs [full-time officers] had to understand the overarching strategy and deliver it. Usdaw needed the managerial capacity to drive central initiatives. It needed to develop a completely new strategic planning process and management capability.
>
> (Parker and Rees 2013, p. 531)

This meant developing performance management tools and an annual strategic organising plan with clear, measureable targets and objectives. A consequence was that USDAW, through some decisive leadership, developed the strategic capacity to grow the union. In its own terms, set against what it hoped to achieve, it was very successful. It experienced significant growth from around 300,000 members in 2000 to just short of 430,000 in 2012 in the four major retailers where it had partnership agreements. It also increased the number of reps in the workplace who were able to support members when they got into difficulties at work. All of these are significant and important achievements, and benefits for the members, and they ensured the survival of the union in a period when other unions were still in decline.

However, if we are to look at this organising success in terms of industrial/structural power – the ability to get the employer to concede better pay for the union's members – there's little evidence that this was achieved through USDAW's organising approach. For example, a simple comparison between Tesco – where USDAW has a partnership agreement and where one third of its membership works – and other similar large retailers where the union isn't recognised doesn't show a wage premium for unionised workers.[3] Clearly, this is not the only measure of union power, but the ability to negotiate and bargain over wages is one of the basic functions of trade unionism, and one of the key direct benefits of being a member of a union (alongside representation in disciplinaries and grievances). Nevertheless, in terms of *organisational change*, USDAW's strategy for re-focusing the union in at least a nominally organising direction was very successful in securing the union's survival by delivering significant growth in membership.

Another union that has been very clear in articulating its leadership strategy and approach to organising is the Rail Maritime and Transport union – although its style is less associated with the TUC's organising model. It's a relatively small union (83,000 members) with a strong class-based orientation in terms of its identity. It describes itself as 'a progressive, democratic and highly professional trade union' … where 'Protecting and bettering our members' pay and conditions is the key RMT objective.'[4] It has a reputation for militancy, for threatening, and undertaking, effective strike action. Because of the structural power of its members, the union has had considerable wins against employers like London Underground, and this has built confidence and increased support from workers. Strikes on the London Underground are incredibly disruptive, causing millions of people to be unable to travel or get to work, and thus having a negative impact on business. This, of course, gives the union's leadership considerable bargaining power, but it also bestows confidence and credibility. The RMT's militant strategy has contributed to an increase in membership, and is capitalised on in the union's approach to organising:

Such an adversarial approach and the material benefits it has accrued has, in turn, contributed to a growth in RMT membership during the period 1999–2007, rising from 56,037 to 75,939 in 2007, representing a 37.3 per cent increase. Even though the absolute numbers are not large, they nevertheless make the RMT one of the fastest-growing unions in Britain, which is no mean achievement in the context of merely stable or even declining membership for many other unions.

(Darlington 2009a, p. 7)

So how was this achieved? This was largely as a result of a culture of leadership among key lay reps that is avowedly left-wing, with an ideological class-based approach to industrial relations which understands that the strength of workers arising from the ability to secure concessions is not achieved by accepting management prerogative – wins have to be fought for through industrial action and demonstrations of structural power. Ralph Darlington, who has studied the RMT in depth, argues that the layers of left-wing leadership within the union have consistently played a strong role in mobilising the wider membership by the political framing of the union's demands. The RMT didn't really buy into the TUC organising agenda in the way other unions did, but instead relied on traditional class-based antagonism with the employer, where the focus was on union activism at the base by shop stewards and ordinary members, largely through the use or threat of industrial action. As one interviewee in Darlington's research explained:

They [the RMT] have built a lot of good trade unionists, they have developed some new people from below, a group of activists. They have good leaflets and political propaganda coming out, and they send people around the system leafleting and signing up new members. They have involved people in action. And that has had an impact in keeping union structures alive at a time when they have been fighting on the defensive all the time. It is quite possible that without this willingness to fight, the union organisation could have become completely passive and simply a rubber stamp for management.

(Darlington 2001, p. 18)

The union rejected the more widely accepted 'organising model' approach whereby specialised organisers (often from outside the union) were employed to rebuild the union. The RMT also stood apart from the managerial form of unionism discussed earlier, where full-time officers are key decision-makers and the membership is relatively passive. In the 1990s, the union adopted a rule change that said that full-time officers would be elected rather than appointed. This meant that union staff became much more accountable to the members, who could remove them if they didn't feel they were representing their best interests. This much more participative form of unionism has strengthened the position of lay representatives in relation to their full-time officers. The union is therefore clear that 'Organising is about more than just recruitment – it's about building an active RMT organisation in the workplace and making sure our organisation is self-sufficient and sustainable.'[5] Importantly, this wasn't just said, it was put into action in workplaces and union branch meetings.

The union's leader when the TUC's turn to organising was evolving was the militant and charismatic Bob Crow. He was elected general secretary in 2002, and built on the RMT's approach by encouraging the strategic capacity of members to exercise their structural power through their self-activity and collective action (Darlington 2009b). As the union's top leader, Crow was the best-known trade unionist of his generation – at a time when trade unionism wasn't on the radar of most people – and he was variously described as 'an old school trade unionist' and 'a dinosaur' (Gall 2017). He was known as one of the most effective negotiators in the UK union movement, consistently improving the pay and conditions of his members, and willing to encourage them to stand up for their rights in the face of concerted attacks from politicians and employers. As a leader, he didn't 'control' the union, but created a culture and environment in which members felt a strong sense of identity with their union and had loyalty and confidence in the union's organising approach. It was the members who became the catalysts for growth of their union – they had the capability to do this. As such, the RMT gained 30,000 members in the seven years after Bob Crow became general secretary (Darlington 2009b). It was through unleashing the creativity of active members and politically conscious shop stewards that the strategic capacity of the union's membership was built.

This form of class-based unionism, promoted by the leadership at all levels, was established as a result of strategic choices for rebuilding the union after it lost considerable membership in the early 1980s. Bob Crow famously said: 'If you fight, you might not win, but if you don't fight, you always lose.'

It was this simplicity of message that resonated with RMT members and solidified the union's identity as militant and participatory. The framing of the union's purpose was done in an overtly political and ideological way: it pushed solidarity and militancy, as opposed to individualism and passivity, acknowledging that industrial relations is, in the end, about strategic power and the ability to use power to challenge managerial prerogative.

The RMT and USDAW could be considered as 'opposites' in terms of their methodology of union rebuilding (and their identity as unions), but most other unions that adopted a new approach to organising in the 'turn to organising' era fall somewhere in between these quite different archetypes. The model promoted by the TUC stressed increasing activity at local level, with greater self-sufficiency of members. While there was a 'toolbox' of tactics in the organising armour to be utilised in different ways depending on particular circumstances, it was almost universally accepted that leadership commitment with a strategic vision was a prerequisite if organising was to be successful (Voss and Sherman 2000).

The largest UK unions have all, at some point, described themselves as 'organising unions' and set up training programmes to equip staff (and in some cases, union reps) with the skills and capability to implement the new agenda. The language of organising pervades all these accounts, but the practice – particularly if considered in terms of power – has resulted in very mixed outcomes. To what extent have unions been able to increase the strategic capacity of their members to realise power in their workplaces, and to what extent has the leadership in unions been able to effect cultural change toward transformative organising? It's useful to compare and contrast the different approaches adopted and the difficulties encountered in some of the larger UK unions following the turn to organising.

To what extent is the RMT's organising model of 'building power through disputes' replicable in other unions' approaches to organising? One union that tried this was the Public and Commercial Services Union (PCS) – the civil service trade union. In 2000, Mark Serwotka was elected general secretary, and in many ways, he is a similar leader to Bob Crow – a great orator and a principled socialist. Throughout his leadership of PCS, he has succeeded in changing the political position of the union to one that is left of centre and identified as radical. He was notoriously part of the so-called 'awkward squad' of public-sector general secretaries that challenged the Labour government in the early part of the twenty-first century. However, the bureaucratic inertia and factionalism within the union has been more difficult to overcome. While the union reportedly grew membership during an early phase of ballots for industrial action (between 2000 and 2008, PCS gained 45,000 new members),[6] these ballots did not, on the whole, lead to significant 'wins', and certainly did not change the balance of power within the civil service. The union continued to attract new joiners by balloting for strike action through to 2013.

In an analysis of PCS's membership figures and strike action ballots over time, Andy Hodder and colleagues (2017) have shown that strike action has a positive impact on increasing union membership even when controlling for a number of variables. However, a negative they found was that this 'strike effect' 'appears to be shifting over time: it is becoming less about recruiting new members and more about retaining existing ones, for reasons that remain unclear' (Hodder et al. 2017, p. 183). Perhaps one explanation could be that the failure to achieve substantive wins following strike action has lessened the willingness of new members to join over time. Another potential reason could be that a consequence of PCS's inability to turn successful ballots into meaningful wins, unlike the RMT, has led to the left-dominated activists in PCS becoming increasingly distanced from the majority of members. Despite the stated objectives of the union, the organising strategy seems to have morphed into balloting to gain members rather than balloting to build power – or to increase the strategic capacity of members in their workplaces.

In 2016, the Trade Union Act required all ballots for industrial action to have at least 50 per cent participation before a union could undertake legitimate industrial action.[7] The legislation was designed by the government to make national industrial action ballots difficult to win. Yet paradoxically, the Act also provided a (potential) organising opportunity for unions not only to build power, but to actualise it in the form of strike action. In the words of Jane McAlevey (2016), it provided unions with the opportunity to undertake 'structure tests' to gauge the support they had among workers and the extent to which they could deliver whatever action was needed to force a recalcitrant employer to concede.

In 2018, after the law on balloting had changed, PCS's leadership called a national ballot of its members for industrial action. Yet the organising work was not as effective as expected, and the ballot missed the threshold. The union repeated the ballot in 2019, perhaps without any assessment of the strategic capacity of the union to deliver and an examination of the previous reasons for failure. There wasn't a 'structure test' or organising plan in place to assess and build membership support, and the ballot, over the same issues, failed for a second time. In a sense, the requirement to have high participation of members in votes for lawful industrial action to take place forces unions to consider the level of collective power there is in particular workplaces, or across the union, to take effective action. Ignoring the issue of power and the degree of support/confidence of members, PCS's strategy of balloting proved ineffective at either increasing recruitment to the necessary levels to increase union density (a proxy indicator of power) or delivering actual power to effect change. It appears that members and potential members were not persuaded in sufficient numbers that industrial action would deliver the pay rise they wanted. In a notable sign of its lack of industrial power (or perhaps strategic thinking by the union's leadership that was aware of the union's weakness), the union launched a campaign in 2020 to get 100,000 signatures on a petition to parliament calling for 'a fair pay rise for government workers' (PCS 2020), which was surely an implicit acknowledgement that it still did not have the organisational capacity to win yet another industrial action ballot over this issue.

In stark contrast to PCS's national organising strategy 'Building, Growing, Winning' (PCS 2019) is the Communication Workers Union (CWU), a union that, in the postal sector, has been involved in a war of attrition with the employer Royal Mail, particularly since privatisation in 2013. The CWU was another union that had little engagement with the TUC's organising model approach, but unlike most other unions faced with a changing industrial environment, it undertook a union renewal strategy, and did so by focusing on workplace organisation of its members. Following the introduction of the Trade Union Act 2015, the CWU was the first union to run a national ballot in October 2017. It saw 89 per cent of members vote for industrial action on a 73.7 per cent turnout. This very high turnout was a result of the level of organisation at workplace level that involved grassroots members led by determined activists. In October 2019, a second ballot saw an even higher 97.1 per cent yes vote on a 75.9 per cent turnout – this 'structure test' demonstrated there was widespread support for industrial action. To the employer, this revealed considerable discontent among workers, and strongly indicated that industrial action would be effective. In essence, it clearly showed the employer the potential collective power of the union.

Feeling threatened by the possible impact on the postal service, Royal Mail, unwilling to resolve the issue by negotiation, resorted to the courts, and successfully managed to win an injunction that invalidated the ballot. Royal Mail challenged the CWU's highly effective workplace organising – which had included encouraging members to vote at work to build visible solidarity – and it was this that the judge ruled amounted to 'improper interference' in the conduct of balloting.

The response from the union was to continue to build its strategic capacity to deliver collective power by continuing workplace organising of members. The union re-balloted, on the same issues, in March 2020, but mindful of the risk of further injunctions, had to scale back its overt organising. Despite this, in the re-run ballot, in March 2020, 94.5 per cent voted for industrial action on a turnout of 63.4 per cent. While ballots for industrial action are not in and of themselves a way of building workplace power, the scale of the turnout is perhaps a good proxy for measuring the extent of workplace confidence and organisation, or to use Jane McAlevey's language: ballots provide the opportunity to undertake an effective structure test that makes visible the extent of the support of union members for issues, and the potential to realise collective power through industrial action.

The Transport and General Workers' Union (now Unite) set out its own 'strategy for growth' in 2005. This was a classic 'organising model' approach with the stated aim of developing workplace leaders to build a collective response to issues in their workplace, and a national strategy targeting a number of key industrial sectors – meat processing plants, low-cost airlines, the contract cleaning industry and logistics. According to the union's head of organising, the strategy to build organisation in these areas comprised 'committed leadership', 'allocation of financial resources' and the 'establishment of a central organising department' (Graham 2007). The latter initially comprised over 100 newly recruited staff in eight organising teams in each of the union's regions.

Unite has reported wins in each of its targeted areas and across each of its measures of success (increased members, recruitment of shop stewards, collective agreements negotiated, increases in pay, and the saving of jobs), but there is no independent verification of this. A number of difficulties in implementing the organising strategy were identified by the leadership with responsibility for the organising department early on: these were a danger that 'normal' recruitment/organising would be reduced as full-time officers referred all this work to the organising department, and that these staff would find it difficult to prioritise organising activities (Graham 2007). In reality, these concerns became evident early on, and today the central organising department – large though it is – remains a bolt-on that hasn't been able to realise the stated aspiration to change the overall culture of the union from that of servicing to organising. In practice, over 15 years since adopting its 'strategy for growth', the full-time officers have little to do with the activities of the organising department (and vice versa), and this division is not conducive to building the strategic capacity needed for effective change and transformation of the union. This is not to undermine the con- siderable effort, nor a number of successful campaigns and wins on behalf of members (in both structures of the union). Without the work of the organ- ising department (now with 130 staff) and the work of full-time industrial officers (400 staff), not to mention the community engagement and leverage work of its community membership, the union's membership and density in certain workplaces would be considerably lower than it is today. It's also the case that as a large private sector union, its membership has been hit signif- icantly by the fall-out from the financial crisis in 2008, such that between 2008 and 2018, the union lost 642,000 members, or 32 percent of its total membership.[8] There is evidence that there is senior leadership support for an organising agenda, but the structural bureaucracy within a union of this size, and the competing power nodes among staff and lay activists, mean that transformational whole-union cultural change has proven elusive.

Similarly, Unison, the largest public-sector union in the UK, has strug- gled to adopt a cultural change toward organising. In many ways, its identity is more 'moderate' and cautious in comparison to Unite, fitting more closely with an identity that is perhaps closest to a managerial form of unionism, where full-time officers exert considerable control over activ- ists and members. As a public-sector union, it is recognised for collective bargaining in its key areas of organisation. Its strategy is therefore to focus primarily on 'infill' recruitment where it already has a presence. Initially, in the early 1990s, the national strategy in Unison was based on regional and branch recruitment targets – 'Winning the Organised Workplace'. Following the turn to organising, the narrative of 'building an organising culture' was adopted and set out in the 'National Organising and Recruitment Strategy'. As with other unions, Unison sponsored staff through the TUC's Organising Academy, and implemented compulsory organising training for its full-time

179

officer staff. Still, the difficulty of shifting full-time officers away from other priorities remained. While changes to the responsibilities of servicing staff were implemented and initial stages of representation for members were moved to shop stewards, this didn't result in a redirection of time to spend on organising, as research showed that 'a combination of existing workload and a commitment to serving among some F-T-Os and lay representatives effectively limited their participation in organising initiatives' (Waddington and Kerr 2015, p. 192).

Building the strategic capacity to effect change requires the activity of members, but Unison has not managed to engage its members (or many activists) to any great extent in organising (or recruitment) activities. Given the multiple layers of management within local government and other sectors that the union organises in, local reps are often called on to lead negotiations and consultation, for example on restructuring, outsourcing and redundancy. Unison has a lay activist culture, but one which is very often 'management-facing' (i.e. consultation and negotiation) rather than 'member-facing' (organising and building for power).

The union has espoused the need for change, but there hasn't been evidence of the necessary leadership capacity throughout the union to make this happen. Like Unite, Unison has a well-entrenched bureaucratic struc-ture and has a significant number of lay representatives on full-time facility release from their employers. Many of these are overwhelmed with case work for their members or engaged in protracted and frequent local nego-tiations, and thus feel they have little time for organising. But also, those reps who have been 'off the tools' (on full-time release) for many years have natural concerns about being required to go back into their substantive posts. In such cases, a focus on organising and building membership may not be attractive, as there is an inherent risk of being challenged in future elections by an influx of new members. Another aspect restraining transfor-mational change to an organising culture is the political nature of Unison, which has close ties to the Labour Party nationally, regionally and locally. A consequence is that militant activity among union activists against their employers – who are, in the main, local government (including a substantial number of Labour-controlled authorities) and the National Health Service – is often restrained by union officials.

Yet there are examples within Unison where strategic thinking in terms of power analysis has shown what is possible with a leadership determined to challenge the power of employers. In 2015, a dispute arose among almost 400 home care workers in Birmingham who were employed by the local Labour-controlled council. These were some of the lowest-paid workers, who faced substantial cuts to their wages. Supported by the union's regional secretary, the workers took 40 days of strike action over a nine-month period, yet this wasn't sufficient to challenge the employer. The union realised the strikes weren't sufficiently effective and the collective power of the workers wasn't proving enough to force the council to back down (it simply did not seem to care if service users did not get their essential service). The council leader was adamant that the cuts would be imposed on these workers. It was therefore recognised that a different strategy was needed. By undertaking a power analysis, the focus shifted to accessing different sources of power.

The target now became the elected councillors. Having decided that what these councillors wanted most was to remain as councillors, the union needed to find a way to threaten that aspiration, and it did. The community was activated through a letter writing campaign designed to put the councillors under pressure to support the care workers.

Over 100,000 leaflets were distributed to the councillors' constituents, and a social media campaign was devised to embarrass the (highly paid) leader of the council and his cabinet. The union built strategic capacity by having high participation of its care workers, but also involved local electors in the campaign. The organising strategy was to threaten the hostile Labour councillors with the loss of their seats at the next election. By identifying its targets – the top three council leaders – and researching the specific self-interests of each of them, the union and the members concerned were able to put their political careers at risk. In effect, they used political and moral power to win the dispute, recognising that in this case, industrial power on its own just wasn't strong enough. The campaign was effective at preventing wage cuts for the low-paid, predominantly women and ethnic minority workers. It was an important victory for a union that prides itself on its commitment to equalities, but it was more than that: the dispute transformed the union's relationship with the local council leadership, which, following the dispute, no longer viewed it as an irritation, but now viewed it as a powerful player which could no longer be ignored.

The GMB is a general union whose membership straddles the public and private sectors. It suffered badly in terms of membership decline following the collapse of manufacturing in the UK. Concerned with financial survival, the union leadership urgently needed an organising strategy that would quickly draw in new members as it was facing a 5 per cent year-on-year decline. As one senior officer recalled in discussing the union's turn to organising: 'we needed to counter a very deep-seated culture that the GMB had which was the notion that you can service people into membership'. There was a prevailing idea that if the union provided a good service to one or two people in a workplace, this would magically lead others to join, but this wasn't delivering results. Yet servicing and negotiating were the main activities of the union's full-time officers. The union's leadership were wary about setting up a separate organising structure because they were concerned that employing specialist organisers would send out the message that full-time officers need not involve themselves in recruitment and organising activity. But the union required all hands on deck if it was to step back from financial collapse – everyone needed to recruit and organise. The national organising plan adopted focused on three low-paid industrial sectors (care, security, and teaching assistants within education) where it was believed there was the greatest potential to pick up membership fast. These were areas untouched and largely unwanted by other unions, but they were all growing sectors with potential membership gains. From 2007, when the organising strategy was in put place and operating in each of the union's regions, to 2017 the GMB increased its membership by 4 per cent.[9] This may not seem a great change, but its previous trajectory would have seen membership fall by 50 per cent over that same timescale.

The union, in its own internal narrative, wanted to develop the strategic capacity of the activists and members to effect change within their own workplaces:

> So getting a 5 per cent pay rise in a factory and then asking people to join afterwards, tends not to work. Saying to people, 'Do you want to participate in a campaign to get a 5 per cent pay increase?', and delaying that process until everyone is involved and consulted is much more attractive, and workers are much more likely to join – so that was the principle that we were pursuing.
>
> (GMB national officer, 2006)

There was a clear understanding in this statement about developing bottom-up organising among the members, and this was written into the national organising strategy and the training of full-time officers. But over the years, the urgent focus on pure recruitment, particularly of teaching assistants – a new role in the classroom that the teaching unions refused to organise – provided low-hanging fruit. It turned out that, financially at least, the GMB didn't need to organise its members at the base, instead it could balance its books through sustained recruitment of classroom assistants, security guards and carers. It should be noted that those working in classrooms are often highly unionised, not necessarily because of any union militancy, but simply because everyone who goes into teaching recognises that at some stage over their career, a child may make an allegation against them (warranted or not), and they will need representation. The GMB's strategic decisions in building membership in these new sectors saved the union from bankruptcy, and in this sense, it was highly effective. However, the more difficult objective – building power – proved elusive as the union was unable to build significant workplace activity to meaningfully challenge the power of employers.

REFLECTIONS ON WHY THE 'TURN TO ORGANISING'
HAS BEEN LIMITED IN ITS SUCCESS

These examples have illustrated the varied picture of organising activity across the UK union movement – they clearly don't tell the whole story, but the chapter has highlighted the considerable difficulties encountered by union leaders seeking to implement organisational change to increase the power of workers. The social, political and economic climate over the last 40 years or so has drastically shifted power away from unions in their traditional heartlands, leaving many of them struggling to remain in exist-ence as membership decline has reduced operating income. There has been an almost universal acceptance from union leaders that 'managing decline' was not the legacy they wished to leave behind, so most have acknowledged that re-focusing on organising was necessary. There is a question, though, as to whether or not the leadership in unions fully appreciated the levels of resource or the cultural change organising requires to build capacity and power at the workplace level. In some cases, unions have simply re-inter-preted 'organising' as recruitment, rather than what it really is – a way of supporting members to build power to improve their pay and conditions through their own self-activity. Unions have certainly struggled to break out of their historical, cultural and structural constraints to develop strategic plans to build the necessary leadership and strategic capacity to facilitate their members winning. The oligarchic tendencies of leadership are clearly evident in most unions, and can, if not challenged, restrict the ability of leaders to implement organisational change.

In many union organising plans, there was – understandably, given the state of union finances – a great deal of focus on target-setting in terms of membership recruitment. Yet if this remains the main focus, this activity cannot on its own build power. To become an 'organising union' requires a strategic vision, articulated by leaders, as to what could be won through the collective action of members. It is the vision of change that then attracts activists and gives confidence and hope to members. People join in the belief that being part of the union is a step toward winning a positive change in the workplace. Missing out the strategic vision, the necessary cultural change, and the building of power is likely to result in organising being interpreted as a mere sales pitch – accompanied by the servicing approach that became the prevalent form of unionism from the 1980s onwards. Indeed, in some cases, it appeared that the role of union members in a number of unions was to become volunteer 'sales staff', recruiting their colleagues, rather than agents of change that could contribute to the strategic capacity of the union to build power. The only participation in their union anticipated of these new recruits was to be the passive recipients of the 'saviour' interventions of reps or full-time union staff if they, as individuals, had a problem at work. This approach reduces trade unions to largely advocacy and insurance-based organisations providing individual services, which is not a model that historically has facilitated the building of collective power.

One of the ways of measuring trade union commitment to organising is the extent to which it invests in building leadership capacity at every level within the organisation. While we have seen that unions utilise the rhetoric of organising and have invested heavily in recruiting so-called specialist organisers, with few exceptions this hasn't translated into a focus on building strategic capacity at workplace level – the very place where it's necessary to create solidarity and a collective identity. There are a number of reasons why this 'blind spot' exists. First, if union leaders only buy into the organising agenda to address membership decline rather than to build union power, there is little need to develop the resource capacity of members. Instead, sparse financial resources could be used to employ additional paid recruiters, in the belief that they will bring in extra cash. Secondly, some unions have an elitist or dismissive attitude toward their members, sometimes viewing them as a 'problem' to be endured rather than a resource that should be nurtured. And finally, of course, there is the fear that if the members were really in charge, they might choose different priorities to those that saw the existing leadership rise through the lay or professional bureaucracies.

Marshall Ganz, currently Senior Lecturer in Leadership, Organizing, and Civil Society at Harvard University, but also a former union organiser with the United Farm Workers in California, neatly summarises the factors necessary for successful organising. He says it requires leadership that has:

> A deep desire for change [which] must be coupled with the capacity to make change. Structures must be created that create the space within which growth, creativity, and action can flourish, without slipping into the chaos of structurelessness, and leaders must be recruited, trained, and developed on a scale required to build the relationships, sustain the motivation, do the strategizing, and carry out the action required to achieve success.
>
> (Ganz 2008, p. 4)

While perhaps easier said than done, this does provide a useful framework for designing a worker-focused organising strategy that is capable of creating the power necessary for workers to win improvements to their working lives, or at least halt the attacks by employers that over the last 50 years have taken away the massive gains unions had achieved since the early days of their formation. We should, therefore, when thinking of trade union renaissance and the (re)building of workers' power, reflect on what different structures (and patterns of thinking), and different types of leaders (and leadership styles) are required to build strategic capacity and thus harness the latent power and creativity of rank-and-file workers, who have hitherto often been allocated the role of passive spectators in the whole process of the 'turn to organising'. The final chapter will reflect on these points, and also consider some of the new forms of unionism that have been challenging conditions in what some claim to be the most difficult-to-organise jobs – those in the so-called 'gig economy'.

9

Winning Power is Possible

Today's anxious, disenfranchised workers wait for the next 'gig' to materi-
alise on a smartphone rather than waiting by the farm or the factory gate.
(Stanford 2017, p. 234)

Chapter 1 began by suggesting that we need to look at the past in order to
understand the present, because the exploitation of workers today has many
echoes of previous times. In the 1880s, when the new unions were forming,
nearly all work was 'precarious', where there was no security of employment
and little employment protection, yet we saw young women matchmakers at
the Bryant & May factory in London organise a strike and win. After three
weeks of striking, all their demands were met: they had petty fines abolished,
an improvement in wages, and a canteen provided by the employer, and
they formalised themselves into a union to help protect themselves against
further exploitation. But it was the dock workers who were the archetypal
'gig workers' of the 1880s. As casual labourers, they would start the day by
hanging around the docks waiting to see who would be chosen to be contracted for a few hours' work, or if lucky, a full day's work. They were at the
mercy of employers who hired and fired at will. There was no job security
or guaranteed wage, and dock workers were subject to zero-hour 'contracts'
similar to those faced by 3 per cent of today's UK workforce.[1] Nevertheless,
it was precarious workers like this who were central to the upsurge in union
activity in the period of new unionism that led to the growth of unions representing the unorganised, and the supposedly 'unorganisable'.

In recent years, there has been considerable focus on the malign influence
on workers of what is referred to as the 'gig economy', particularly so-called
'platform workers'. Driven by digital technology, increasing numbers of
workers are allocated jobs (or gigs) through economic agents (intermediar-
ies),[2] 'providing virtual spaces for matching labour supply and demand via
online technologies based on algorithmic management' (Vandaele 2018, p.

5). In most cases, workers are not paid for their time, but receive payment by completed job – in effect a piece rate. Workers may also be highly monitored – again using digital technology that continually tracks their movements – allowing managers to control and discipline workers or 'independent contractors' who are not considered to be performing to expected standards (Moore et al. 2018). In addition, figures suggest that up to another 4.6 million people in the UK regularly experience what is referred to as 'precarious scheduling', which is described as 'flexible working with limited hours dictated by management, often with little notice, and to the detriment of employees' home lives and mental health' (Wood and Burchell 2017). There are also around 1.5 million temporary workers,[3] many of whom have little job security, adding to around 10 million of the UK labour force who are considered to be in precarious employment.

These forms of 'non-standard' employment – short-term, flexible and independent work – are not new to the economy, and indeed, were the common form of employment in the past. Casual, seasonal and contract labour was universal when capitalism first emerged, and it was only through political reform and workers combining that this began to change. The standard employment relationship, comprising full-time employment at a place of work, with employment benefits (sick pay, holiday pay and pensions) and regulated by labour law, emerged in the late nineteenth century, but only became 'standard' after the Second World War. Its existence, then, is only relatively recent in modern capitalism, and it came about both because of the struggle of workers to secure stable employment and because, at times, it suited the needs of capital and the state to have a stable and reliable workforce. As Jim Stanford explains:

> The attendance and performance requirements of capital-intensive enterprises made it too risky to allow workers choice or discretion in working hours. Similarly, the job-specific skill requirements of mass production technologies enhanced the benefits to employers of a stable workforce, thus encouraging them to offer permanent jobs.
>
> (2017, p. 390)

It was a combination of social, economic and political circumstances that fed into a post-war consensus of reformed managerial capitalism and the 'rise of a broader, redistributive understanding among employers, the state and workers', leading to the move away from a reliance on casualisation. As a result, 'norms about what constituted fair treatment on the part of employers changed: workers came to expect stable employment and associated entitlements and benefits as normal features of work' (Stanford 2017, p. 390). It should, however, be noted that the 'standard employment relationship' was not standard for all sections of the labour force. Women's work has often been more precarious than that of men, and that of minority ethnic workers – along with immigrants – has often shown a similar tendency. Today, it is jobs done by people in these demographic groups that have some of the lowest wages in the labour market, and where the greatest levels of precarious work are to be found. Home care workers are predominantly female, ethnic minority and migrant – sometimes all three – and have little contact with fellow workers as they spend their time travelling between clients. Cleaners, many of whom work for sub-contractors, find they don't have the same benefits as those they work alongside in the buildings they clean – they also tend to be predominantly women and migrants. Hospitality, agriculture, retail, taxi drivers and security guard, are other jobs that tend to be done by an immigrant workforce, where job insecurity and non-standard working is the norm. As Judy Fudge (2017) makes clear, the shift away from the 'standard employment relationship' makes it more difficult for workers to assert their rights and to challenge managerial prerogative:

> As the pillars (other institutions and political alliances that support them) upon which this normative model of employment, known as the standard employment relationship, have weakened there has been a proliferation of employment and work relationships that fall outside the norm and, consequently, beyond the scope of labour law and its associated labour standards and techniques of regulation, such as collective bargaining.
>
> (Fudge 2017, p. 374)

The other key thing the above workers have in common is that the sectors they work in are largely un-unionised. As such, they have little or no protection from over-exploitation, from exposure to health and safety risks, from unlawful deductions of wages, from discrimination and from arbitrary dismissal.

ORGANISING THE 'DIFFICULT TO ORGANISE'

Unions have often considered these groups of workers (non-standard workers) to be 'difficult to organise', and while there have been a few attempts by mainstream unions to recruit in some of these sectors, the actions have been largely piecemeal and ineffective. High turnover of staff, difficulties in accessing workplaces (if indeed there is a traditional workplace), issues relating to communication (i.e. languages) and the resourcing of organising in these sectors have meant that unions have tended to ignore these workers, and instead have focused on recruiting the 'low-hanging fruit' of non-members in already unionised workplaces. At times, however, groups of workers in these sectors – particularly migrants – have approached unions for help, and have joined hoping they could get support for their issues, but they have often been left wanting. As a consequence, migrant members have, on occasion, left as a group to form, or join, new independent unions,[4] where the workers have had significant wins. Davide Però, who has spent many years researching migrant worker organising, explains the formation of what he refers to as 'indie unions' as resulting of the lack of, or inadequate, support for migrant workers within the established or mainstream unions: 'their gestation, emergence and growth are directly linked to first-hand, negative experiences with mainstream unions, especially on issues of representation, autonomy, cooperation, bureaucracy and the development of policy and collective initiatives' (2019, p. 906).

Both Unison and Unite have, over time, taken such groups into membership, but not in significant numbers, and the members have often felt that they were inadequately supported, and have complained that bureaucratic structures have prevented rapid or innovative organising approaches when dealing with the issues members have faced. In one case, a group of migrants set up the Latin American Workers Association and took their members into the Transport and General Workers' Union (now Unite) in the early 2000s, where they were provided with office space in which to represent the 1,000 members who joined. Through their collective identity as migrants from Latin America, as low-paid precarious workers and as people who were racialised, they built a strong solidarity network – what Gabriella Alberti and Davide Però describe as a 'community of struggle'. These authors reported that the Latin American Workers Association gave its members a sense of pride and identity:

an empowering feeling that they were shaping their lives and those of low-paid working people more generally, despite the disadvantageous and exclusionary conditions they faced. It embedded them in a solidarity circuit that was at once a 'community of coping' (Korczynski 2003) and a community of struggle in which class and ethnicity were interwoven, making them feel stronger as well as cared about.

(Alberti and Però 2018, p. 703)

This was an intensely political group of workers (in part derived from the background to their, often involuntary, decisions to migrate and leave their home countries) whose approach to issues was, in some cases, more militant than their host union. This led to tensions over organisational practices, particularly around the autonomy of the Latin American Workers Association to act on behalf of precarious migrant workers, but also the conservatism of the union's bureaucracy and its perceived failure to act, and to act quickly. In 2012, the tensions resulted in a break-up, and members of the Latin American Workers Association went on to form the Independent Workers of Great Britain (IWGB).

Similarly, a group of low-paid migrant workers (cleaning, catering, maintenance, porters and security staff) at the University of London's central administrative building and library did likewise. Migrant workers at this workplace joined the UK's largest union, Unison, which has members across the higher education section, mainly in admin roles and support staff. The union was, at the time they joined, supporting Citizens UK (a broad-based community association), which was leading the Living Wage Campaign, and the union successfully negotiated its implementation at the university in 2012. This resulted in a substantial pay increase for these outsourced workers and union recognition by the employers (the contractors supplying labour to the university). Emboldened by this success, the migrant workers began making further demands that they be given the same benefits in terms of pensions, holiday pay and sick leave as the 'in-house' staff. The workers wanted their union to agree they be allowed to conduct a much more high-profile and lively organising campaign where they would target not only their employer, but also the employer's client (the University of London where they worked). It appears that Unison officers rejected these proposals, and when this was followed by the union declaring branch officer elections void due to alleged procedural issues, the migrant workers felt the union wasn't providing them with the support they needed to win on their issues (Alberti and Però 2018). Like the Latin American workers in the Transport and General Workers' Union, these migrant members in Unison also left, as a group, to join the IWGB:

> At the origin of the conflict between the migrant workers and the recognized trade union there were factors that related to union democracy, institutional issues and internal norms. In this case, the uneven ways in which the branch was run, decisions were taken and power distributed in favour of the long-term British officers had special weight.
>
> (Alberti and Però 2018, p. 706)

These two short quotes, which are the findings of in-depth research by the authors into the organising of, and by, migrant workers, reveal a range of issues about union structure, bureaucracy and organisational form, strategic capacity-building, internal power nodes within unions, and differences between bottom-up and top-down organising approaches, and not least the intersection of race and class and the multi-layered experience of discrimination and how these are taken up (or not) in unions. These are issues to which we will return, but before that, we will consider the ways new independent unions have been organising and how they have been utilising power. As low-paid, precarious, outsourced and easily replaced migrant workers, it might appear that they have few power resources at their disposal. Yet these unions have shown that despite their small size (just several thousand members between them), and with little finance, they have managed to identify and utilise sources of power to secure a number of significant wins, including through direct action that has inflicted reputational damage on a number of high-profile employers operating in the gig economy and the contract cleaning, catering and security sectors – places where mainstream unions have largely been absent.

BREAKING AWAY: THE DEVELOPMENT OF INDEPENDENT UNIONS

A number of very small independent unions have formed since the breakaway of migrant worker members from the two mainstream unions mentioned above. The Independent Workers of Great Britain, formed in

2012, and United Voices of the World (UVW), formed in 2014, are the two most notable of these.[5] These are tiny unions compared to the super-unions Unite and Unison. The IWGB has around 4,000 members and the UVW approximately 5,000, but although membership is important, an organiser from UVW commented that they have never been particularly focused on membership numbers as they see membership as a very unreliable proxy of strength; instead, the focus is on activism of rank-and-file workers. Both these unions are formed of predominantly migrant workers, mostly from Latin America, but also from Africa – with the addition of smaller numbers of black and white British workers. The main sectors they have been organising in are cleaning, security guards, private hire drivers and couriers, where much of this form of work is precarious, and where workers are nominally self-employed or indirectly employed via contractors.

One of the first successful campaigns, which began in January 2013, was led by the IWGB at the University of London. Here, members organised and then mobilised for three claims (the '3 Cosas Campaign'): sick pay, holiday and pensions – as outsourced workers, they demanded equal treatment to 'in-house' staff. With only rank-and-file members, this was a bottom-up campaign reliant on the self-activity of workers themselves. As Alberti (2016a) explains, the organising approach embraced a mix of community mobilisation, informal bargaining tactics, direct action and legal cases to force the employer to comply with their demands. The wider university community made up of students and academics was drawn into direct actions such as sit-ins and occupations – as was the Latin American community in London and many others who were concerned about the growing exploitation of low-paid precarious migrant workers. The strategic use of social media also drew people to noisy street protests to gain publicity, and it was used effectively to appeal for financial support. Despite their perceived lack of structural power – these were a small number of outsourced workers who arguably could easily be replaced – the workers also took strike action with very visible picketing. By summer 2014, following a serious of strikes that gained widespread publicity, the university was suffering reputational damage, and the contractor that employed the workers ceded to the worker's demands.

The power on which these workers were able to draw was their own associational power, but also that of a community of interest outside the workplace – people who were free to protest in a way in which unions are sometimes restricted by industrial action legislation. Mainstream unions have become very cautious of autonomous rank-and-file actions, particularly when unpredictable direct action and community engagement are involved, but it is these actions that provided the additional leverage that these workers – with otherwise low structural power – needed if they were to win. Union members were able to mobilise a strong social justice narrative and activate a wide base of support, imaginatively utilising moral, associational and coalitional power to 'change the rules of the game', which were, arguably, specifically designed to make it difficult for outsourced workers to challenge managerial prerogative and win. As Gabriella Alberti concluded from her following of this dispute throughout its duration:

> Most surprisingly the 3 Cosas campaign has showed how the inventiveness of new media labor struggles and the imaginative power of solidarity leveraged across a range of formal and informal action can bring important victories to those considered unorganizable as they trouble the 'orderly' space of our marketized universities and strive for a collective voice in the ruins of traditional representation.
>
> (2016a, p. 100)

In another case, a group of workers who might appear to have few infrastructural resources on which to draw succeeded in challenging the online platform food delivery company Deliveroo when it announced it was changing its payments to riders. The company issued notice in 2016 that it was changing the way workers were paid – from a flat hourly rate of £7 per hour (with a £1 bonus per completed delivery) to piece rate delivery of £3.74 (and no hourly rate) (Cant 2019). Clearly, if drivers didn't receive any orders, they would earn no money, and this could have resulted in a considerable drop in pay. What happened next was clearly not on the employer's risk register. It didn't occur to it that a group of disparate, non-unionised, 'self-employed' workers would take 'unofficial' strike action in protest. As supposed independent contractors, the riders could lawfully just stop working without notice, and this is what they did when they heard about the company's plans. Food delivery requires a 'just-in-time' system to meet the needs of customers, so when drivers refused to work, the company's operation fell apart. Food orders went undelivered across London, the service was in chaos, and Deliveroo didn't have a contingency plan, so effectively power was in the hands of the riders, and they used this structural power to force the company to back down and revert to the status quo.

Following assistance from the IWGB, which crowdsourced cash to support the strikers, many of the riders joined the union, and were able to continue their strike for another three days until they won their initial demands. They did not win union recognition, which was added to the workers' claim during the dispute. In some ways, the fact that the company refused to recognise the riders as 'workers' made their industrial action easier to undertake, as they weren't subject to the rules and regulations in the legislation relating to balloting, such as notification of when the strikes would take place. Lack of structures or the requirement to follow procedures worked to the advantage of this group of precarious workers in this particular case. However, this hasn't stopped the IWGB pushing for employment status for these workers – the advantage being that they would then become entitled to a minimum wage, holiday pay, sick pay and pensions provided by their employer. In targeting other 'gig economy' employers, the IWGB has focused on a company's clients to provide leverage for the demands of its members – again overcoming the relatively weak structural power for some groups of workers. In one reported case, four clients gave an ultimatum to eCourier that they would take their business elsewhere, which resulted in couriers receiving on average a 28 per cent pay increase (Roberts 2018).

More recently, in 2019, members of the United Voices of the World undertook a series of strike actions at hospitals in London, the government's Ministry of Justice, the HQ of the TV companies Channel 4 and ITV and three London Universities. These actions followed a previous success at the London School of Economics, where in 2017 the employer ended the outsourcing of its cleaning staff, bringing workers back in-house on the same terms and conditions as its directly employed staff. UVW members, who are predominantly migrants in low-paid precarious jobs, took strike action, again creating associational power through the involvement of staff and students at the university. In early 2020, UVW had a significant win at St Mary's Hospital when, after a successful ballot, the workers staged nine days of strikes, and planned a further five days when the hospital committed to negotiations. Union members celebrated their success when the Hospital Trust announced that around 1,000 contracted-out cleaners, caterers, porters and other service staff would be brought back in-house as full National Health Service employees. Again, it was lively demonstrations, strikes, pickets, blockades and occupations, as well as signed support from 50 doctors in the hospital, that built the associational power and strategic capacity of the union to deliver this victory. This was achieved through a particular form of union organising. The UVW is structured non-hierarchically – it doesn't have a general secretary – and meetings are participatory, where members are encouraged/expected to play a role in decision-making over strategy and tactics. Its largely horizontal make-up is designed to ensure that decisions are decided from the bottom up, and agreed as far as possible collectively in mass meetings. While there are a few paid staff,[6] a lot of the union's resources are provided voluntarily – especially legal support. The UVW's organising practice is to look for and create opportunities for solidarity, alliances beyond the workplace, political engagement and, importantly in order to foster a collective culture, through socialising.

It is the sensitivity to, and centrality of, the lived experiences of low-paid migrant workers that distinguishes the independent unions from mainstream unions – and this is one of the key reasons why members join and have trust in their union. As Davide Però (2019, p. 41) explains, this is 'expressed through their [indie unions'] strong attention to workers' linguistic and cultural specificities, and characterized by systematic inclusionary practices'. As such, union meetings are lively affairs, inclusive spaces where simultaneous translations take place, and where Jane McAlevey's (2016) notion of 'whole worker organising' is expressly part of a deep organising approach. Language skills are taught, food shared and assistance with housing, migration status and other issues beyond the workplace is incorporated into union activities. Personal growth and empowering workers to act are also central, allowing people who have experienced lack of respect and degradation as a result of their migrant status to 'overcome fear, build self-esteem and confidence, and take pride in who they are and what they can do at work and beyond' (Però 2019, p. 44). These 'communities of coping' that are developed as a result of mutual support and socialising then lead to the strengthening of 'communities of struggle' and resistance, giving members confidence to act on the associational power they have built through their active participation in their union.

While these independent unions are still small, they demonstrate that bottom-up, deep participatory organising of members can work, and work well, for unions. Not only that, they show that even without structural power that forces employers to concede demands (e.g. because workers have a strong position in the labour market and can't easily be replaced), these precarious union members can still win. The independent unions have succeeded in building organisational capacity in radically different ways to the mainstream unions. First, indie unions have utilised strong associational power in a strategic way by involving their members in devising strategies, but also widening the scope by organising beyond the workplace – drawing in allies as supporters and activists, while also targeting the employer's customers to create the possibility of reputational damage. The lesson is that winning power is possible with strategic thinking and what Jane McAlevey (2016) would refer to as 'super-majority' participation of members in taking industrial and other action. It's also the case that small organisations, unencumbered by the structures of bureaucracy that bedevil much larger enterprises, are able to act in a much more nimble and unconstrained manner.

The form of organising adopted by these newly formed independent unions does raise the question of whether or not trade unionism in the twenty-first century requires a *fundamental* rethinking about its structure, form, internal culture and strategic direction. The structure of unionism in the UK still largely reflects that established in the 1880s, and while it has, at times, served its members well, many unions in their current form are not delivering the type and scale of wins (with a few notable exceptions, e.g. GMB's equal pay strike in Scotland in 2019 and the RMT's numerous strikes on the railways) that are needed to give hope and confidence to workers whose pay, terms and conditions are, in general, falling rather than rising. Neither have unions shown the capacity – as old industries decline or disappear – to intervene effectively in new industries where even skilled jobs are increasingly designed as contingent labour. Without a belief in the possibility of transformative change, why would members join and participate in a union, and without a positive and realistic vision from leaders, how can there be a union renaissance?

RETHINKING TRADE UNIONISM FOR THE FUTURE

It is nearly 40 years since the UK union movement acknowledged that it needed to figure out a way to regain the power it once had in order to be able to effect positive change for workers. Yet despite 'new unionism' and the 'turn to organising', less than a quarter of all workers in 2020 belong to a trade union, and only 26 per cent are covered by collective bargaining agreements. What are the reasons why the actions so far have not resulted in a revitalisation of the union movement, and why has it proven so difficult to increase union organising, membership and density? Before exploring these questions, it's important to acknowledge that without the considerable effort put in by committed union leaders and organisers, trade unions would be in a much more perilous state than they currently are. I have had the pleasure to meet many trade union leaders, activists, staff and members over my time as a researcher and activist, and have witnessed the considerable effort and commitment that have gone into attempts to rebuild the union movement. Not every trade union officer, organiser, activist or leader is a working-class hero, but many are, and it is not through lack of effort or commitment on the part of many that union renewal has floundered. My reflections on why organising has proven so challenging is based on these encounters and my research, but also on input from my academic colleagues whose own research and thinking has provoked much discussion and debate on this topic.

In its current state, the UK labour movement can do little to alter the macro-economic factors that have contributed to its decline. It has been argued that union membership and strength are related to the business cycle – when the economy is prospering and there is low unemployment and wages are increasing, workers are less concerned about the need for protection, but when there is accelerating inflationary pressure, workers are more inclined to look for unions to bargain on their behalf (Bain and Price 1987; Mason and Bain 1993). Similarly, the potential for union growth can be constrained by socioeconomic, political and legal factors, as well as employer policies. While the changing nature of the economy and the structure of the labour market are largely beyond the control of unions at this current time and the political climate is not favourable, this does not mean that unions do not have agency. Roger Undy and colleagues (1981), writing early on in the debates about the way forward for unions, argued that one of the primary conditions for union rebuilding was a national union leadership oriented and committed to growth as a priority.

Leadership: Form, Type and Diversity

Clearly, leadership from the top is important in creating a culture that allows organisational change to take place. This requires vision, the building of strategic capacity and the development of what Marshall Ganz refers to as a 'story of us'. The 'story of us' is the creation of a *shared* organisational narrative that taps into the 'values that equip us with the courage to make choices under conditions of uncertainty', that is, to be able to exercise our own agency (Ganz 2011). The ability to communicate a union's values effectively is an important first step in motivating people to join and become active. If a union is 'marketed' as a service, then that is what members will believe it to be.

The narrative or message that is communicated matters because it can set out an expectation of what it means to be a member of a union. I am frequently struck by the way in which union members tend to refer to 'the union' as if it's an external body, rather than referring to it as 'our union'. It's common to hear members say, 'The union ought to …' or 'What's the union doing about this?' or even 'What do we pay our union dues for?' This suggests people perceive the union to be an organisation or body separate from themselves, where there's an expectation that things should be done *for* them. Members who think in terms of 'our union' are more likely to see the union as belonging to them and feel that they need to participate and to shape the direction of the organisation. Therefore, a leadership wanting to build strategic capacity will need to create a 'story of us' that encourages high participation, provides vision and hope, and helps solidify a sense of collective identity – it is, as Marshall Ganz says, 'a critical function of leadership'. Too often, though, this has been missing from union organising narratives: a cursory look at union websites shows that the key message is still about providing services: 'what we can do to help you'. This is why organising is often perceived to be someone else's job – not the role of everyone in the union. In many unions, organising departments have been an 'add-on' to the main business of the union – therefore, organising hasn't been seen as *the* main business of the union.

So transformational leadership from the top is important in driving change and creating the capacity and willingness to act, but there also needs to be a focus on the type and form of leadership throughout the organisation, among staff and lay representatives. Great leaders don't create followers, they are able to develop more leaders – and leaders need to be representative of the people they are organising, but in unions this often isn't the case. Despite the fact that union membership is higher among women than it is for men,[7] this is not reflected in leadership positions (TUC 2018).

The oligarchic tendencies in unions tend to generate particular routes to leadership that consolidate power in the hands of like-minded people – often white men. Among the lay leadership of unions, particularly those with positions that attract facility time,[8] there is a reluctance to give up these roles, and they will use their positions and the union's resources to stave off challenges to their power (Kelly and Heery 1994). In 2018, there was a call from a female union president to rectify the gender imbalance in trade union leadership positions. Lynn Henderson, president of the Scottish TUC, launched 'Step Aside, Brother', which was a call for men to think about the diversity of union structures and to consider vacating at least some of their multiple leadership positions and leaving space for women to come through. The call did, as Henderson (2018) reported, 'hit a few raw nerves':

> because most of our good committed comrades think they either have no power or responsibility to make the change. 'Step Aside Brother' seeks a conscious and deeply political critique and offers a choice to men occupying multiple union positions to act for the collective good.

As Gill Kirton and Geraldine Healy (2012, p. 343) have noted, 'the structural progress of women in leadership positions is 'mediated by an enduring gendered oligarchy and an associated struggle to access power resources'. This leads to self-replicating leadership that doesn't reflect, or help to increase, the diversity of membership, and this matters if unions want to build inclusive organisations. In their book *Gendering and Diversifying Trade Union Leadership*, Sue Ledwith and Lise Lotte Hansen (2013) write about how the lack of diversity in leadership positions within unions works against transformational change because it limits the capacity for strategic thinking.

The power relations in unions are not only gendered, though, they are also racialised, and this feeds into the particular social processes and cultural practices that influence who is encouraged or elected into leadership positions. Without the ability to draw on the lived experiences of a diverse group of leaders, the tendency is for committees or leaders to adopt familiar repertoires of action even when these are no longer effective. There are, consequently, fewer opportunities for organisational learning. Richard Hyman informs us that the inherited identity of unions thus shapes the direction of union renewal because they rarely overturn their past character and purpose: 'Within trade unions, particularly those long established, the widespread respect for precedent and protocol means that the traditions of all the dead generations frequently inhibit learning' (2007, p. 202).

Diversity of leadership is therefore not simply about 'looking good' or satisfying targets, it is about harnessing the latent talent within the membership. It is about understanding that drawing on diversity of opinion leads to greater creativity and innovation. Too often in organising practice, knowledge about strategy, tactics and power is drawn from too narrow a pool of (similar) leaders, leading to replication of ineffective strategies and tactics. One of the great strengths of the independent unions is that their leaders are from many diverse cultures and backgrounds. It's the very different lived experience of their membership, from which their leadership is drawn, and the lack of adherence to particular forms of action that have taken employers by surprise. These unions, as new organisations, are less constrained by 'traditional' industrial action, and are able to draw on the diverse culture of their membership to innovate. As political theorist of community organising Saul Alinsky said in his book *Rules for Radicals* (1972), whenever possible, go outside the expertise of your adversary by finding ways to increase insecurity, anxiety and uncertainty, because power is not only *what* you have, but what the enemy *thinks* you have, and if you can surprise them by taking unexpected actions, then you start to change the power dynamic. But this not only requires a diverse and strategic leadership, it also requires a learning and reflective culture within an organisation.

Organisational Learning: The Lack of Political Education

When unions dedicate time and resources to developing a culture of education and implementing organisational learning, they are more able to adapt to change. They also have greater ability to react quickly and, importantly, strategically. To avoid repeatedly adopting forms of action that no longer work, unions that are learning organisations are able to grow their capacity as a result of past failures and can figure out how to adapt their structures and procedures to apply new knowledge about strategies and tactics to move forward. Learning environments where staff and members are both teachers *and* students and where there is a continual exchange of information from the bottom to the top, and vice versa, provide a process that allows unions to be continually reviewing how and where power has shifted, and how

different types of power might be harnessed to outmanoeuvre their opponents. Yet one thing that is noticeably absent from those unions that have
adopted the 'turn to organising' is education and training as an embedded
element of union strategy. While there have been training programmes for
staff organisers (and in some cases, lay reps as well), there seem to have
been few attempts to use education and training as a means to build capacity
among members. It is notable that in the early days of the TUC's Organising
Academy, there was time allocated in the training programme to debate and
discuss the strategic issues facing the trade union movement, but that over
time this element was reduced, and organisers were asked to reflect on this
in their personal training logs instead:

> Largely as a result of this, there has been a notable shift toward reflect-
> ing on and assessing organizing practice, rather than the more conceptual
> and strategic discussions that happened in previous years ... it is very
> notable that there has been a shift to more skill-based training rather than
> discussion of the strategic or theoretical issues relating to organizing.
>
> (Simms et al. 2013, pp. 48–49)

There has been huge and long-standing debate in the trade union
movement about union-provided education and training. Union educators
have been divided on the acceptance of government funding for the training
of shop stewards, with opponents arguing that it restricts the type of material
that can be taught in classes, watering down courses to more technical and
skills-based training rather than a form of working-class political studies
that educates workers on critical strategic thinking and leadership development (Fisher 2017). Once again, we can return to the Donovan Report
(1968) to understand the push toward skills-based training, and away from
the more political content of trade union courses. In the report's Section 709
on training, it stated:

> to prepare union officers at all levels for the reconstruction of industrial
> relations will make heavy demands on the available resources, despite a
> considerable expansion in facilities since the war, in which the TUC has
> played a notable part.
>
> (Donovan Report 1968, p. 190)

The report continues that trade unions should concentrate on developing courses for officers and shop stewards:

> The need for shop stewards training is immense. There are about 175,000 shop stewards, of whom more than two-thirds have received no training of any kind. ...Additional resources undoubtedly required. They should be used to develop competent teachers and adequate syllabuses with a view to using training of shop stewards as part of a planned move to more orderly industrial relations based on comprehensive and formal factory or company agreements. This is where shop stewards training will be able to make its biggest contribution.
>
> (Donovan Report 1968, pp. 190–191)

We can see in this the germ of the move toward the professionalisation of full-time officers, where their role has increasingly been to 'manage' workplace activism. The de-politicisation of trade union education has provided union representatives with skills in bargaining and representation of members, but it hasn't assisted with the development of critical thinking around social, political and economic issues – the very areas where unions need to develop capacity in getting workers to figure out collectively how to build power to resolve their own issues and to act accordingly.

Access to effective union training and development in organising techniques is, at this time, limited, and it will remain so if unions remain reliant on government funding that restricts the material that can be taught to stewards. In the past, many trade unions provided political education that equipped union stewards to become workplace leaders who were able to articulate injustice and exploitation beyond that of the bread-and-butter issues in the workplace. Political education afforded union reps with the capacity to initiate a wider examination of class politics and the power dynamics in unions, society and the employment relationship. It also offered space for discussion of ideas and tactics that would build sufficient power to make employers listen to the demands of workers.

A lot of the training around organising frequently ignores peer-to-peer organising teaching, the political context of power relations, and the role of the vested interests that so often undermine our efforts – in truth, what many trade unions are providing is not education, but skills-based training that delivers a toolbox of tactics to be deployed in the same way in every circumstance. What is needed, however, is a form of political education, open to members as well as union reps, that helps to build the strategic capability and capacity of grassroots activism to create power resources and effect change. To quote a well-known phrase from Sun Tzu's *Art of War* (1910), strategy without tactics is the slowest route to victory, but tactics without strategy is the noise before defeat.

If unions are to be able to effectively challenge the growing disparity of power that drives inequality and exploitation of workers, they need to show that through organising collectively, workers can win. But without political education that develops critical thinking and an ability to assess the successes (and failures) of the past and the present, workers are left without a vision of a credible path to winning, and consequently they are left without hope, and are thus most likely to remain passive or detached from the labour movement. As long-time African-American civil rights organiser Ella Baker once said: 'Give light and the people will find a way.'

Another neglected element of trade union education which is important in terms of organising is a focus on its role in encouraging democratic participation in union branches and the wider structure of the organisation. As experienced labour educator and ex-director of research and education at the TGWU John Fisher has observed:

> Breathing life into this [democratic participation], however, has not often shown itself to be the first priority of union leadership. One of the functions of trade union education is to build the necessary knowledge and confidence amongst the membership to encourage them to take part in committees and other activities of the organization, and to make democracy a reality, rather than a mere form.
>
> (2017, p. 36)

While there are still a few specific trade union political education programmes (run by Unite, the CWU, GMB and RMT), these are limited to very small number of members – often just 10–12 per year. If there is to be transformative change in unions, then teaching members to organise has to be at the centre of any rebuilding strategy, and that requires members having the collective ability to analyse the power and acknowledge the forces at work within the situation they wish to change. Without developing this capacity within the membership, unions will not be able to build the capacity required to grow and assemble the power that is necessary for workers to win.

Transformative wins are not something that can be delivered by staff, they can only be won by the members themselves. Leadership, vision, diversity and participatory democracy are all essential elements in creating a vibrant union that has the confidence to be led by its members. Unions that act *on behalf* of the membership rather than *through* the membership will always limit their ability to deliver one of the most important power resources available to workers: the capacity to withdraw their labour when challenging employers and the state. Further, without creative input from the lifetime of accumulated knowledge and understanding of their members, and without focusing on the issues that concern them most, the scope of union activity may constrain itself to addressing sectional industrial interests, to the detriment of wider social issues. Should there be, therefore, an alternative vision of trade unionism that at its heart is about really building the capacity of workers to increase collective control over the way that work (but not just work) is organised in society?

What Should Unions Be Organising For?

This is a question as old as trade unions themselves. The primary purpose of trade unions is job regulation through collective bargaining to improve the working conditions of its members, but it has been much more than this at different times and in different societies. Alan Flanders, (1972, p. 30) describes unions as a mixture of (social) movement and organisation, where 'the relationship between the two is the key to understanding the dynamics of their growth'. In terms of movement, this is a group with common purpose organising to have their voices heard, and acting collectively to effect change. In terms of organisation, this is a body that is structured in a way to order the duties and responsibilities of people in order to be able to realise the ideals of the movement. Flanders maintains that trade unions need to be dynamic membership organisations if their power is to be maintained beyond a fleeting existence – to flourish, he says, 'they must renew their vigour by keeping the spirit of movement alive in their ranks'. If they don't they are likely to become stale and ineffective:

A trade union that had none of the characteristics of movement, which was thrown back entirely on the bonds of organization, would be in a sorry state. To sum up, trade unions need organisation for their power and movement for their vitality, but they need both power and vitality to advance their social purpose.

(Flanders 1972, p. 31)

This vision of trade unionism with a social purpose (rather than just workplace regulation and advancing the sectional 'self-interest' of a minority of workers) has been either lost or undervalued for some time. Yet in the current social, economic and political climate, it seems that there are at least possibilities for union renaissance if a vision of unionism includes a much wider social purpose that can excite and energise well beyond its current ranks. As one example, climate change has become an issue of great concern for the majority of people in the UK. A representative survey conducted in 2019 showed that around two-thirds of people agreed the climate emergency was the biggest issue facing the world at this time (Carrington 2019). A growing broad-based movement of campaigners has been calling for a 'green new deal' – a plan to virtually eliminate greenhouse gas emissions by transforming the economy, creating a fair or 'just transition' to secure the future and livelihoods of workers and their communities in the move to a low-carbon economy.

The movement for climate change action, though, has been led primarily by young people, in particular schoolchildren – not the union movement. The UK Student Climate Network, set up by volunteers in late 2018, has co-ordinated monthly Friday strikes to demand systemic change in order to halt the climate crisis. By September 2019, it estimated that around 850 demonstrations had taken place, including when 350,000 students and adults went on strike in September 2019 demanding urgent action on the climate crisis. At the TUC's annual Congress in 2019, a motion on climate change and just transition stated: 'we must keep the pressure up. Greta Thunberg and the school students have led the way but educators and the trade union movement as a whole must now act to ensure that they don't fight alone'. Yet despite the congress motion and a TUC report (2019, p. 7) that stated 'workers and communities across the UK most affected by the move toward low-carbon industries must have a central voice in how this is implemented. The best and most obvious way to achieve this is by working with trade unions', there is little evidence of how the TUC or the wider movement plan to see this aspiration translated into practice.

A number of unions have put together guidance and courses on how union reps can bargain over carbon reduction in the workplace, for example by reviewing employer policies on environmental concerns and assessing the extent to which they can identify levers for change, but otherwise activity is limited in this area. A transformational union vision in this area would be one that connected young people concerned about climate change with the union movement. Union statistics show that only 4.4 per cent of union members are under 25. Having taught employment relations to university students for many years, I am no longer surprised to find that most young people are not even aware what trade unions are, or even that they still exist. A social movement for a green new deal, however, needs to include the labour movement because it is workers who have the knowledge to make just transition a reality. Workers in the energy-intensive sectors have the skills and expertise that are required to help jobs transition to lower-carbon models if they are given the support to do so.

There are very understandable and valid concerns from unions about the loss of their members' jobs and livelihoods where these are closely tied to a high-carbon economy, but the long-term interest of workers does not always coincide with the continuation of their existing jobs – something that has meant that unions have, at times, defended the continuation of dangerous and environmentally unfriendly jobs. Rather than giving support to industries that are literally choking the planet, more needs to be done to create the pressure necessary to create new green jobs in these sectors as the carbon industry jobs simply won't be around in the long term. Unions should be acting with workers in these industries and organising for a just transition now, otherwise the main role of unions in these circumstances will be to assist with managing decline within these industries. Such an approach will eventually result in a devastating loss of jobs in these communities. The coal industry is one such industry that has never recovered – from almost a million jobs in the UK at its height, it now has under 1,000.[9] The National Union of Mineworkers, which we saw in earlier chapters was once a powerful force, had a membership of 170,000 at the beginning of the 1980s (and 950,000 in the 1920s), but with the devastation of the industry, it now has fewer than 100 working members. The transformation in the coalfields was brutal – some would say vengeful – with absolutely no commitment from successive governments to train the pre-existing workforce to transition into the new high-value jobs that could have been attracted into those areas.

There is much that unions could do to avoid such catastrophes. They could be the catalysts for workers to analyse the options in threatened industries to develop just transition plans for a low-carbon future that minimises the burden on the workforce. Unions need to be working with their members (and the affected communities) *now* to anticipate the effects of the reduction in carbon-producing jobs and build the power to demand forward-thinking strategies that include plans that incorporate new skills training and future livelihoods for the existing workforce.

A model for such an approach was developed by trade unionists at Lucas Aerospace in the mid-1970s. As an alternative to arms production and mass redundancies, the workers put together an alternative corporate plan for 'socially useful products and new forms of employee development' (Wainwright and Elliot 1982). The incredibly detailed plan put forward 150 product ideas that could be produced using the existing skills of the work-force. It is worth noting the company's statement on receipt of the workers' plan:

> The authors of the report suggest that there would be a contraction in the aerospace components industry as a result of successive Defence cuts, a trend which they regard as desirable. On this premise, they believe that the Company should be protecting the jobs of its employees by diversi-fying into socially acceptable/useful products such as those indicated in the report.
>
> (Wainwright and Elliot 1982, p. 114)

This was an eminently sensible approach from the union stewards and their members – it was also a socially and morally just way forward. Yet it was rejected by the company even though it clearly indicated that aerospace work was in decline. The workers, however, found that they did not have the power or leverage to force the company to accept the plan:

> While individual Trade Unions and the Labour Government supported the Combine's Plan in principle, there was neither the structures in place, nor the political will, to put pressure on Lucas Aerospace management to

negotiate with the Combine to implement the Plan. An opportunity was lost to make a company receiving public money accountable to the community in which it served.

(Salisbury 2020)

The company succeeded in its tactics of dividing the 11,000 workers across its 17 sites; unfortunately, in this they were ably assisted by some union officials. It is said that management had figured out the strength of the shop stewards' combine and had decided to crush it using 'soft and hard measures' (Wainwright and Elliot 1982). Although ultimately unsuccessful, the Lucas Plan nevertheless offers a model for unions, climate change campaigners and local communities to consider today.[10] It also raises valid questions about the future of the world of work, which has come into much sharper focus in 2020.

This book was written in the period of 'lockdown' during the Covid-19 pandemic. The resulting crisis has caused many people to radically re-evaluate the world of work as workers are laid off in many industries, and the structures of employment have fundamentally changed since many workers have been confined to working from home. The outcome from this is still too early to determine, but the UK's Office for National Statistics has predicted that unemployment could rise by 10 per cent. While this forecast is bleak, it provides an opportunity for unions to rethink how their structures and organisations might be reconfigured to meet the challenges ahead. It is difficult to build traditional workplace power when the economy is in crisis and jobs are being lost in huge numbers, so it's time to think about a renewed role for unions to reconnect with the communities in which their members live and to form coalitions with social justice partners to be able to draw on their combined power resources:

What is now required is a new social contract with a moral purpose. It would be based around strengthening public services and other human necessities sometimes known as the foundational economy, while creating green jobs aimed at cutting carbon emissions. Jobs would be socially productive and environmentally sustainable – not 'bullshit jobs' such as public relations or corporate law or telemarketing.

(Dobbins 2020)

Unions with a Social Purpose: In the Community as Well as in the Workplace

It is not only on environmental matters that trade unions could, and should, be leading the way. Unions have often been at their strongest and had greatest power when they have been embedded in communities. The history of trade union formation in the UK is inextricably linked to the places and spaces in which people lived and worked. In the early days of the formation of jour-neymen's associations in the late eighteenth century, and even, in some places, well into the second half of the twentieth century, most workers lived in the vicinity of their work. This meant that communities and workers were closely bound together in their localities in a way that is much less evident today. Trade union historian Malcolm Chase (2000, p. 4), has observed that until the nineteenth century, trade unions occupied a more central place in the associational life of their members, where they would engage in self-help initiatives outside the workplace and in the local communities in which they were situated. He explains:

> Unions were far from simply being an expression of new solidarities engendered by industrialisation. Rather, they reflected and perhaps inten-sified, behaviours that were common place in the communities beyond them .... The communities in which they [trade unionists] lived and worked had their own networks, structures and therefore capacities to organise. ... Trade union consciousness and community consciousness were virtually coterminous in the handicraft trades and there is no reason to suppose that this was not the case across a wide range of industries.
> (Chase 2000, p. 47)

However, these strong links between trade union consciousness and com-munity consciousness have been severely weakened, and in many places no longer exist. As unions developed structural power and became incorporated into industrial relations machinery, the links between unions and commu-nity became less conscious, and even more so when structural changes in the economy saw the demise of larger workplaces and the accompanying community identities – pit villages, steel towns, 'potteries', manufacturing etc. The Thatcher governments' onslaught succeeded in undermining trade union power, and trade union membership halved (Holgate 2015).

As we have seen from earlier chapters, during this period unions became more inward-looking and more focused on servicing their surviving membership, and thus less visible in the wider community (Kelly and Heery 1994). But there are new hopes and possibilities for trade union expansion – but only if there is a willingness to take these on board. The rapid development of mutual aid groups that formed across the UK when the government ordered people to stay at home to stop the spread of Covid-19 was inspiring. Tens of thousands of voluntary community groups were formed to support vulnerable and shielding neighbours.[11] This has been a large-scale mobilisation of the very best in people that has contributed to rebuilding community in a way not seen for decades. It shows that the 'individualism' that we were told was a dominant feature of modern society was not as embedded as we had been led to believe.

In times of crisis, the human instinct is to reach out to those around us and to work together. The UK government's Lifestyle Survey into the impacts of the coronavirus pandemic on people, households and communities has shown that '73% of UK residents were confident that they could turn to others in their community for help during the pandemic, and 81% felt that people were doing more to help others than before the outbreak' (Anderson 2020). Research is considering the potential of the mutual aid groups to foster ongoing community organising and the breaking down of societal barriers, particularly those relating to class and other forms of inequality such as race, gender and disability:

> By facilitating meaningful contact between advantaged and less advantaged groups, CMAGs [Covid Mutual Aid Groups] have the potential to lead to an increase in intergroup solidarity, particularly on class lines, effectively depleted by neoliberal policies over the past 40 years. If participation in these groups is viewed through the lens of activism, it may lead to greater empowerment, self-esteem, politicisation, as well as sustained commitment, for example. Initial humanitarian motivations to become involved (i.e. to help vulnerable neighbours) could become politicised as new understandings of injustice and inequality are developed, which might in turn motivate solidaristic behaviours and attitudes.
>
> (O'Dwyer 2020)

Of course, it is not certain that new forms of solidarity and power resources will develop through these community-organised mutual aid groups, but again there is considerable scope for trade unions to play a role in making that outcome more likely. Similarly, websites and social media sites like Facebook have discussion forums where users share advice and information on work and employment, creating an online community space where people can share advice and get guidance.

Steve Williams, Brian Abbott and Ed Heery have been studying the role of civil society organisations (CSOs) and the extent to which these are engaging with the world of paid work and intervening in employment relations as 'other actors' beyond the traditional actors of unions, managers and the state. These authors explain that 'CSOs not only attempt to shape the behaviour of employers through the forging of direct, collaborative relationships, but also try to do so indirectly, with interactions of various kinds with the state being integral' (Williams et al. 2017, p. 103). CSOs are able to influence corporate policy and practice through lobbying and campaigning activities. While these organisations don't have the same levers of collective or associational power as unions, they can focus on creating change through the use of civil governance and regulation – using institutional power by pursuing test cases in employment law or 'enforcement' of corporate social responsibility – by the lever of moral power.

While there have been a number of studies about how CSOs and unions might collaborate effectively to broaden the base of trade union activity and to increase the power of workers more generally, there is little evidence of much constructive work in this area. I have written elsewhere that the terrain on which CSOs and trade unions are operating is often contested, and that both CSOs and trade unions have shown a lack of understanding and, on some occasions, a lack of concern for each other's way of working, meaning they do not engage with each other or they work in opposition (Holgate 2009; Holgate and Wills 2007). Yet others have found successful collaborations showing that where there is a will there is often a way of joint working that can benefit each party and improve the working lives of a much broader constituency, as well as the wider community (Tattersall 2010). As Heery and his colleagues note, many CSOs are operating as institutions of worker representation, or certainly in the terrain or employment relations, 'but their form of representation, in this as so many other things, departs from that developed classically by trade unions' (Heery et al. 2012,

p. 24). Despite this, it should not be beyond trade unions to build sustaina-ble alliances with social movements, lobbying groups and charities (and vice versa) if there is a will to do so.

Too often in the period of managerial unionism that dominates the labour movement today, unions have recruited on the basis of individual-ism – to be there for you if you, as an individual, have a problem at work. However, people are not mobilised solely on the basis of a calculation of self-interest – whether that is through the benefits of collective bargaining or individualised services. Other reasons advanced for people joining unions are ideological, where there's a political identification with the values of col-lectivism – where there is class-consciousness and an commitment to the transformation of inequality or social order (Moore 2010). Stephen Deery and Helen Cieri (1991, p. 62), for example, suggest that 'the explanation for union membership may lie in the general value system of the individual, the antecedents of which can be traced to societal and family variables'. So ori-entation toward union membership doesn't even need to arise from political consciousness; if unions are able to articulate the value systems that drive people to volunteer (as in the mutual aid groups), then there are opportuni-ties not only to recruit, but to rebuild the activist base of trade unions.

Early on in debates around the 'turn to organising' there were voices calling for a return to a social movement approach to trade unionism based on member involvement and activism (Clawson 2003; Johnston 1995; Turner and Hurd 2001). It was argued that unions should embrace social movement unionism to build a broad base of power resources necessary to transform and revitalise the union movement to combat economic and social inequality (Turner and Hurd 2001, p. 21).

One union that has purposefully attempted to look outward in this way into communities is Unite, the UK's largest union. In 2011, the union intro-duced 'Unite Community', a new membership scheme 'to ensure those pushed to the margins of society can benefit from collective power'. Around 50 community branches have been formed, mainly, but not exclusively, of retired trade unionists who volunteer their time to organise campaigns in their geographical localities. The activities the 50,000 recruited members have been organising around mainly relate to welfare cuts – the attacks on disability benefits, and benefit sanctions (for being late for welfare appoint-ments or being ill). Community members have set up peer support groups to help claimants facing sanctions, and have been successful in challenging these at appeals. Other actions have been around the sell-off of social housing, ethical procurement and living wage campaigns, domestic violence, organising and supporting food banks for people experiencing poverty crises, and removal of disabled passes on public transport. Unite Community members have won thousands of pounds for people who were not claiming benefits to which they were entitled, and volunteers have also won bedroom and council tax appeals, helping people stay in their own homes (Holgate 2018). In essence, the Unite Community section of Unite has been operating in similar ways to the early pre-union friendly societies of the early 1800s and the mutual aid groups formed 200 years later in 2020 in the coronavirus pandemic. It is, however, despite very promising outcomes, still too small and under-resourced an initiative to be truly transformative, but it does illustrate the potential for unions to expand their remit and to draw in people from diverse backgrounds and constituencies.

The #MeToo and #BlackLivesMatter movements also demonstrate how issues relating to systemic sex and race discrimination are of serious concern to so many people. While it was specific incidents such as the exposure of sexual abuse cases in 2017 and the murder of George Floyd in 2020 that sparked a world-wide response to these events, the outpouring of anger in protests on the streets also reflected the endemic nature of sexism and racism in society – and the workplace. It's true that many unions have admirable statements on equality issues, and that day-in and day-out union representatives deal with inequality in the workplace, but this is, most often, on an individual case-by-case basis. Yet this is not enough. Unions should have harnessed the energy and commitment expressed by tens of thousands of their members – outside their union framework – to protest against racism and sexual harassment and directed it toward rebalancing power in the workplace, winning not just 'paper policies' from employers, but cultural changes in the workplace.

May 2020 was the 50th anniversary of the UK's Equal Pay Act, which established the principle of equal pay for equal work, yet too often women are still paid less than men even when doing the same job. The gender pay gap is, in 2020, 17 per cent, and it is estimated by the Fawcett Society that at current rates of narrowing, it will take another 60 years to achieve equal pay between men and women. For many years, trade unionists believed that pursuing equal pay for work of equal value cases was 'too difficult' because of the time and expertise involved in undertaking the job comparison process. It was not until 'no win–no fee' lawyers started to win many millions of pounds for low-paid women workers that unions, belatedly, began to develop legal strategies to address gender pay discrimination at work.

One excellent collective effort by members of the GMB union was the Glasgow equal pay strike in 2019. Following a ballot of home care, school cleaning and catering staff across Glasgow, workers overwhelmingly (98 per cent) voted for and took industrial action which led to the settlement of 14,000 equal pay claims. There is, however, a lesson here. Trade unions should not assume they have the 'franchise' on representing workers' interests, and if they fail to have a strategic vision to address blatant inequality, they may find 'new actors' moving onto 'their turf'. Initially, this campaign was led from outside the union movement, and it was only following criticism from members that the union became more proactive. As the regional officer in Glasgow said:

> our union was being attacked by our own members in North Lanarkshire over equal pay, and we were quite rightly being called out in the national media for this too … we let ourselves down because we stopped acting as a proper trade union should, by campaigning – in the workplace, in the media and on the streets.
>
> (Smith 2019)

Similarly, the ethnic pay gap[12] not only highlights in-job discrimination, but also that it is occupational and industrial segregation that is the main cause of lower pay among minorities. Black workers are disproportionately located in lower-paid jobs – cleaning, care, catering, security, public transport and private hire – the very occupations that are the least unionised and where there is some of the greatest exploitation and sexual and racial harassment. Black ethnic groups are currently experiencing mortality rates from Covid-19 that are twice those of white people. This is unlikely to be, as some have suggested, due to genetic predisposition, but far more likely to be a consequence of existing social and economic disparities. Indeed, the occupations with the highest death rates are security guards, taxi drivers, bus and coach drivers, chefs and retail workers[13] – all jobs undertaken by a disproportionately high percentage of ethnic minorities. It is in many of these jobs that trade unions have often had a poor record of organising.

Yet it is in these so-called 'hard to organise' workplaces that many millions of pounds have been won for the low-paid workers through leverage-based 'living wage' campaigns, where often faith and community groups – and 'moonlighting' trade unionists[14] – have created and used new forms of moral power to win pay increases that the trade union movement had not attempted to win (Bunyan 2016; Heery et al. 2017; Holgate 2009). It is, of course, easy to criticise these 'external' campaigns by non-union organisations as insufficient (e.g. it's argued that organisations external to the workplace have no mechanisms following the 'wins' to ensure enforcement or to prevent reductions in other terms and conditions to compensate for the increase), but that criticism is only valid if unions have a proven better strategy. In the absence of trade union capacity to win for low-paid workers, we can expect more and more of the traditional 'territory' of trade unions to be whittled away by charities, pressure groups and no win–no fee lawyers (Deakin et al. 2015).

One strategic approach from unions to combine all these issues is to think in terms of what Jane McAlevey (2016) refers to as 'whole worker organising'. By this, she means that organising campaigns need to be relational, transformational and community-based (in the broadest sense), but also that organising needs to be 'deep'. The wider notion of deep organising (rather than shallow mobilising)[15] requires 'union activists and staff to see the "whole worker" with their complex, overlapping and sometimes contradictory interests, concerns and identities' (Holgate et al. 2018, p. 609). This means unions not separating out the issues that affect the lives of workers into those that 'belong' in the workplace and those that are in the 'community'. Instead, what is needed is a more intersectional approach to organising if workers are to feel confident that their issues won't be marginalised, or not even understood. It is necessary to raise the expectations of workers – in effect, to be more aspirational, and able to create a sense of hope and a belief in the possibilities of change through collective action. Jane McAlevey explains that, in attempting to raise expectations, a deep organising approach is more likely to ask workers 'Which key things would you like to change about your work?' rather than 'Do you think you should have a pay rise?' In the 'whole-worker' organising model, unions therefore need to be organisations that aspire to improve the lived experience of the working class *as a whole*, not just those privileged to be in organised workplaces. This approach provides the potential to broaden the base of support and increase the power and leverage available to workers by drawing on the organic links between workplaces and communities.

IS UNION RENAISSANCE POSSIBLE?

The answer is yes, but only if unions are prepared for transformative change, and as Marshall Ganz (2008, p. 530) has said: 'a deep desire for change must be coupled with the capacity to make change'. Yet many unions are constrained structurally and organisationally by their past – and the present – which creates obstacles to the type of organisational learning and power analysis necessary for the innovation, organisational change and transformation that are necessary if we are to see a union renaissance. Meeting the challenges posed by loss of membership and power requires much more than adopting a toolbox of organising tactics or creating organising departments that are an adjunct to 'traditional' trade union practice. What is required is rethinking of the current structures of power in society – not just in the industrial arena – to consider what sort of tactics are needed to organise, and then mobilise, around these in the most effective way. But it also requires a deep internal focus on how to make this happen with a leadership that can understand and drive forward a union's strategic capacity for transformative change.

Without an ability to lead organisational change throughout the union, unions will remain wedded to their traditions and routines, which are no longer effective, as well as the sectional interests that work against a unified approach. Oligarchic tendencies work against innovation as sections of unions operate in silos in order to maintain internal power structures. Only a strong, thoughtful leadership that is prepared to reconceptualise what trade unions are actually organising for can overcome these restrictions, and then re-orientate unions so their purpose is a true and inclusive social movement operating for the benefit of the working class as a whole. Diversity, it all its forms, is the essence of an inclusive organisation, and is essential in creating innovation and change. If groups of people feel marginalised because their issues are not taken up, or if people are made to feel the organisation doesn't belong to them, people are less likely to join or to be active. The base of power available to unions is therefore automatically reduced.

Traditionally, unions have tied themselves to traditional class politics with industrial action in the form of strikes as the ultimate threat to force employers into agreement. This is still one of the most effective weapons in the armoury of unions, but the declining power of the union movement has, at this particular time, removed this as a credible threat for many unions, weakening their ability to act to defend their members' jobs and terms and conditions. Unions need not resign themselves to managing decline; there are strategic choices available to rebuild capacity and power if there is a willingness to do so. But this involves creating a vision (a 'story of us') and framing messages that connect with members and potential members. It needs a form of participatory democracy in unions that has widespread involvement of members. There needs to be a rethinking of union structures that too often constrain rather than facilitate change and nimble responses to changing circumstances. There is a need to understand the role that 'new actors' can play in the union movement, instead of seeing them as separate or as a threat. Rather than thinking of new actors as just additional players in shaping employment relations, we need to think much more broadly about the role these new actors are playing, and could play, in linking communities with workplaces, and vice versa. There needs to be a new imagination and much more strategic thinking to build the forms of external solidarities that can increase the power resources of unions.

The focus of this book has been on power, because without it the working class's ability to fight against injustice and exploitation and for a better world will not be realised. Power, though, is not usually conceded voluntarily to workers; it generally has to be captured through struggle. As Frederick Douglass, ex-slave, abolitionist, social reformer and writer, once said:

> If there is no struggle, there is no progress. Those who profess to favor freedom, and yet depreciate agitation, are men who want crops without plowing up the ground. They want rain without thunder and lightning. They want the ocean without the awful roar of its many waters. This struggle may be a moral one; or it may be a physical one; or it may be both moral and physical; but it must be a struggle. Power concedes nothing without a demand. It never did and it never will.
>
> (Douglass 1999, p. 367)

For struggles to win, union demands need to connect and be deeply felt by members – people have to believe the issues are worth the fight, the sacrifice worth making, and that there is at least a reasonable likelihood of winning. Struggles are most likely to win when workers have formidable collective organisation and where they have a relationship of trust with their fellow workers – and this means high active participation of members in the day-to-day running of their union. Relying on others to undertake the struggle for you generally doesn't work, and it certainly doesn't work long-term. Taking power requires agency, and it is the realisation of the *capacity* to change things through the self-activity of members themselves that makes unions powerful, not merely the existence of collectivism itself.

There is therefore a stark choice for trade unionists today – to continue doing what the movement has done for the last 40 years and continue to see a decrease in power, leading to a further growth in inequality, an increase in precarity, a loss of hope within our communities and a consequent increase in the confidence of right-wing, authoritarian ideas, or to organise to change the current circumstances in which we find ourselves. The stakes are high. It's not just about whether there's an annual pay award that matches inflation, winning job security, career development and safe workplaces, eradicating discrimination from employment and pay practices or defending hard-won pension rights. Quite literally, the very future of the world depends on the ability of working-class communities to build sufficient power – in the next few years – to defeat the suicidal short-termism of the fossil fuel industry. The challenges for the labour movement are immense, but to borrow a phrase, we are the 99 per cent, and we could do worse than reflect on the prescient advice of Eric Hobsbawm that was highlighted in Chapter 1:

> if the labour and socialist movement is to recover its soul, its dynamism, and its historical initiative ... [we need] to recognise the novel situations in which we find ourselves, to analyse it realistically and concretely, to analyse the reasons, historical and otherwise, for the failures as well as the successes of the labour movement, and to formulate not only what we would want to do, but what can be done.
>
> (1978, p. 286)

Another world really is possible, one where equality and social justice is the norm, but we have no time to waste. The forward march of labour was halted – indeed, it went into reverse for decades – but the lesson we have learned from the original 'gig economy' workers of the 1880s is that organising works. We are today, once again, seeing that it's the most precarious of workers demonstrating that, despite their circumstances, they can find and use a range of power resources to win. To transform the world, we need to inspire, to provide hope and to organise to build a movement that has the strategic capacity to realise the power we have as a collective force – and to do so for the many, not the few.

Notes

CHAPTER 1

1. This was a reference to the 'new unionism' of the 1880s, when the union movement grew at a faster rate than at any other time in its history. There was a surge in trade unionism among the unskilled and semi-skilled, and the development of more general unions (as opposed to craft unions). There was also a uniting of common interests around the campaign for an eight-hour day.

CHAPTER 2

1. These are iconic disputes in the UK labour movement. Grunwick was a strike over union recognition in 1974–75 by mainly Asian women. For an account of the dispute, see Anitha and Pearson (2018). Warrington was a particularly violent dispute in 1983, when print workers walked out on strike because of the use of non-union labour to undercut pay; see Dickinson (1984). Wapping was another violent dispute that occurred in 1986 in east London. Again, print workers were violently attacked by the police in a 54-week lock-out by the employer, News International; see Ewing and Napier (2009).
2. Under section 181 (2) of the Trade Union and Labour Relations (Consolidation) Act 1992, an employer is obliged to disclose information: (a) without which a union would be materially impeded in collective bargaining and (b) which it would be in accordance with good industrial relations practice to disclose. However, a precondition has to be satisfied. Section 181 (1) provides that the bargaining must be about matters in relation to workers in respect of which the union is recognised by the employer. However, these powers have seldom been used, and even less enforced.

CHAPTER 3

1. For an account of the Tolpuddle Martyrs, see www.tolpuddlemartyrs.org.uk [accessed 12 April 2021].
2. The 1871 Bank Holiday Act made paid bank holidays compulsory.

CHAPTER 4

1. The franchise was much wider in local elections than it was in general elections, such that working-class men and women were able to vote from 1888 onward.

2. *Daily Mail*, 3 November 1913, quoted in Kosmin (1978, p. 433).
3. In 1918, the Labour Party adopted the 'party objects', which included the celebrated 'clause four', which read: 'To secure for the producers by hand and brain, the full fruits of their industry, and the most equitable distribution thereof that may be possible, upon the common ownership of the means of production and the best obtainable system of popular administration and control of each industry or service'. This was deleted in 1995 under Prime Minister Tony Blair's leadership.
4. The 1968 Ford machinists' strike had an influence on the 1970 Equal Pay Act. The government's minister for labour, Barbara Castle, intervened in the dispute in an attempt to resolve it, and two years later put forward legislation designed to make pay inequality unlawful. Fifty years later, this still has not been achieved.
5. The liquidation of the shipyards did not take place overnight. It took months for different waves of workers to be issued with redundancy notices. Those made redundant and who continued working were paid from the 14 unions' fighting fund. Money came in from union movements across the world.
6. Although the 1979 figures here only refer to the first few months of that year (in the actual period of the Winter of Discontent), it is nevertheless useful to provide a comparison (despite very different times). In the whole of 2018 there were just 273,000 working days lost due to labour disputes, the sixth-lowest annual total since records began in 1891 (Office for National Statistics 2019).
7. In the 1970s, much of the UK's electricity supplies came from coal and coke. The three-day week meant the government decreed that commercial users of electricity were limited to three specified consecutive days of consumption each week.
8. For details of this strike, the trial and the connections between the employers and the Conservative government, see www.shrewsbury24campaign.org.uk [accessed 12 April 2021].

CHAPTER 5

1. There were worries by men about their jobs been done by women while they were away at war and the consequences of the devaluing of their labour when they returned.
2. This Act was repealed by the Labour government in 1946, but elements of it were re-legislated by the Conservative governments after 1979.
3. The main difference between the two approaches was that the former saw the law as the main instrument for reform, as opposed to better collective bargaining procedures set out in the Donovan Report.
4. Initially, there were 137 strikers out of a workforce of around 500. While a few more workers joined the dispute, the strike was not supported by the majority of the workforce, many of whom were fearful of losing their jobs.

5. For a detailed exposé of how the police embedded undercover officers within unions and left-wing groups and acted as *agents provocateurs*, see Chamberlin and Smith (2015).

6. This report was written by the MP Nicholas Ridley for the Conservative Research Department in 1977 and leaked to *The Economist* in May 1978 – the year before the Conservatives came to power. It was written for a discussion in the Nationalised Industry Policy Group. See Ridley (1977).

7. Note the reference here to the 1972 miners' strike and the blockade at the Saltley Coke Depot in Birmingham which led to victory for the union in that dispute.

8. 'As assistant MI5 director in charge of F2 branch, targeting trade unions, [Stella] Rimington supervised the most ambitious counter-subversion operation ever mounted in Britain. Under her guidance, MI5 infiltrated Arthur Scargill's inner circle, oversaw the country's largest-ever bugging and telephone-tapping effort in cooperation with GCHQ, coordinated the legal onslaught against the NUM and helped organise the strike-breaking effort' (Milne 2000).

9. The Act's Part 2 introduced secret pre-strike ballots. To ensure industrial action enjoyed immunity from actions in tort, a trade union could only start industrial action if the action had been approved by a simple majority in a secret ballot held not more than four weeks before.

10. IPSOS MORI polling recorded that in 1978, 82 per cent of the general public and 72 per cent of trade union members felt that unions had too much power. But, perhaps demonstrating a degree of cognitive dissonance, 78 per cent of the public in 1978 also felt that trade unions are essential to protect the interests of workers – almost the same percentage as in 2017 (77 per cent) See IPSOS MORI (2017) 'Attitudes to trade unions 1975–2014', available at: www.ipsos.com/ipsos-mori/en-uk/attitudes-trade-unions-1975-2014 [accessed 7 April 2021].

CHAPTER 6

1. Source: International Monetary Fund, World Economic Outlook Database, April 2019.

2. It was also the case that some trade union leaders took this view themselves and were keen to take back control of collective bargaining in a more centralised way through union staff.

3. Three-way negotiations and discussions between government, employer bodies and trade union bodies.

4. Pendulum arbitration is where the arbitrator takes the final offers from the two parties and makes a decision based upon them. In this case, the arbitrator does not try to reach a compromise or suggest an alternative, but chooses one of these offers as the settlement. The approach is designed to encourage settlement prior to arbitration.

5. The unions had assumed that the Labour Party would be returned to government in the next general election, as the Conservatives had difficulties managing the economy since 1979. Yet following the Falklands War, Margaret Thatcher's popularity increased and the Conservatives gained their biggest parliamentary majority of the post-war era, defeating Labour with a 47.4 per cent majority (just 27.6 per cent of the vote went to Labour).
6. One of the authors was the former head of research at the TUC and GMB and a management consultant, and the other the Industrial Editor of *The Times*.
7. This particular piece of research was from the largest sample of partnership agreements at that time in Britain, involving 126 agreements drawn from an estimated total of 248 agreements signed between 1990 and 2007.
8. It is notable that the wage premium associated with unionised workplaces is not evident when comparing unionised and non-unionised companies of a similar size and market share.
9. While there was often considerable inflation of union members prior to merger (to boost each side's bargaining power), and in some cases dual membership, nevertheless the figures after merger represented a more accurate figure of union membership.
10. New Labour policy and practice were influenced by the political thinking of Anthony Giddens's 'Third Way' theory, which was an attempt to provide a 'middle way' or synthesis between capitalism and socialism. Blair was an advocate of a new form of capitalism whereby the markets, properly managed, would deliver economic efficiency and social justice. Those on the labour movement left criticised New Labour for its breaking its links between trade unions and the state.

CHAPTER 7

1. In 2018, the US Supreme Court ruled that unions collecting fees from non-members in the public sector violated the First Amendment right to free speech. This overturned the 1977 decision in *Abood* v. *Detroit Board of Education* that had allowed such fees. This was a landmark case that seriously threatened union finances. See Heilman (2018).
2. The majority of USDAW's membership are covered by nationally negotiated voluntary recognition agreements in the four major retail giants.

CHAPTER 8

1. Another interpretation is that the purpose of unions should be to maintain or improve the conditions of the lives of *all workers*.
2. Each union has different titles for general full-time officer positions (the role of support officer to union branches – which generally includes negotiating with employers, representing members and undertaking employment tribunals).

While recruitment and organising are also expected in the role – and commonly included in job titles – these parts of the job are subsidiary to the former day-to-day tasks of full-time officers.

3. The basic shop assistant role at Tesco pays £9 per hour. At the other three where USDAW has recognition, the figures are: Sainsbury £9.20, Asda £9.18 and Morrisons £9. And in places where USDAW does not have recognition, the figures are: Aldi £9, Lidl £9, Iceland £9.21, Marks & Spencer £9 and Waitrose £9.35. Figures as of May 2020, reported in E. Mundbodh, 'Britain's best paying supermarkets – find out how much you could earn an hour', *Daily Mirror*, 28 May 2020, available at: www.mirror.co.uk/money/britains-best-paying-supermarkets-aldis-13890309 [accessed 12 April 2021].

4. 'About us', *RMT*, available at: www.rmt.org.uk/about/ [accessed 12 April 2021].

5. 'Organising strategy', *RMT*, available at: www.rmt.org.uk/member-benefits/resources/organising-strategy/ [accessed 12 April 2021].

6. Figures from the UK's Certification Officer, available at: https://webarchive.nationalarchives.gov.uk/20110708094736/http://www.certoffice.org/Publications/Annual-Reports.aspx [accessed 12 April 2021].

7. The Trade Union Act 2016 introduced a 50 per cent turnout requirement. In certain important public services, such as emergency medical services, certain teaching services and passenger rail services, there is the additional requirement that 40 per cent of members entitled to vote must vote in favour of striking.

8. Figures from the UK's Certification Officer's Annual Reports for 2007–2008 and 2017–2018, available at: https://webarchive.nationalarchives.gov.uk/20110708094736/http://www.certoffice.org/Publications/Annual-Reports.aspx [accessed 12 April 2021]. It should be noted that these figures are likely to be an overestimation, but they are probably a comparable overestimation.

9. Personal correspondence with GMB head of organising.

CHAPTER 9

1. The UK's Department of Business, Innovation and Skills defines zero-hour contracts as 'an employment contract in which an employer does not guarantee the individual any work and the individual is not obliged to accept any work offered'; 'Dataset: EMP17: People in employment on zero hours contracts', available at: www.ons.gov.uk/employmentandlabourmarket/peopleinwork/employmentandemployeetypes/datasets/emp17peopleinemploymentonzerohourscontracts [accessed 12 April 2021].

2. The Office for National Statistics estimated the size of the gig economy workforce in 2017 to be 4.4 per cent of the population; Department for Business, Energy & Industrial Strategy, The Characteristics of Those in the Gig Economy: Final Report, February 2018, available at: https://assets.publishing.service.gov.uk/government/uploads/system/uploads/attachment_data/file/687553/The_characteristics_of_those_in_the_gig_economy.pdf [accessed 12 April 2021].

3. Employment figures from the UK's Office for National Statistics, 'Dataset: EMP07: Temporary employees', available at: www.ons.gov.uk/employment andlabourmarket/peopleinwork/employmentandemployeetypes/datasets/ temporaryemployeesemp07?fbclid=IwAR29Er42tjeUr1ZIxmvTIP2sc2rnEzlR3 VWyEZxuOMaSwoEyGNNeERtIh3A [accessed 12 April 2021].

4. There are three independent unions that have been formed in London since 2010: the Independent Workers of Great Britain (around 4,000 members); United Voices of the World (around 5,000 members) and the Cleaners and Allied Independent Workers Union (around 1,000 members).

5. Other independent unions include the Cleaners and Allied Independent Workers Union (1,353 members in 2019) and the International Workers of the World (about 2,000 members).

6. The UVW annual return for 2019 to the UK's Certification Officer, who keeps a register of all unions, shows that £101,263 was paid out in staff costs out of an annual income of £156,624 – of which £130,000 came from members' dues.

7. 'Women make up 49.5 per cent of UK employees. Since 2002, union density has been higher among female employees than male employees and in 2017 it was 25.6 per cent compared with 20.9 per cent for men. ... In 2017, 54.6 per cent of union members were women, despite accounting for just 49.5 per cent of employees' (TUC 2018).

8. Facility time is a percentage of time (sometimes up to 100 per cent) granted by employers to union reps/shop stewards so that they are able to carry out trade union duties.

9. 'Number of people employed in the coal mining industry in the United Kingdom (UK) from 1920 to 2019 (in 1,000s)', available at: www.statista. com/statistics/371069/employment-in-coal-mining-industry-in-the-united-kingdom-uk/ [accessed 12 April 2021].

10. For a discussion on the ideas around a new Lucas Plan, see https://lucasplan. org.uk/ [accessed 12 April 2021]. In 2018, a film was made that features interviews with a number of the shop stewards who put together the plan, The Plan That Came from the Bottom Up by Steve Sprung, is available at: http:// theplandocumentary.com/ [accessed 12 April 2021].

11. The extent and distribution of mutual aid groups can be seen at https:// covidmutualaid.org/ [accessed 12 April 2021].

12. Capturing the data for the ethnic pay gap is complicated by a number of factors. One is that there is considerable disparity between different ethnic groups. Secondly, the majority of companies do not collect data on the ethnicity of employees, and thirdly, of those that do, 95 per cent have not analysed their ethnic pay gap; see PricewaterhouseCoopers, Taking the Right Approach to Ethnicity Pay Gap Reporting, March 2019, available at: www.pwc.co.uk/human-resource-services/assets/pdfs/ethnicity-pay-gap-report.pdf [accessed 12 April 2021].

13. Data from the Office for National Statistics, 'Coronavirus (COVID-19) related deaths by occupation, England and Wales: deaths registered between 9 March and 25 May 2020', May 2020, available at: www.ons.gov.uk/peoplepopulationandcommunity/healthandsocialcare/causesofdeath/bulletins/coronaviruscovid19relateddeathsbyoccupationenglandandwales/deathsregisteredbetween9marchand25may2020 [accessed 12 April 2021], and Public Health England, Disparities in the Risk and Outcomes of COVID-19, August 2020, available at: https://assets.publishing.service.gov.uk/government/uploads/system/uploads/attachment_data/file/892085/disparities_review.pdf [accessed 12 April 2021].
14. Trade unionists operating outside their union structures.
15. 'Mobilizing is most often limited to activating an existing base of support (usually union members in the case of industrial relations), whereas deep organizing involves engaging and activating people who may not initially agree but who, through a process of collective organizing and the development of grassroots leaders, begin to self-identify as part of a community with a shared objective in seeking to challenge injustice' (Holgate et al. 2018, p. 600).

Bibliography

Ackers, P. 2014. 'Game changer: Hugh Clegg's role in drafting the 1968 Donovan Report and redefining the British industrial relations policy-problem'. *Historical Studies in Industrial Relations* 35: 63–88.

Alberti, G. 2016a. 'Mobilizing and bargaining at the edge of informality: The "3 Cosas Campaign" by outsourced migrant workers at the University of London'. *WorkingUSA* 19: 81–103.

Alberti, G. 2016b. 'Moving beyond the dichotomy of workplace and community unionism: The challenges of organising migrant workers in London's hotels'. *Economic and Industrial Democracy* 37: 73–94.

Alberti, G. and Però, D. 2018. 'Migrating industrial relations: Migrant workers' initiative within and outside trade unions'. *British Journal of Industrial Relations* 56: 693–715.

Alinsky, S. 1972. *Rules for Radicals: A Pragmatic Primer for Realistic Radicals*. New York: Vintage.

Anderson, E. 2020. 'Volunteering, mutual aid and lockdown has shifted our sense of "happiness"'. *The Conversation*, 6 July. Available at: https://theconversation.com/volunteering-mutual-aid-and-lockdown-has-shifted-our-sense-of-happiness-141352 [accessed 23 July 2020].

Anitha, S. and Pearson, R. 2018. *Striking Women: Struggles and Strategies of South Asian Women Workers from Grunwick to Gate Gourmet*. London: Lawrence & Wishart.

Attlee, C. 1937. *The Labour Party in Perspective*. London: Victor Gollancz, Left Book Club.

Babic, M., Fichtner, J. and Heemskerk, E.M. 2017. 'States versus corporations: Rethinking the power of business in international politics'. *The International Spectator* 52: 20–43.

Bain, G. and Price, R. 1987. 'The determinants of union growth' in McCarthy, W. (ed.) *Trade Unions*. London: Penguin, pp. 243–271.

Banks, R. 1969. 'The reform of British industrial relations: The Donovan Report and the Labour government's policy proposals'. *Relations industrielles/Industrial Relations* 24: 333–382.

Barrow, C. 1997. *Industrial Relations Law*. London: Cavendish Publishing.

Bassett, P. and Cave, A. 1993. *All for One: The Future of the Unions*. London: Fabian Society.

Bevir, M. 1997. 'Labour Churches and ethnic socialism'. *History Today* 47: 50–55.

Beynon, H. 1973. *Working for Ford*. London: Penguin.

Boston, S. 1987. *Women Workers and the Trade Unions*. London: Lawrence & Wishart.

Bridgford, J. and Stirling, J. 1988. 'Ideology or pragmatism? Trade union education in France and Britain'. *Industrial Relations Journal* 19: 234–243.

British Library 2020. 'Female Chartists'. Available at: www.bl.uk/learning/ histcitizen/21cc/struggle/chartists1/historicalsources/source7/femalechartists. html [accessed 13 March 2020].

British Universities Film & Video Council 1983. 'Violence at Messenger Group works picket'. News report, 30 November. Available at: http://bufvc.ac.uk/tvan-dradio/lbc/index.php/segment/0014700243021 [accessed 27 April 2020].

Brookes, M. 2019. *The New Politics of Transnational Labor: Why Some Alliances Succeed*. Ithaca, NY: Cornell University Press.

Brown, W., Deakin, S., Hudson, M. and Pratten, C. 2001. 'The limits of statutory trade union recognition'. *Industrial Relations Journal* 32: 180–194.

Buchan, A. 1972. *The Right to Work: The Story of the Upper Clyde Confrontation*. London: Calder & Boyars.

Bunyan, P. 2016. 'The role of civil society in reducing poverty and inequality: A case study of the Living Wage Campaign in the UK'. *Local Economy: The Journal of the Local Economy Policy Unit* 31: 489–501.

Burgmann, M. and Burgmann, V. 1998. *Green Bans, Red Union: Environmental Activism and the New South Wales Builders Labourers' Federation*. Sydney, Australia: University of New South Wales Press.

Cant, C. 2019. *Riding for Deliveroo: Resistance in the New Economy*. Oxford, UK: Wiley.

Carrington, D. 2019. 'Climate crisis affects how majority will vote in UK election – poll'. *The Guardian*, 30 October. Available at: www.theguardian.com/ environment/2019/oct/30/climate-crisis-affects-how-majority-will-vote-in-uk-election-poll [accessed 12 April 2021].

Carruth, A. and Disney, R. 1988. 'Where have two million trade union members gone?'. *Economica* 55: 1–19.

Castle, B. 1969. *In Place of Strife: A Policy for Industrial Relations*. White Paper, Cmnd 3888. London: Her Majesty's Stationery Office.

Chamberlin, P. and Smith, D. 2015. *Blacklisted: The Secret War between Big Business and Union Activists*. Oxford, UK: New Internationalist.

Chase, M. 2000. *Early Trade Unionism: Fraternity, Skill and the Politics of Labour*. Aldershot, UK: Ashgate.

Clawson, D. 2003. *The Next Upsurge: Labor and the New Social Movements*. Ithaca, NY: Cornell University Press.

Clegg, H. 1985. *A History of British Trade Unions Since 1889: Volume 2, 1911–33*. Oxford, UK: Oxford University Press.

Coates, D. 1983. 'The question of trade union power' in Coates, D. and Johnston, G. (eds) *Socialist Arguments*. Oxford, UK: Martin Robertson, pp. 55–82.

Conn, D. 2012. 'Miners' strike: How the bloodiest battle became the "biggest frame-up"'. Available at: www.theguardian.com/politics/2012/nov/22/miners-strike-orgreave-bloodiest-battle [accessed 9 March 2020].

Conservative Political Centre 1968. *Fair Deal at Work – the Conservative Approach to Modern Industrial Relations*. London: Conservative Political Centre.

Crehan, K. 2002. *Gramsci, Culture and Anthropology*. Berkeley, CA: University of California Press.

Crehan, K. 2016. *Gramsci's Common Sense: Inequality and Its Narratives*. Durham, NC: Duke University Press.

Creighton, S. 1999. *From Exclusion to Political Control: Radical and Working Class Organisation in Battersea 1830–1918*. London: Agenda Services.

Crosby, M. 2005. *Power at Work: Rebuilding the Australian Union Movement*. Annandale, Australia: Federation Press.

Dahl, R.A. 1957. 'The concept of power'. *Behavioral Science* 2: 201–215.

Danford, A., Richardson, M. and Upchurch, M. 2002. '"New unionism", organising and partnership: A comparative analysis of union renewal strategies in the public sector'. *Capital & Class* 26: 1–27.

Darlington, R. 2001. 'Union militancy and left-wing leadership on London Underground'. *Industrial Relations Journal* 32: 2–21.

Darlington, R. 2009a. 'Leadership and union militancy: The case of the RMT'. *Capital & Class* 33: 3–32.

Darlington, R. 2009b. 'Organising, militancy and revitalisation: The case of the RMT union' in Gall, G. (ed.) *Union Revitalisation in Advanced Economies: Assessing the Contribution of Union Organising*. London: Palgrave Macmillan, pp. 83–106.

Darlington, R. and Lyddon, D. 2001. *Glorious Summer: Class Struggle in Britain 1972*. London: Bookmarks.

Darlington, R. and Upchurch, M. 2012. 'A reappraisal of the rank-and-file versus bureaucracy debate'. *Capital & Class* 36: 77–95.

Davis, K. 1991. 'Critical sociology and gender relations' in Davis, K., Leijenaar, M. and Oldersma, J. (eds) *The Gender of Power*. London: SAGE Publications, pp. 65–86.

Deakin, S., Fraser Butlin, S., McLaughlin, C. and Polanska, A. 2015. 'Are litigation and collective bargaining complements or substitutes for achieving gender equality? A study of the British Equal Pay Act'. *Cambridge Journal of Economics* 39: 381–403.

Deery, S. and Cieri, H. 1991. 'Determinants of trade union membership in Australia'. *British Journal of Industrial Relations* 29: 59–73.

Department for Business, Energy & Industrial Strategy 2019. *Trade Union Membership 2018: Statistical Bulletin*. London: Department for Business, Energy & Industrial Strategy.

Department for Business Innovation and Skills 2014. *Trade Union Membership: Statistical Bulletin*. London: Department for Business Innovation and Skills.

Dickens, L. 2008. *Legal Regulation, Institutions and Industrial Relations*. Warwick Papers in Industrial Relations 89. Coventry, UK: Industrial Relations Research Unit, University of Warwick.

Dickinson, M. 1984. *To Break a Union: The Messenger, the State and the NGA*. Chicago, IL: Booklist Publications.

Dobbins, T. 2020. 'Jobs crisis: The case for a new social contract'. *The Conversation*, 21 July. Available at: https://theconversation.com/jobs-crisis-the-case-for-a-new-social-contract-143024 [accessed 12 April 2021].

Donovan Report 1968. *Royal Commission on Trade Unions and Employers' Associations: 1965–1868*. London: Her Majesty's Stationery Office.

Douglass, F. 1999. *Frederick Douglass: Selected Speeches and Writings*, ed. Y. Taylor and P.S. Foner. Chicago, IL: Lawrence Hill Books.

Downing Street papers 1983. 'Cabinet papers'. The National Archive. Available at: www.nationalarchives.gov.uk [accessed 8 March 2020].

Drake, B. 1984. *Women in Trade Unions*. London: Virago.

Dromey, J. and Taylor, G. 1978. *Grunwick: The Workers' Story*. London: Lawrence & Wishart.

Dundon, T. 2002. 'Employer opposition and union avoidance in the UK'. *Industrial Relations Journal* 33: 234–245.

Ellem, B., Goods, C. and Todd, P. 2019. 'Rethinking power, strategy and renewal: Members and unions in crisis'. *British Journal of Industrial Relations* 58: 424–446.

England, J. and Weeks, B. 1981. 'Trade unions and the state: A review of the crisis' in McCarthy, W. (ed.) *Trade Unions*. London: Penguin, pp. 406–432.

Ewing, K.D. and Napier, B.W. 2009. 'The Wapping dispute and labour law'. *Cambridge Law Journal* 45: 285–304.

Fairbrother, P. 2000. 'British trade unions facing the future'. *Capital & Class* 71: 47–78.

Fairbrother, P. 2008. 'Social movement unionism or trade unions as social movements'. *Employee Responsibilities and Rights Journal* 20: 213–220.

Fairbrother, P. and Yates, C. 2003. *Trade Unions in Renewal*. London: Continuum.

Findlay, P. and Warhurst, C. 2011. 'Union learning funds and trade union revitalization: A new tool in the toolkit?'. *British Journal of Industrial Relations* 49: s115–s134.

Fine, J. 2005. 'Community unions and the revival of the American labor movement'. *Politics and Society* 33: 153–199.

Fisher, J. 2005. *Bread on the Waters : A History of TGWU Education, 1922–2000*. London: Lawrence & Wishart.

Fisher, J. 2017. 'What do we mean by "trade union education"?' in Seal, M. (ed.) *Trade Union Education: Transforming the World*. Oxford, UK: New Internationalist, pp. 22–37.

Flanders, A. 1972. 'What are trade unions for?' in McCarthy, W. (ed.) *Trade Unions*. London: Pelican, pp. 26–34.

Fox Piven, F. and Cloward, D. 2000. 'Power repertoires and globalisation'. *Politics and Society* 28: 413–430.

Freedland, J. 2020. 'As fearful Britain shuts down, coronavirus has transformed everything'. *The Guardian*, 20 March. Available at: www.theguardian.com/world/2020/mar/20/as-fearful-britain-shuts-down-coronavirus-has-transformed-everything [accessed 3 April 2021].

Freedom Association. 2020. 'History'. Available at: www.tfa.net/history [accessed 20 April 2021].

Friedman, H. and Meredeen, S. 1980. *The Dynamics of Industrial Conflict: Lessons from Ford*. London: Croom Helm.

Fudge, J. 2017. 'The future of the standard employment relationship: Labour law, new institutional economics and old power resource theory'. *Journal of Industrial Relations* 59: 374–392.

Gall, G. 2003. *Union Organizing: Campaigning for Trade Union Recognition*. London: Routledge.

Gall, G. 2006. *Union Recognition: Organising and Bargaining Outcomes*. London: Routledge.

Gall, G. 2007. 'Trade union recognition in Britain: An emerging crisis for trade unions?'. *Economic and Industrial Democracy* 28: 78–109.

Gall, G. 2017. *Bob Crow: Socialist, Leader, Fighter: A Political Biography* Manchester, UK: Manchester University Press.

Gall, G. 2018. 'Gregor Gall: Unions could become extinct unless they start winning strikes'. *The Scotsman*, 7 September 2018.

Gallie, D., Penn, R. and Rose, M. 1996. *Trade Unionism in Recession*. Oxford, UK: Oxford University Press.

Ganz, M. 2008. 'Leading change: Leadership, organization, and social movements' in Nitin Nohria, R.K. (ed.) *Handbook of Leadership Theory and Practice*. Cambridge, MA: Harvard University Press, pp. 527–564.

Ganz, M. 2011. 'Public narrative, collective action, and power' in Odugbemi, S. and Lee, T. (eds) *Accountability through Public Opinion: From Inertia to Public Action*. Washington, DC: The World Bank, pp. 273–289.

Geary, J. and Trif, A. 2011. 'Workplace partnership and the balance of advantage: A critical case analysis'. *British Journal of Industrial Relations* 49: s44–s69.

Gennard, J. 1984. 'The implications of the Messenger Newspaper Group dispute'. *Industrial Relations Journal* 15: 7–20.

Gennard, J. 2009. 'Trade union merger strategies: Good or bad?'. *Employee Relations* 31: 116–120.

General, Municipal, Boilermakers and Allied Trades Union 1991. *A New Agenda: Bargaining for Prosperity in the 1990s*. London: General, Municipal, Boilermakers and Allied Trades Union.

Graham, S. 2007. 'Organising out of decline – the rebuilding of the UK and Ireland shop stewards movement'. Available at: http://employees.org.uk/annual-report-TGW.html [accessed 20 April 2021].

Gramsci, A. 1971. *Selections from the Prison Notebooks*. New York: Harper and Row.

Hall, M. 2005. 'Assessing the information and consultation of employees regulations'. *Industrial Law Journal* 34: 103–126.

Hansard 1983. 'Messenger Newspaper Group – NGA Dispute'. *HL Deb* 1 December, vol. 445, cc834-58. Available at: https://api.parliament.uk/historic-hansard/lords/1983/dec/01/messenger-newspaper-group-nga-dispute [accessed 27 April 2020].

Healey, J. and O'Grady, F. 1997. 'New unionism in the 1990s'. *Soundings* 6: 172–178.

Heery, E. 1996. 'The new new unionism' in Beardwell, I.J. (ed.) *Contemporary Industrial Relations: A Critical Analysis*. Oxford, UK: Oxford University Press, pp. 175–202.

Heery, E. 1998. 'The relaunch of the Trades Union Congress'. *British Journal of Industrial Relations* 36(3): 339–360.

Heery, E. 2002. 'Partnership versus organising: Alternative futures for British trade unionism'. *Industrial Relations Journal* 33(1): 20–35.

Heery, E. 2011. 'Debating employment law: Responses to juridification' in Blyton, P., Heery, E. and Turnbull, P. (eds) *Reassessing the Employment Relationship*. London: Palgrave Macmillan, pp. 71–93.

Heery, E. 2015. 'Unions and the organising turn: Reflections after 20 years of Organising Works'. *The Economic and Labour Relations Review* 26: 545–560.

Heery, E., Abbott, B. and Williams, S. 2012. 'The involvement of civil society organizations in British industrial relations: Extent, origins and significance'. *British Journal of Industrial Relations* 50: 47–72.

Heery, E., Delbridge, R., Salmon, M., Simms, M. and Simpson, D. 2001. 'Global labour? The transfer of the organising model to the United Kingdom' in Debrah, Y. and Smith, I. (eds) *Globalisation, Employment and the Workplace*. London: Routledge, pp. 41–68.

Heery, E., Delbridge, R., Simms, M., Salmon, J. and Simpson, D. 2003. 'Organising for renewal: A case study of the U.K.'s organising academy'. *Research in the Sociology of Work* 11: 79–110.

Heery, E., Hann, D. and Nash, D. 2017. 'The Living Wage Campaign in the United Kingdom'. *Employee Relations* 39: 800–814.

Heery, E. and Kelly, J. 1994. 'Professional, participative and managerial unionism: An interpretation of change in trade union'. *Work, Employment and Society* 8: 1–22.

Heery, E. and Simms, M. 2008. 'Constraints on union organising in the United Kingdom'. *Industrial Relations Journal* 39: 24–42.

Heery, E. and Simms, M. 2011. 'Seizing an opportunity? Union organizing campaigns in Britain, 1998–2004'. *Labor History* 52: 23–47.

Heery, E., Simms, M., Delbridge, R., Salmon, J. and Simpson, D. 2000a. 'The TUC's Organising Academy: An assessment'. *Industrial Relations Journal* 31: 400–415.

Heery, E., Simms, M., Delbridge, R., Salmon, J. and Simpson, D. 2000b. 'Union organizing in Britain: A survey of policy and practice'. *International Journal of Human Resource Management* 11: 986–1,007.

Heery, E., Simms, M., Simpson, D., Delbridge, R. and Salmon, J. 2000c. 'Organising unionism comes to the UK'. *Employee Relations* 22: 33–57.

Heilman, H. 2018. 'Janus v. AFSCME and the future of American unions'. *Perspectives on Work* 22: 56–59.

Henderson, L. 2018. 'Please step aside brothers'. *Scottish Left Review* 118. Available at: www.scottishleftreview.scot/please-step-aside-brothers/ [accessed 12 April 2021].

Herod, A. 1997. 'From a geography of labor to a labor of geography: Labor's spatial fix and the geography of capitalism'. *Antipode* 29: 1–31.

Herod, A. 1998. *Organizing the Landscape: Geographical Perspectives on Labor Unionism*. Minneapolis, MN: University of Minnesota Press.

Heyes, J. 2009. 'Recruiting and organising migrant workers through education and training: A comparison of community and the GMB'. *Industrial Relations Journal* 40: 182–197.

Hinton, J. 1973. *The First Shop Stewards' Movement*. London: George Allen & Unwin.

Hinton, J. 1983. *Labour and Socialism: A History of the British Labour Movement 1867–1974*. Brighton, UK: Wheatsheaf Books.

Hobsbawm, E. 1978. 'The forward march of labour halted?'. *Marxism Today* September: 279–286.

Hodder, A., Williams, M., Kelly, J. and McCarthy, N. 2017. 'Does strike action stimulate trade union membership growth?'. *British Journal of Industrial Relations* 55: 165–186.

Holgate, J. 2005. 'Organising migrant workers: A case study of working conditions and unionisation at a sandwich factory in London'. *Work, Employment and Society* 19: 463–480.

Holgate, J. 2009. 'Contested terrain: London's Living Wage Campaign and the tension between community and union organising' in McBride, J. and Greenwood, I. (eds) *The Complexity of Community Unionism: A Comparative Analysis of Concepts and Contexts*. Basingstoke, UK: Palgrave Macmillan, pp. 49–74.

Holgate, J. 2013. 'Faith in unions: From safe spaces to organised labour?'. *Capital and Class* 37: 239–262.

Holgate, J. 2015. 'Community organising in the UK: A "new" approach for trade unions?'. *Economic and Industrial Democracy* 36: 431–455.

Holgate, J. 2018. 'Trade unions in the community: Building broad spaces of solidarity'. *Economic and Industrial Democracy*, 29 March. Available at: https://doi.org/10.1177/0143831X18763871 [accessed 12 April 2021].

Holgate, J. and Simms, M. 2008. *Ten Years On: The Impact of the Organising Academy on the UK Union Movement*. London: Trades Union Congress.

Holgate, J., Simms, M. and Tapia, M. 2018. 'The limitations of the theory and practice of mobilization in trade union organizing'. *Economic and Industrial Democracy* 39: 599–616.

Holgate, J. and Wills, J. 2007. 'Organising labor in London: Lessons from the Living Wage Campaign' in Turner, L. and Cornfield, D. (eds) *Labor in the New Urban Battlefields: Local Solidarity in a Global Economy*. Ithaca, NY: ILR Press, pp. 211–223.

Hoskyns, J. and Strauss, N. 1977. 'Stepping Stones'. London: Margaret Thatcher Foundation. Available at: https://c59574e9047e61130f13-3f71d0fe2b653c4f00f32 175760e96e7.ssl.cf1.rackcdn.com/5B6518B5823043FE9D7C54846CC7FE31.pdf [accessed 30 April 2020].

Howell, D. 1987. 'Goodbye to all that? A review of literature on the 1984/5 Miners' Strike'. *Work, Employment and Society* 1: 388–404.

Hunt, T. 2006. 'The charge of the heavy brigade'. *The Guardian*, 4 September. Available at: www.theguardian.com/theguardian/2006/sep/04/features5 [accessed 7 April 2021].

Hyman, R. 1979. 'The politics of workplace trade unionism: Recent tendencies and some problems for theory'. *Capital & Class* 3: 54–67.

Hyman, R. 2001. *Understanding European Trade Unionism: Between Market, Class and Society*. London: SAGE Publications.

Hyman, R. 2007. 'How can trade unions act strategically?'. *Transfer: European Review of Labour and Research* 13: 193–210.

Ibsen, C. and Tapia, M. 2017. 'Trade union revitalisation: Where are we now? Where to next?'. *Journal of Industrial Relations* 59: 170–191.

Jenkins, J. 2007. 'Gambling partners? The risky outcomes of workplace partnerships'. *Work, Employment and Society* 21: 635–652.

Jenkinson, J. 1981. 'The 1919 race riots in Britain: A survey' in Lotz, R. and Pegg, I. (eds) *Under the Imperial Carpet: Essays in Black History 1780–1950*. Crawley, UK: Rabbit Press, pp. 182–207.

Johnston, P. 1995. *Success While Others Fail: Social Movement Unionism and the Public Workplace*. Ithaca, NY: ILR Press.

Johnstone, S. and Wilkinson, A. 2016. *Developing Positive Employment Relations: International Experiences of Labour Management Partnership*. London: Palgrave Macmillan.

Jones, E. 1867. 'Democracy vindicated: A lecture delivered to the Edinburgh Working Men's Institute on the 4th January 1867 by Ernest Jones, Barrister, in reply to Professor Blackie's lecture on democracy, delivered on the previous evening'. Available at: https://minorvictorianwriters.org.uk/jones/b_jones_democracy.htm [accessed 4 April 2021].

Joyce, P. and Wain, N. 2014. *Palgrave Dictionary of Public Order Policing, Protest and Political Violence*. London: Palgrave Macmillan.

Judd, D. and Surrige, K. 2013. *The Boer War: A History*. London: I.B. Tauris.

Kelly, J. 1996. 'Union militancy and social partnership' in *The New Workplace and Trade Unionism: Critical Perspectives on Work and Organization*. London: Routledge, pp. 77–109.

Kelly, J. 1998. *Rethinking Industrial Relations: Mobilization, Collectivism and Long Waves*. London: Routledge.

Kelly, J. 1999. 'Social partnership in Britain: Good for profits, bad for jobs and unions'. *Communist Review* 30: 310.

Kelly, J. 2015. 'Trade union membership and power in comparative perspective'. *Economic and Labour Relations Review* 26: 526–544.

Kelly, J. and Badigannavar, V. 2011. 'Partnership and organizing: An empirical assessment of two contrasting approaches to union revitalization in the UK'. *Economic and Industrial Democracy* 32: 5–27.

Kelly, J. and Frege, C. 2004. *Varieties of Unionism: Struggles for Union Revitalization in a Globalizing Economy*. Oxford, UK: Oxford University Press.

Kelly, J. and Heery, E. 1994. *Working for the Union: British Trade Union Officers*. Cambridge, UK: Cambridge University Press.

Kirton, G. and Healy, G. 2012. *Gender and Leadership in Unions*. London: Routledge.

Koçer, R.G. 2018. 'Measuring the strength of trade unions and identifying the privileged groups: A two-dimensional approach and its implementation'. *Journal of Mathematical Sociology* 42: 152–182.

Korczynski, M. 2003. 'Communities of coping: Collective emotional labour in service work'. *Organization* 10: 55–79.

Kosmin, B. 1978. 'J. R. Archer: A Pan Africanist in the Battersea labour movement'. *New Community* 7(1): 430–436.

Kotter, J. 1996. *Leading Change*. Boston, MA: Harvard Business Review Press.

Labour Party 1997. *New Labour Because Britain Deserves Better*. Available at: www.labour-party.org.uk/manifestos/1997/1997-labour-manifesto.shtml [accessed 10 April 2021].

Laybourn, K. 1997. *A History of British Trade Unionism, c. 1770–1990*. Stroud, UK: Sutton Publishing.

Laybourn, K. and Shepherd, J. 2017. *Labour and Working-class Lives: Essays to Celebrate the Life and Work of Chris Wrigley*. Manchester, UK: Manchester University Press.

Ledwith, S. and Hansen, L.L. 2013. *Gendering and Diversifying Trade Union Leadership*. Abingdon, UK: Routledge.

Lévesque, C. and Murray, G. 2010. 'Understanding union power: Resources and capabilities for renewing union capacity'. *Transfer: European Review of Labour and Research* 16: 333–350.

Lindop, F. 1998. 'The dockers and the 1971 Industrial Relations Act, Part 2: The arrest and release of the "Pentonville Five"'. *Historical Studies in Industrial Relations* 6: 65–100.

Lukes, S. 2004. *Power: A Radical View*. London: Palgrave.

Machin, S. 2000. 'Union decline in Britain'. *British Journal of Industrial Relations* 38: 631–645.

Machin, S. and Wood, S. 2005. 'HRM as a substitute for trade unions in British workplaces'. *Industrial and Labor Relations Review* 58: 201–218.

Mann, T. 1886. *What a Compulsory Eight-hour Day Means to the Workers*. London: Modern Press. Available at: www.marxists.org/archive/mann-tom/1886/eight hours1886.htm [accessed 4 April 2021].

Marsh, D. 1992. *The New Politics of British Trade Unionism: Union Power and the Thatcher Legacy*. London: Macmillan.

Martin López, T. 2014. *The Winter of Discontent: Myth, Memory and History*. Oxford, UK: Oxford University Press.

Martínez Lucio, M. and Weston, S. 1992. 'The politics and complexity of trade union responses to new management practices'. *Human Resource Management Journal* 2: 77–91.

Marx, K. 1977. *Selected Writings*, ed. D. McLellen. Oxford, UK: Oxford University Press.

Mason, B. and Bain, G.S. 1993. 'The determinants of trade union membership in Britain: A survey of the literature'. *Industrial and Labor Relations Review* 46: 332–351.

McAlevey, J. 2003. 'It takes a community: Building unions from the outside in'. *New Labor Forum* 12: 23–32.

McAlevey, J. 2016. *No Shortcuts: Organising for Power in the New Gilded Age*. Oxford, UK: Oxford University Press.

McBride, J. and Greenwood, I. 2009. *The Complexity of Community Unionism: A Comparative Analysis of Concepts and Contexts*. Basingstoke, UK: Palgrave Macmillan.

McGaughey, E. 2017. *Democracy or Oligarchy? Models of Union Governance in the UK, Germany and US*. King's College London Law School Research Paper No. 2017-35. Available at: https://ssrn.com/abstract=2995297 or http://dx.doi.org/10.2139/ssrn.2995297 [accessed 10 April 2021].

McGowan, J. 2008. '"Dispute", "battle", "siege", "farce"? – Grunwick 30 years on'. *Contemporary British History* 22: 383–406.

McIlroy, J. 1988. *Trade Unions in Britain Today*. Manchester, UK: Manchester University Press.

McIlroy, J. 2008. 'Ten years of New Labour: Workplace learning, social partnership and union revitalization in Britain'. *British Journal of Industrial Relations* 46: 283–313.

McIlroy, J. and Campbell, A. 1999. 'Organizing the militants: The Liaison Committee for the Defence of Trade Unions, 1966–1979'. *British Journal of Industrial Relations* 37: 1–31.

Michels, R. 1915. *Political Parties: A Sociological Study of the Oligarchical Tendencies of Modern Democracy*. Translated into English by Eden Paul and Cedar Paul from the 1911 German source. New York: The Free Press.

Milkman, R. 2000. *Organizing Immigrants: The Challenge for Unions in Contemporary California*. Ithaca, NY: ILR Press.

Milne, S. 2000. 'What Stella left out: The truth about MI5's role in the miners' strike will not come out in Rimington's memoirs'. *The Guardian*, 3 October. Available at:

www.theguardian.com/comment/story/0,3604,376455,00.html [accessed 7 April 2021].

Monks, J. 1993. 'A trade union view of WIRS3'. *British Journal of Industrial Relations* 31: 227–233.

Monks, J. 1999. 'My biggest mistake – John Monks: Why my union wars ended'. *The Independent*, 13 April. Available at: www.independent.co.uk/news/business/my-biggest-mistake-john-monks-why-my-union-wars-ended-1087086.html [accessed 10 April 2021].

Moore, C. 2013. *Margaret Thatcher: The Authorized Biography*. London: Penguin.

Moore, P., Upchurch, M. and Whittaker, X. 2018. *Humans and Machines at Work: Monitoring, Surveillance and Automation in Contemporary Capitalism*. London: Palgrave Macmillan.

Moore, R. 1974. *Pitmen, Preachers and Politics: The Effects of Methodism in a Durham Mining Community*. Cambridge, UK: Cambridge University Press.

Moore, S. 2010. *New Trade Union Activism: Class Consciousness or Social Identity?* Basingstoke, UK: Palgrave Macmillan.

Moss, J. 2015. '"We didn't realise how brave we were at the time": The 1968 Ford sewing machinists' strike in public and personal memory'. *Oral History* 43: 40–51.

Murphy, C. 2016. 'Fear and leadership in union organizing campaigns: An examination of workplace activist behavior'. *SAGE Open*, 21 January. Available at: https://journals.sagepub.com/doi/full/10.1177/2158244015623932 [accessed 12 April 2021].

Murray, G. 2017. 'Union renewal: What can we learn from three decades of research?'. *Transfer: European Review of Labour and Research* 23: 9–29.

Musson, A.E. 1959. 'The Great Depression in Britain, 1873–1896: A reappraisal'. *Journal of Economic History* 19: 199–228.

Nissen, B. 2004. 'The effectiveness and limits of labor–community coalitions: Evidence from south Florida'. *Labor Studies Journal* 29: 67–89.

O'Dwyer, E. 2020. 'COVID-19 mutual aid groups have the potential to increase intergroup solidarity – but can they actually do so?'. Available at: https://blogs.lse.ac.uk/politicsandpolicy/covid19-mutual-aid-solidarity/ [accessed 23 July 2020].

Office for National Statistics 2019. *Labour Disputes in the UK: 2018*. London: Office for National Statistics. Available at: www.ons.gov.uk/employmentandlabourmarket/peopleinwork/workplacedisputesandworkingconditions/articles/labourdisputes/2018 [accessed 31 March 2021].

Palmer, G. 1986. 'Donovan, the Commission on Industrial Relations and Post-liberal Rationalisation'. *British Journal of Industrial Relations* 24: 267–296.

Parker, C. and Rees, J. 2013. 'Membership growth at a time of union decline: Usdaw, organizing and leadership'. *Transfer: European Review of Labour and Research* 19: 521–538.

PCS 2019. *National Organising Strategy 2019*. London: Public and Commercial Services Union. Available at: www.pcs.org.uk/sites/default/files/site_assets/conference/2019/LoRes-9876-ADC2019-national-organising-strategy-part1.pdf [last accessed 7 July 2020].

PCS 2020. 'PCS members secure a parliamentary debate on fair pay'. Available at: www.pcs.org.uk/news/pcs-members-secure-a-parliamentary-debate-on-fair-pay [accessed 20 April 2021].

Pelling, H. 1963. *A History of British Trade Unionism*. Harmondsworth, UK: Penguin.

Però, D. 2019. 'Indie unions, organizing and labour renewal: Learning from precarious migrant workers'. *Work, Employment and Society* 29: 932–949.

Phizacklea, A. and Miles, R. 1978. 'The strike at Grunwick'. *New Community* 6: 268–278.

Pierson, S. 1960. 'John Trevor and the Labor Church Movement in England 1891–1900'. *Church History* 29: 463–478.

Raw, L. 2009. *Striking a Light: The Bryant and May Matchwomen and Their Place in History*. London: Bloomsbury.

Reid, J. 1976. *Reflections of a Clyde-built Man*. London: Souvenir Press.

Ridley, N. 1977. 'Economy: Report of Nationalised Industries Policy Group (leaked Ridley report)'. Available at: www.margaretthatcher.org/document/110795 [accessed 7 April 2021].

Roberts, Y. 2018. 'The tiny union beating the gig economy giants'. *The Guardian*, 1 July. Available at: www.theguardian.com/politics/2018/jul/01/union-beating-gig-economy-giants-iwgb-zero-hours-workers [accessed 4 April 2021].

Rogaly, J. 1977. *Grunwick*. Harmondsworth, UK: Penguin.

Rose, F. 2000. *Coalitions across the Class Divide: Lessons from the Labor, Peace and Environmental Movements*. Ithaca, NY: IPR Press.

Ross, R. 2012. 'Trade unions and workers' education: 1945–1995'. Available at: www.unionhistory.info/britainatwork/narrativedisplay.php?type=tuand workereducation [accessed 5 March 2020].

Rowbotham, S. 1975. *Hidden from History: 300 Years of Women's Oppression and the Fight against It*. London: Pluto Press.

Rudder, B. 1993. *Builders of the Borough: A century of achievement by Battersea and Wandsworth Trades Union Council from 1894–1994*. London: Battersea and Wandsworth Trades Union Council.

Ruggie, J.G. 2018. 'Multinationals as global institution: Power, authority and relative autonomy'. *Regulation & Governance* 12: 317–333.

Russell, B. 1986. *Power: A New Social Analysis*. London: George Allen & Unwin.

Salisbury, B. 2020. 'Story of the Lucas Plan'. Available at: https://lucasplan.org.uk/story-of-the-lucas-plan/ [accessed 12 April 2021].

Samuels, P. and Bacon, N. 2010. 'The contents of partnership agreements in Britain 1990–2007'. *Work, Employment and Society* 24: 30–448.

Sanders, C. 2014. 'Why the positional leadership perspective hinders the ability of organizations to deal with complex and dynamic situations'. *International Journal of Leadership Studies* 8: 136–150.

Saville, J. and Briggs, A. 1971. *Essays in Labour History 1886–1923*. London: Macmillan.

Schmalz, S., Ludwig, C. and Webster, E. 2018. 'The power resources approach: Developments and challenges'. *Global Labour Journal* 9: 113–134.

Seal, M. 2017. *Trade Union Education Transforming the World*. London: New Internationalist.

Shepherd, J. 2013. *Crisis? What Crisis? The Callaghan Government and the British 'Winter of Discontent'*. Manchester, UK: Manchester University Press.

Silver, B.J. 2003. *Forces of Labor: Workers' Movements and Globalization Since 1870*. Cambridge, UK: Cambridge University Press.

Simms, M. 2003. 'Organising front-line service workers: Evidence from four union campaigns' in White, G., Corby, S. and Stanworth, C. (eds) *Regulation, Deregulation and Re-regulation: The Scope of Employment Relations in the 21st Century*. London: University of Greenwich.

Simms, M. 2006. 'The transition from organising to recognition: A case study' in Gall, G. (ed.) *Union Recognition: Organising and Bargaining Outcomes*. London Routledge, pp. 167–180.

Simms, M. 2015. 'Accounting for greenfield union organizing outcomes'. *British Journal of Industrial Relations* 53: 397–422.

Simms, M. and Holgate, J. 2010a. 'Organising for what? Where is the debate on the politics of organising?'. *Work, Employment and Society* 24: 157–168.

Simms, M. and Holgate, J. 2010b. 'TUC Organizing Academy 10 years on: What has been the impact on British unions?'. *International Journal of Human Resource Management* 21: 355–370.

Simms, M., Holgate, J. and Heery, E. 2013. *Union Voices: Tactics and Tensions in UK Organizing*. Ithaca, NY: Cornell University Press.

Simms, M., Holgate, J. and Hodder, A. 2018. *Organising Innovation: Unions, Young Workers and Precarity*. London: Unions21.

Smith, D. and Sloane, K. 1969. 'The British Royal Commission on Trade Unions and Employers' Associations, 1965–1968'. *University of Western Australia Review* 9: 1–49.

Smith, G. 2019. 'Glasgow equal pay – celebration for our women, reflection for our union'. Available at: www.gmbscotland.org.uk/campaigns/equal-pay/overview [accessed 12 April 2021].

Smith, P. 1999. 'The "Winter of Discontent": The hire and reward road haulage dispute, 1979'. *Historical Studies in Industrial Relations* 7: 27–54.

Snape, E. 1994. 'Reversing the decline? The TGWU's Link Up campaign'. *Industrial Relations Journal* 25: 222–233.

Snape, E. 1995. 'The development of 'managerial unionism' in Britain: A research note'. *Work, Employment and Society* 9: 559–568.

Speer, P.W. and Hughey, J. 1995. 'Community organizing: An ecological route to empowerment and power'. *American Journal of Community Psychology* 23: 729–748.

Stanford, J. 2017. 'The resurgence of gig work: Historical and theoretical perspectives'. *Economic and Labour Relations Review* 28: 382–401.

Staton, B. 2020. 'The upstart unions taking on the gig economy and outsourcing'. *The Financial Times*, 19 January.

Stewart, A. 2016. 'Battle of Orgreave: A bloody battle which transformed industrial relations'. Available at: www.itv.com/news/2016-10-31/battle-of-orgreave-a-bloody-battle-which-transformed-industrial-relations/ [accessed 9 March 2020].

Stirling, J. 2005. 'There's a new world somewhere: The rediscovery of trade unionism'. *Capital and Class* 87: 43–64.

Stockhammer, E. 2013. *Why Have Wage Shares Fallen? A Panel Analysis of the Determinants of Functional Income Distribution*. Geneva, Switzerland: International Labour Office.

Storey, J., Bacon, N., Edmonds, J. and Wyatt, P. 1993. 'The "New Agenda" and human resource management: A roundtable discussion with John Edmonds'. *Human Resource Management Journal* 4: 63–70.

Streeck, W. and Hassel, A. 2003. 'Trade unions as political actors' in Addison, J. and Schnabel, C. (eds) *International Handbook of Trade Unions*. Cheltenham, UK: Edward Elgar, pp. 335–365.

Stuart, M., Cook, H., Cutter, J. and Winterton, J. 2010. *Evaluation of the Union Learning Fund and unionlearn*. Leeds, UK: Centre for Employment Relations Innovation and Change at Leeds University Business School.

Sun Tzu 1910. *Sun Tzu: The Art of War*. Leicester, UK: Allandan Online Publishing.

Tattersall, A. 2010. *Power in Coalition: Strategies for Strong Unions and Social Change*. Ithaca, NY: Cornell University Press.

Taylor, G. 2018. 'Internecine strife in trade union organisations: Status, competition and the effect of industry rationalisation and neo-liberalism'. *Labor History* 59: 162–184.

Taylor, R. 2000. *The TUC: From the General Strike to New Unionism*. London: Trades Union Congress.

Terry, M. 2000. *Redefining Public Sector Unionism: Unison and the Future of Trade Unions*. London: Routledge.

Terry, M. 2003. 'Partnership and the future of trade unions in the UK'. *Economic and Industrial Democracy* 24: 485–507.

TGWU 1998. *Organising for Change: Recruitment and Organisation*. London: Transport and General Workers' Union.

Thompson, W. and Hart, F. 1972. *The UCS Work-in*. London: Lawrence & Wishart.

Thorne, W. 2014. *My Life's Battles*. London: Lawrence & Wishart.

Thorne, W. 2018. *My Life's Battles (Classic Reprint)*. London: Forgotten Books.

Thornett, A. 1998. *Inside Cowley: Trade Union Struggle in the 1970s: Who Really Opened the Door to the Tory Onslaught?* London: Porcupine Press.

Tilly, C. 1995. 'Contentious repertoires in Great Britain, 1758–1834' in Traugott, M. (ed.) *Repertoires and Cycles of Collective Action*. Durham, NC: Duke University Press, pp. 15–42.

Towers, B. 1985. 'Posing larger questions: The British miners' strike of 1984–85'. *Industrial Relations Journal* 16: 8–25.

TUC 1999. *Congress Report*. London: Trades Union Congress.

TUC 2018. *TUC Equality Audit*. London: Trades Union Congress.

TUC 2019. *A Just Transition to a Greener, Fairer Economy*. London: Trades Union Congress.

Turnbull, D. 2005. 'Organising migrant workers: The experience of the TGWU international catering workers' branch' in Gibbons, S. (ed.) *Organising Migrant Workers in Trade Unions*. London: International Centre for Trade Union Rights, pp. 12–16.

Turner, L. and Hurd, R. 2001. 'Building social movement unionism: The transformation of the American labor movement' in Turner, L., Katz, H. and Hurd, R. (eds) *Rekindling the Movement: Labor's Quest for Relevance in the 21st Century*. Ithaca, NY: ILR Press, pp. 9–28.

Undy, R. 1993. 'Trade union mergers: Causes and consequences'. *Management Research News* 16: 20–21.

Undy, R. 2008. *Trade Union Merger Strategies: Purpose, Process, and Performance*. Oxford, UK: Oxford University Press.

Undy, R., Ellis, V., McCarthy, W. and Halmos, A.M. 1981. *Change in Trade Unions*. London: Hutchinson.

US Department of Labour 2020. 'News release. Bureau of Labor Statistics'. Available at: www.bls.gov/news.release/pdf/union2.pdf [accessed 14 June 2020].

USDAW 2002. *Sustainable Organising: Power to Usdaw Reps!* Manchester, UK: USDAW.

Vandaele, K. 2018. *Will Trade Unions Survive in the Platform Economy? Emerging Patterns of Platform Workers' Collective Voice and Representation in Europe*. ETUI Research Paper – Working Paper 2018.05. Available at: https://ssrn.com/abstract=3198546 or http://dx.doi.org/10.2139/ssrn.3198546 [accessed 12 April 2021].

Voss, K. and Sherman, R. 2000. 'Breaking the iron law of oligarchy: Union revitalization in the American labor movement'. *American Journal of Sociology* 106: 303–349.

Waddington, J. 1992. 'Trade union membership in Britain, 1980–1987: Unemployment and restructuring'. *British Journal of Industrial Relations* 30: 287–324.

Waddington, J. and Kerr, A. 2000. 'Towards an organising model in UNISON? A trade union membership in transition' in Terry, M. (ed.) *Redefining Public Sector Unionism: Unison and the Future of Trade Unions*. London: Routledge, pp. 231–266.

Waddington, J. and Kerr, A. 2015. 'Joining UNISON: Does the reform of a union organising strategy change how members perceive their recruitment?'. *Industrial Relations Journal* 46: 187–207.

Waddington, J. and Whitston, C. 1997. 'Why do people join unions in a period of membership decline?'. *British Journal of Industrial Relations* 35(4): 515–546.

Wainwright, H. and Elliot, D. 1982. *The Lucas Plan: A New Trade Unionism in the Making?* London: Allison & Busby.

Waldinger, R., Erikson, C., Milkman, R., Mitchell, D., Valenxuela, A., Wong, K., et al. 1998. 'Helots no more: A case study of the Justice for Janitors campaign in Los Angeles' in Bronfenbrenner, K., Friedman, S., Hurd, R.W., Oswald, R.A. and Seeber, R.L. (eds) *Organizing to Win: New Research on Union Strategies*. New York: Cornell University Press, pp. 102–122.

Wearmouth, R. 1937. *Methodism and the Working Class Movements of England 1800–1850*. London: Epworth Press.

Wearmouth, R. 1948. *Some Working Class Movements of the Nineteenth Century*. London: Epworth Press.

Wearmouth, R. 1954. *Methodism and the Struggle of the Working Class*. Leicester, UK: Edgar Backus.

Wearmouth, R. 1957. *The Social and Political Influence of Methodism in the Twentieth Century*. London: Epworth Press.

Wets, J. 2019. *Cultural Diversity in Trade Unions: A Challenge to Class Identity?* London: Routledge.

White, M. 1989 'Liberties with freedom: The Freedom Association's notions of cricket'. *The Guardian*, 24 January.

Williams, S., Abbott, B. and Heery, E. 2017. 'Civil governance in work and employment relations: How civil society organizations contribute to systems of labour governance'. *Journal of Business Ethics* 144: 103–119.

Wills, J. 2004. 'Trade unionism and partnership in practice: Evidence from the Barclays–Unifi agreement'. *Industrial Relations Journal* 35: 329–343.

Winship, C. and Mehta, J. 2010. 'Moral power' in Steven, H. and Stephen, V. (eds) *Handbook of the Sociology of Morality*. New York: Springer, pp. 425–438.

Winterton, J. and Winterton, R. 1989. *Coal, Crisis and Conflict: The 1984–85 Miners' Strike in Yorkshire*. Manchester, UK: Manchester University Press.

Wood, A.J. and Burchell, B. 2017. '"Precarious scheduling" at work affects over four million people in UK – far more than just zero-hours'. Cambridge, UK: Cambridge University. Available at: www.cam.ac.uk/research/news/precarious-scheduling-at-work-affects-over-four-million-people-in-uk-far-more-than-just-zero-hours [accessed 12 April 2021].

Wright, E. 2000. 'Working-class power, capitalist-class interests, and class compromise'. *American Journal of Sociology* 105: 957–1,002.

Wrigley, C. 1974. 'Liberals and the desire for working-class representatives in Battersea, 1886–1922' in Brown, K. (ed.) *Essays in Anti-labour History*. London: Palgrave Macmillan, pp. 126–158.

Wrigley, C. 2009. 'Trade unionists and the Labour Party in Britain: The bedrock of success'. *Revue Française de Civilisation Britannique* 15(2): 59–72.

Wrong, D. 1979. *Power: Its Forms, Bases and Uses*. Oxford, UK: Basil Blackwell.

Index

Thanks to our Patreon Subscribers:

Lia Lilith de Oliveira
Andrew Perry

Who have shown generosity and
comradeship in support of our publishing.

The Pluto Press Newsletter

Hello friend of Pluto!

Want to stay on top of the best radical books
we publish?

Then sign up to be the first to hear about our
new books, as well as special events,
podcasts and videos.

You'll also get 50% off your first order with us
when you sign up.

Come and join us!

Go to bit.ly/PlutoNewsletter